The Translator
Studies in Intercultural Communication

Volume 5, Number 2, 1999

Dialogue Interpreting

Special Issue

Guest Editor
Ian Mason
Heriot-Watt University, Edinburgh, UK

St JEROME
PUBLISHING

COVER DESIGN

Steve Fieldhouse
Oldham, UK
+44 161 620 2263

Printed & bound by Biddles Limited
Guildford, Surrey GU1 1DA, UK

THE TRANSLATOR

STUDIES IN INTERCULTURAL COMMUNICATION

Volume 5, Number 2, 1999

EDITOR

Mona Baker (UMIST, UK)

EDITORIAL BOARD

Dirk Delabastita (Facultés Universitaires Notre-Dame de la Paix, Belgium)
Ian Mason (Heriot-Watt University, UK)
Christiane Nord (Polytechnic of Magdeburg, Germany)
Anthony Pym (Universitat Rovira i Virgili, Spain)
Miriam Shlesinger (Bar-Ilan University, Israel)
Lawrence Venuti (Temple University, USA)

REVIEW EDITOR

Myriam Salama-Carr (University of Salford, UK)

INTERNATIONAL ADVISORY BOARD

Annie Brisset (University of Ottawa, Canada)
Franco Buffoni (Università di Cassino, Italy)
Michael Cronin (Dublin City University, Ireland)
Basil Hatim (Heriot-Watt University, UK)
Kinga Klaudy (University of Budapest, Hungary)
Ingrid Kurz (Universität Wien, Austria)
Paul Kussmaul (Johannes Gutenberg-Universität Mainz, Germany)
Carol Maier (Kent State University, USA)
Kirsten Malmkjær (University of Cambridge, UK)
Roberto Mayoral Asensio (Universidad de Granada, Spain)
Alastair Niven (The British Council, UK)
Yetunde Ofulue (United Bible Societies, Nigeria)
Franz Pöchhacker (University of Vienna, Austria)
Douglas Robinson (University of Mississippi, USA)
Juan Sager (UMIST, UK)
Christina Schäffner (Aston University, UK)
Candace Séguinot (York University, Canada)
Sonja Tirkkonen-Condit (University of Joensuu, Finland)
Else Vieira (Universidade Federal de Minas Gerais, Brazil)

St. Jerome Publishing
Manchester, UK

THE TRANSLATOR

Volume 5   Number 2   November 1999

Dialogue Interpreting
Guest Editor: Ian Mason, UK

Contents

Revisiting the Classics

Book Reviews

Course Profile

Dialogue Interpreting

Recent Publications

Conference Diary

Transcription conventions

[ ] [ ]	Simultaneous or overlapping talk
,	Continuing intonation (rising or level tone)
.	Terminating intonation (falling tone)
?	Questioning intonation (rising tone)
…	Open-ended intonation (fading or ambiguous tone)
e: or e:::	Long or lengthened vowel sound
(.)	Short pause
(2)	Two-second pause
+	Un-timed brief pause
/	Abandoned utterance
(looks up)	Non-verbal feature
boldface	Emphasis, stressed syllable or loudness
º º	Uttered quietly or as an aside
(xxx)	Inaudible
→	Line in transcript referred to in discussion
italics	English back-translation of talk in other languages

NB – Contributors make use of few, many or all of these conventions, depending on the relative delicacy of transcription needed for the analysis.

The Translator. Volume 5, Number 2 (1999), 147-160   ISBN 1-900650-21-5

Introduction

IAN MASON
Heriot-Watt University, UK

It is now more than twenty years since Ranier Lang (Lang 1978) observed the work of an interpreter in a Papua-New Guinea courtroom and published findings which effectively constituted the beginnings of empirical research into the work of the dialogue interpreter. At the same time, Brian Harris (Harris 1978) was drawing our attention to evidence of the behaviour of 'natural' interpreters, bilinguals with no training as interpreters, who were – and still are – frequently called upon to act as interpreters in a variety of professional contexts. What they observed were phenomena not generally found, or considered as applying to, the work of conference interpreters, hitherto the only object of research interest in interpreting studies. Role conflict, in-group loyalties, participation status, relevance, negotiation of face – all of these being issues which are now recognized objects of enquiry – were implicitly or explicitly present in these early studies. We now know far more about these and other issues, thanks to the work of a small but increasingly important body of research carried out over the years since then. What are these studies? What insights into the work of the interpreter do they afford us? And what is the current state of our knowledge and understanding of the phenomenon investigated in this volume?

In order to set the scene for the studies brought together here, we need to define our terms, especially those used in the title of this special issue of *The Translator.* We then need to sum up the 'state of the art', the stage we have reached in investigating dialogue interpreting and how the studies in this volume add to our understanding of the process. This in turn leads us to consider new directions in dialogue interpreting research, the as-yet-uncharted areas which are bound to receive attention in years to come, in what is a burgeoning field of research.

1. Defining the field

For the purposes of this issue, dialogue interpreting includes what is variously referred to in English as Community, Public Service, Liaison, Ad Hoc or Bilateral Interpreting – the defining characteristic being interpreter-mediated communication in spontaneous face-to-face interaction. Included under this heading are all kinds of professional encounters: police, immigration and welfare services interviews, doctor-patient interviews, business negotiations, lawyer-client and courtroom interpreting, and so on. Dialogue interpreting is

ISSN 1355-6509   © *St Jerome Publishing, Manchester*

thus to be distinguished from Conference Interpreting (both simultaneous and consecutive), which is typically monologic and does not involve face-to-face interaction (although dialogue encounters do take place on the fringe of conference activity). It should be noted that our definition includes the simultaneous mode, when used in face-to-face encounters (see, for example, Riddick 1998)[1] but, strictly speaking, excludes telephone interpreting. The latter however is an instance of dialogue and shares so many characteristics with the forms of interpreting considered in this volume that an investigation of the difference in communicative outcomes between telephone and face-to-face interaction (Wadensjö, this volume) is of particular interest. By the same token, signed-language interpreting (Brennan, this volume) is not strictly conducted face-to-face – or rather, the face-to-face relationship is between producer and receiver of signs instead of between the 'principal' participants or interlocutors. But all parties are present and active in the exchange so that this mode falls within the general interpersonal category we are considering.

Of course, one can cut up the interpreting cake in many different ways, and equally valid in its own right is the situational distinction, often made, between conference and community interpreting. For example, in terms of power and distance – two variables of prime importance in the investigation of interpreting, whereas conference interpreting often, or even typically, involves equal-to-equal relations, in community encounters there is almost always a power differential, which in itself places a range of additional constraints on the interpreter. Likewise, the stressful and sensitive situations in which community encounters take place are less familiar to the conference interpreter. But whereas situational descriptions can account for a number of important factors, it is the interpersonal dimension which, we submit, is the prime determiner of the range of concerns which dialogue interpreters experience in their day-to-day work. A glance at the issues listed below, as they emerge from studies carried out over the last two decades, shows quite conclusively the centrality of face-to-face dialogue in the interpreters' dilemmas, role-adopting and decision-making processes.

Within these boundaries, a wide range of user variables may be involved. As already observed, the **mode** may be consecutive or (less frequently) simultaneous. Where simultaneous mode is involved, it may be conducted by *chuchotage* (typical of some courtroom interaction), signing (signed-language interpreting) or via headsets and microphones. **Fields** include all those mentioned above, most research hitherto focusing on either courtroom interaction (e.g. Berk-Seligson 1990, Hale 1997, Morris 1989, 1995) or police and immigration interviews (Wadensjö 1992, 1998). Medical consultations are also the subject of a number of studies (e.g. Englund-Dimitrova 1997) and are prominent in this volume. It is, of course, the particularly sensitive and face-threatening nature of much of this interaction which sets these fields apart from other, less investigated fields such as business meetings or diplomatic negotiations, an issue we shall return to below. But tensions arise in these encounters too and the interpreter may feel herself to be under just as much pressure. In general, wherever a particular outcome is of vital importance to one or both parties, pressures on the interpreter increase and go well beyond those experienced in routine conference simultaneous work. Finally, addresser/addressee relationships (**tenor**) may vary and deserve much greater attention than merely recording that there is a power differential between the principal participants. The interpreter herself may enjoy greater or lesser prestige within the exchange, demoted to the role of 'speak when I say so' or promoted to the role of genuine intercultural mediator and counsellor. For Anderson (1976: 218), the interpreter, as the sole bilingual in an exchange, enjoys "the advantage of power inherent in all positions which control scarce resources". In some cases, principal participants may be observed virtually to ignore their interlocutor, addressing all their remarks and questions directly to the interpreter. In other cases, however, primary participants conduct dialogue with each other directly, almost as if no interpreter were present; in such cases they may short-circuit the process, over-riding the interpreter's turn where they are able to understand each other without the latter's assistance. All of these attitudes, perceptions of attitudes, displays of deference or condescension are bound to surface in the linguistic and paralinguistic features of the exchange, the way they are (or are not) translated and, most importantly, the observable outcomes of the event.

2. The state of the art

Within this diversity, what are the findings of studies conducted so far into dialogue interpreting? It is, of course, impossible within the confines of this introduction to include mention of (let alone do justice to) all the work that has been done and all of the observations made. For although the research field is in its infancy, it is now attracting a lot of attention and many of the studies have been scrupulously thorough. Nevertheless, there is a striking convergence between very different studies in terms of what they reveal about dialogue interpreting encounters, and it is this consensus which we shall attempt to describe here. The consensus is best captured in a number of recurring themes, identified by various scholars in the context of different kinds of interpreted events.

The first of these is the gross mismatch between, on the one hand, commonly held perceptions (among the public at large and users of interpreting services alike) of the dialogue interpreter as a kind of 'translating machine' which simply transfers language products from one language into another and, on the other, the observable reality of a situation in which meaning is subject to constant negotiation, literal translations lead to misunderstandings while, conversely, attempts by interpreters to convey intended meaning may sometimes lead them into hot water; and there is constantly shifting ground as the speech event unfolds. This issue is not a new one. It was Reddy (1979) who coined the term 'conduit metaphor' to describe commonly held assumptions about language communication, noting that the way we talk about language ('getting one's message across'; 'sending the wrong message'; 'I can't get through to him', etc.) reveals what is tacitly assumed about the nature of communication. It is interpreters who find themselves at the sharp end of the consequences of such mistaken assumptions. Roy (1990) shows how the pervasiveness of the conduit metaphor and and its applicability to dialogue interpreting have led to confusion among interpreters about the nature of their own role. Often it is assumed that what is missing is a code of ethics; but, as Roy (1990:84) observes, quoting a view put forward and warmly applauded at a conference of practitioners, "Interpreters don't have a problem with ethics, they have a problem with the role". Berk-Seligson (1988, 1990) draws attention to the fact that training for court interpreters in the United States explicitly enjoins them to translate closely and accurately. Standards of Professional Conduct include statements such as "The interpretation should be as close to verbatim and literal in content and meaning as possible".[2] She is then able to show how relaying complex English passive constructions, used by attorneys in a very deliberate way to avoid attributing blame in their cross-examinations, is highly problematic in a language such as Spanish, in which the standard passive is dispreferred but a variety of alternative formulations are available, none of which is a literal translation of the English passive. Morris (1995) documents the tension which results from the legal profession's insistence that interpretation (a specific judicial process) should be the exclusive domain of lawyers and judges and that translation – the activity allotted to the court interpreter – should consist of verbatim rendition of utterances and nothing more than that. Specifically, interpreters may not mediate by relaying their own understanding of speaker meanings and intentions: this must be left to the court.

Roy (1993), observing a very different kind of encounter – that between an academic in a university and a Deaf doctoral student – is able to explode the 'conduit' myth by showing that it is simply untenable as an account of the interpreter's actual behaviour in resolving problems of overlapping talk. In effect, the interpreter's decisions about who will be awarded the next turn appear to depend on his or her sociolinguistic competence in deciding what is appropriate within the social situation of an interview between student and professor. In other words, the interpreter is not a neutral and uninvolved machine but rather an active participant in the talk exchange, fulfilling a crucial role in coordinating others' talk – a central theme in the research of Wadensjö (e.g. 1992, 1997; see below).

In the courtroom, however, interpreters do not enjoy such latitude. Hale (1997) adduces telling examples of the ways in which the literal translations

which court interpreters are exhorted to produce may be seriously misleading. Thus, when a Spanish-speaking witness insists:

> Yo soy una persona educada/ siempre he sido educado/ Yo puedo
> probar que soy una persona educada

and is interpreted:

> I'm an educated person/I've always been educated/I can prove I'm
> an educated person

those present in the courtroom, including monolingual speakers of English,
may feel that the translating machine is functioning properly, but the magis-
trate's response to the last offer ('No thank you!') shows that something has
gone wrong: the repeated claim is seen as irrelevant to the current communicative situation. But in fact, the witness, by referring to his respectable
upbringing (*educación*), is implying that he would never behave in a particular manner, previously referred to in the exchange. Pragmatic meaning,
derivable only through matching of words uttered to the sociocultural and
sociotextual context in which they are uttered, cannot possibly survive the
injunction to translate literally in this way. Yet pragmatic meaning can be
shown to be central even to monolingual exchanges in the courtroom, where
presupposition, implicature and inference are exploited by defence and prosecution lawyers (cf. Berk-Seligson 1990:22-25).

The pretence of the interpreter's invisibility cannot, however, be sustained.
Whereas cross-examination or any question-and-answer session may for part
of the time proceed as if the interpreter were no more than a mechanical
device assisting a two-way exchange between primary interlocutors, many
studies document the multiple ways in which attention is inevitably drawn to
the interpreter's presence. These include correction of interpreters' errors by
other bilingual participants in an exchange (Morris 1995:33-34), untrained
and very nervous witnesses who persist in addressing the interpreter directly
instead of addressing all their answers to the judge or attorney who has asked
them a question (Berk-Seligson 1988), officials such as immigration or police officers who address remarks to the interpreter which they do not intend
them to translate (Wadensjö 1992:238-39), and other courtroom witnesses
who, under extreme pressure, turn on the interpreter who has relayed a threatening question posed by a prosecuting lawyer (Harris 1981:198).

Such incidents as these bring us to the second major preoccupation of
researchers in recent years, namely the participation framework (Goffman
1981) of dialogue interpreting encounters. Keith (1984) was the first study to
draw attention to the relevance of Goffman's work to the analysis of liaison
interpreting and to make use of the concept of 'footing' to characterize the
interpreter's and speaker's relationship to each other. But it is Wadensjö's

(1992, 1998) analysis of 'footing' that has had a major impact on our understanding of the interpreter's status and role within a speech exchange. Footing (Goffman 1981:227; see also Metzger, this volume) is defined as "the alignment of an individual to a particular utterance, whether involving a production format, as in the case of the speaker, or solely a participation status, as in the case of the hearer". That is, participants adopt different – and shifting – roles and attitudes vis-à- vis each other and vis-à-vis what is uttered. "Participants over the course of their speaking constantly change their footing, these changes being a persistent feature of natural talk" (ibid:128). Speakers may behave as 'principal', showing commitment to and ownership of what is expressed; as 'author', responsible for the thoughts expressed and the words uttered; or merely as 'animator', a sounding-box or talking machine. Correspondingly, there are reception roles, in the sense of the set of attitudes assumed by or ascribed to an individual towards the utterances of other parties. Wadensjö (1992:124) classifies these as the roles of 'responder' – listening in anticipation of speaking as a primary participant or 'principal'; 'recapitulator' – listening in order to repeat or give an account of what was said as 'author'; and 'reporter' – an assumed or ascribed role of listening in order to repeat words heard without assuming any responsibility for them. An interpreter may, at various stages in an exchange, adopt all three such roles. For example,

> as *responder*: (to a courtroom witness who has addressed the interpreter directly) 'Please address your remarks to the attorney, not to me'.

> as *recapitulator*: (relaying the request: 'Ask him to spell his name, please') 'Please spell your name'.

> as *reporter*: (following a primary party's injunction: 'Spell your name, please') 'Spell your name, please'.

It is important to realize that these stances are not just the result of a free choice on the part of the interpreter but also a reaction to what is assumed by the principal parties as being the appropriate interpreter role. Evidence for this comes from the way the primary interlocutors address each other. As Wadensjö (1997:48) observes, there are four possibilities here: third-person (he, she), first-person inclusive (we), second-person (you) or avoidance (no address forms used). The choice is not necessarily consciously made and, as many authentic samples quoted in the literature show, the shift of footing reflected in a shift of pronoun of address is commonplace in interpreter-mediated exchanges of this kind. Thus, the footing of each party is subject to constant renegotiation, with the stance of the primary interlocutors often influencing the interpreter's style. Harris (1981) cites a case of a court interpreter deliberately opting for the indirect, third-person style throughout a trial with the explicit aim of creating a certain distance between herself and what, in the context of a war crimes trial, was bound to be a particularly stressful and sensitive set of exchanges. But even when such distance is created, the exchange remains essentially a three-party interaction. Thus, as Wadensjö (1992: 4), following Simmel (1964), observes, such events must be seen as triadic as well as dyadic. Indeed, a major contribution by Wadensjö (e.g. 1992, 1995) to our understanding of dialogue interpreting is her investigation of the interpreter's role as a *coordinator* of others' talk.

The dynamics of the interaction are, it seems, subject to negotiation not only by means of linguistic cues but also through the strong influence of paralinguistic features: gaze, posture, gesture. By such means, primary parties can signal inclusiveness or exclusiveness vis-à-vis the interpreter. On the basis of his observation of court interpreting in Papua New Guinea, Lang (1978:241) concluded:

> Although his official role is that of a passive participant as far as the origination of primary conversation is concerned, the realisation of that role depends on the active cooperation of his clients and the extent to which they wish to include him as an active participant not only linguistically but also gesturally, posturally and gaze-wise. Likewise it is the interpreter who can by these means actively involve himself, or abstain from such involvement.

Lang was here writing, of course, of non-trained interpreters operating in an unregulated (save by tradition) courtroom situation. In many countries nowadays, the role of the court interpreter is pre-defined, even if prescribed behaviour and actual behaviour are frequently at variance, creating a constant tension (see, for example, Pym in this volume). But in many other situations, no rules have been laid down and one may observe constant shifts of footing, posture and so on within a single institution or a single exchange. For example, in a televised documentary on illegal immigration shown in the UK on Channel Four (*Cutting Edge*, 'Illegal Immigrants', 30 September 1997), it can be seen that, in interview, some immigration officers seek to make eye contact with the interpreter while others direct their gaze solely towards the immigrant being interviewed. Some of the persons interviewed make eye contact with the interpreter only, averting their gaze throughout from the officer interviewing them, while interpreters seek to establish eye contact with both primary parties. Naturally, such matters as seating arrangements, often regarded as peripheral, exert a strong influence on who faces – or is forced to face – whom.

One interesting concomitant of all of these uncertainties among participants is the phenomenon, well known to dialogue interpreters, of 'ownership' of meaning. Thus, a particular lexical choice selected by the interpreter to relay one interlocutor's meaning may be taken up or challenged by the other interlocutor as if it emanated not from the interpreter but from the other speaker. Wadensjö (1992:74) cites the example of a medical consultation involving Russian and Swedish in which the doctor suggests, in Swedish, that a thyroid problem has been 'worrying' the patient; this is then relayed to the patient by the interpreter, using a Russian word which relays the dual notion 'disturbing/worrying'. But the patient objects to the term, stating that the thyroid has not been 'disturbing/worrying' her; it has just got bigger. The objection is, of course, to a lexical item selected by the interpreter, not by the doctor. How then can the objection be relayed back to the doctor in a manner which is coherent with the doctor's original utterance in Swedish? The interpreter's response, here back-translated into English, shows her awareness of the problem that has arisen and the need to handle it: 'No, it is not that I feel worried or it hurts, but it seems to have grown bigger'. This expanded rendition attempts to make more explicit for the doctor the locus of the patient's disagreement. In other cases, the lexical item(s) at issue may be altogether more crucial. Krouglov (this volume) cites the case of a murder investigation in which a key lexical item uttered by a suspect is interpreted in three different ways by three different interpreters. Fortunately, the fact that the source of each of the three renditions (I'll kill you/I'll get you/I will stitch you up) was one lexical item was picked up and indicated to the police investigators, who thus avoided attributing to the suspect one particular lexical choice made by the interpreter.

Other phenomena investigated in research carried out include the interpreter's role and status as a cross-cultural mediator. Reporting on the relative dominance of one language over the other in bilinguals, Anderson (1976:213) states that "[i]n general, it is expected that the greater the linguistic dominance the more likely an interpreter will identify with the speakers of the dominant language, rather than with clients speaking his "other" language". It has been observed, for example, that, in a situation of unequal power distribution such as Latin American accused persons or witnesses in a United States courtroom (Berk-Seligson 1988, 1990), interpreters are sensitive to in-group loyalties towards relatively powerless participants whose language and culture they share. Indeed, the neutrality of the dialogue interpreter, referred to in instruction manuals and codes of practice, is not nearly as unproblematic as is often assumed. Wande (1994) reports similar findings from a research project involving Swedish/Finnish community interpreting. In other situations, the interpreter may easily be perceived by powerless parties to be an agent of an oppressive institution. Barsky (1994) documents in some detail the loss of status, even of identity, of applicants for asylum whose voice is heard only through the official interpreter. In order to succeed in gaining refugee status, applicants are obliged to construct an identity for themselves as appropriate refugees, all other aspects of their personal history being deemed irrelevant to the Convention Refugee hearing. Yet applicants are unfamiliar with the particular Western image they have to construct and, in a situation in which interpreters are required to translate 'accurately' and 'faithfully', "variation between the speakers' intended meaning and the text that emerges is, by the very nature of the procedure, inevitable" (Barsky 1994:41). Another study of interpreting across a wide cultural divide is Baker (1997), who analyses the performance of an interpreter in a televised interview by Trevor Macdonald, the British political interviewer, of Saddam Hussein just before the commencement of the Gulf War. In this case, the injunction to translate 'accurately' comes not from the employing institution but rather from the highly sensitive nature of the event, watched by millions of viewers and potentially influential on the evolution of diplomatic relations and the possible outbreak of war. In such circumstances, as Baker argues, interpreters will want to minimize the threat to themselves involved in either committing a highly visible error or through incurring the wrath of two primary participants whose interpersonal relations deteriorate as the interview proceeds. Consequently, the interpreter seeks to relay at all times the closest semantic sense of the words used by Saddam, even offering several alternatives, ostensibly to 'play it safe' and cover his own back; for example:

> Let us... we must rather... we must choose or take or adopt a single criterion or a single standard.

As Baker (1997:117) points out, repetition and hesitation of this kind are not a feature of Saddam's speech so that a monolingual Western viewer is liable to form a false impression of the coherence of his speech.

These studies of cross-cultural interaction involve well trained interpreters who, for all their expertise, are influenced in their interpreting behaviour by situational constraints: role conflict (cf. Anderson 1976), in-group loyalties, stress in a sensitive situation, perceptions of power and distance, and so on. Another fertile strand of research has been into the performance of what Brian Harris calls natural, i.e. untrained, interpreters. Indeed, it can be convincingly argued that, if we wish to understand the basic (cognitive and non-cognitive) mechanisms involved in the process of dialogue interpreting, then we should investigate not the results of training, based as it is on sets of normative assumptions about what constitutes appropriate behaviour, but rather the spontaneous behaviour of bilinguals who can and do interpret in a wide variety of social situations, prior to any norms of behaviour inculcated by training. This point should not, of course, be construed as in any way implying that it is appropriate for untrained individuals to interpret in community interpreting situations which demand professional expertise. The deleterious consequences of relying on children, for example, to act as interpreters in sensitive and stressful medical situations are well known in the profession. Studies included in this volume (Cambridge; Pöchhacker and Kadric) bear witness to what is at stake when untrained staff serve as interpreters in medical consultations. But the investigation of such situations can indeed provide insights into the nature of the very issues outlined so far in this introduction to the field.

As suggested above, awareness of different client needs and expectations in cross-cultural encounters can be a powerful influence on interpreter behaviour. An early study of natural interpreting, Harris and Sherwood (1978), relates the case of a business negotiation conducted between an Italian immigrant to Canada and an English-speaking Canadian, interpreted by the former's bilingual daughter. Both primary parties behave according to their own cultural norms and when, at a crucial point in the negotiation, the Italian – appropriately, within his own cultural expectations – calls the other man a fool, the untrained interpreter exhibits both bi-cultural awareness and an instinctive move to save face all round:

> Father: Digli che è un imbecille!
> Daughter (to 3rd. party):   My father won't accept your offer.

What the natural (as opposed to the trained) interpreter may not have considered is how such a move can backfire. In this case, the father, whose English is apparently good enough for him to monitor his daughter's performance, immediately interjects (in Italian): "Why didn't you tell him what I told you?".

The natural interpreter's awareness of the need to preserve face is among the issues investigated by Knapp-Potthof and Knapp (1986), in an experiment involving discussions between Germans and Koreans, interpreted by a Korean student in her mid-twenties. They found that, whereas the interpreter does not relay many markers of politeness from German into Korean (e.g. *vielleicht*, 'perhaps'; *mal*, 'just'), she also introduces her own politeness strategies which "strongly suggest that [she] is very much concerned with saving her own face" (Knapp-Potthof and Knapp 1986:198). For example, when the German speaker asks to know the age of his interlocutors, the interpreter introduces this intrusive question by saying "what interests him" and "what he wants to know", thus disowning responsibility for any threat to face in the question. It is significant that these deictic transformations had not occurred previously in the interpreter's output and are clearly linked to this particular speech act. Many other examples are available in the evidence presented by these analysts, who conclude (1986:199) that the interpreter "regards her role as that of an independent, active party in the interaction, who, too, has a face to lose". We return to the issue of face below but, for the moment, let us note the similarity of these conclusions to those reported in many other independent studies.

3. Research directions

The articles in this volume speak for themselves and I shall not attempt to summarize them here. What is striking though is the number of common themes, issues and interrelated observations in a variety of different dialogue interpreting settings. At one and the same time, these observations provide corroborative evidence for many of the hypotheses advanced and attested in earlier work and point to new directions in interpreting research. Reference has already been made to some of these topics but at this point let us try to identify some of the most salient strands.

3.1 Participation framework

Franz Pöchhacker and Mira Kadric's observation of a natural interpreter in a medical setting picks up many of the themes alluded to above. Let us highlight just one incident which contributes to our understanding of shifts of footing. In the data, a shift from first-person to third-person style is clearly initiated by one of the primary parties when she says: 'do you understand me? Tell him to ...'. The shift of addressee from patient to interpreter seems to coincide with a sudden loss of confidence in direct therapist-patient interaction and an appeal to the interpreter to act as intermediary. This incident highlights not only the fact that primary participants are often influential in determining the interpreter's footing, as suggested above, but also that shifts of footing are motivated rather than random. Thus, in the data presented here by Helen Tebble, it is striking that a shift of footing by a doctor coincides with having to announce relatively bad news to a patient: the distancing effect of asking the interpreter to address the patient is an option which participants are instinctively aware of. Likewise, in the courtroom interaction which is the object of Mary Brennan's investigation, a lawyer's shift of footing in questioning ('Did he actually see ...', instead of 'Did you see ...') is probably traceable to the fact that the lawyer cannot establish eye contact with the Deaf witness, who is bound to face the interpreter rather than the questioner. Cecilia Wadensjö, whose previous work on footing was referred to above, is able to show here how participation framework is inevitably and radically affected by the different situational context of telephone interpreting. Such comparative studies are of great relevance to users of interpreting services who need to know more of the communicative effects of different forms of provision. From our perspective, these studies, taken together, open up a rich vein of future research: what motivates shifts of footing? How does the participation framework respond to the situational constraints of particular modes and settings?

3.2 Lexical choice and discoursal value

The way in which an interpreter chooses to relay a particularly salient lexical item has been shown to have repercussions on later talk and especially on the attribution of responsibility for use of the term to an interlocutor who has not, in fact, used it. Mary Brennan shows how a lawyer, cross-examining a witness, takes up the exact terms used by the interpreter but not by the person interpreted. Given what is at stake in courtroom interaction, it will be appreciated that such decisions can have far-reaching consequences (see also Anthony Pym's discussion of the key terms *hit* and *slap* in an exchange from the O. J. Simpson trial). The issue of interpreting in sensitive contexts, investigated by Baker (1997, see above) also surfaces in the work presented here by Helen Tebble, Jan Cambridge, Cecilia Wadensjö and Alex Krouglov. What happens, in cross-cultural contexts, to the discoursal value of lexical selections? A hospital doctor addressing a patient may well refer to a 'problem with the waterworks' rather than a 'genito-urinary tract' problem; the discourse adopted is one which acts as an appropriate sign (informality, friendly bedside manner) within its culture; if used cross-culturally without interpreter mediation, it may meet with a look of blank incomprehension or, worse, result in offence being taken. Of similar discoursal significance is the key term discussed by Alex Krouglov ('I'll kill you/I'll stitch you up'), which belongs in the source language to a non-standard dialect. Such lexicalizations are marked – in the sense of unexpected and therefore dynamic – and are bound to take on additional discoursal values within their own culture; how can such values be relayed and, if they cannot, is the interpreter then drawn into assuming the role of expert witness by explaining what is involved? How, indeed, do interpreters negotiate appropriate discourses and genres (cf. Hatim and Mason 1997) across cultural boundaries, especially in situations of unequal access by all parties to what is culturally sanctioned within particular settings?

3.3 Visibility and audience design

The fact that primary parties, who are not entirely monolingual, often monitor their interpreter's performance is well attested in the literature and an issue discussed by Anthony Pym in this volume. In the O. J. Simpson trial, the interpreter is called upon not because the witness knows no English but rather because, in a courtroom whose language is English, the Hispanic witness is at a disadvantage and must be seen to be offered linguistic protection. Moreover, many officers of the court know Spanish so that, as Pym observes, "despite apparent invisibility, the interpreters are being checked on all sides". The interpreter is therefore aware of being highly visible and is bound to design her output for various categories of receivers. Following Bell (1984), we may distinguish between direct addressees (e.g. the witness, the counsel), auditors (ratified participants who are not being directly addressed, e.g. counsel for the defence while prosecuting counsel is cross-examining), overhearers (who are present but not ratified participants, e.g. the public), and eavesdroppers (whose presence the participants are not currently aware of, e.g. the analyst, observing the trial on television). Francesco Straniero Sergio illustrates similar diversity of receiver groups in a very different setting, that of the television chat show. In media interpreting of this kind, the influence exerted on the interpreter's audience design is even more apparent. The extent to which each of the categories (addressee, auditor, overhearer) influences interpreter style – in contrast to, say, the interpeter in the private medical consultation – is an obvious area for future research to investigate.

3.4 Power and face

There is a sense in which power within the speech event resides with the interpreter who, as gate-keeper, controls the attribution of turns at talk (cf. Anderson 1976, cited above). As bi-cultural and bilingual, the interpreter may also enjoy certain other forms of power within the interaction by virtue of his/her knowledge. But it is the overall power dynamic formed among the triad of primary parties and interpreter within a particular social setting which acts as main determinant of how the event proceeds. In the medical consultation, asymmetrical power relations may result in important information being skewed or overlooked. All parties seem tacitly to acknowledge the right of the doctor to control the exchange. Englund-Dimitrova (1997) shows how a doctor, by interrupting the interpreter's turn, potentially misses an important response by a patient. Similarly, Mary Brennan notes in her paper in this volume how the sign language interpreter's turn management is usurped when speakers ignore some of the actions of signers and take their turn before the relay of meaning is complete. In the illuminating data studied by Mira Kadric and Franz Pöchhacker, it is apparent that the natural interpreter feels able to take unwarranted initiatives of her own when addressing the ten-year-old boy patient but would be much less likely to offer directive advice to the therapists who are the other primary parties in the interaction. Above all, there seems to be evidence, in accordance with previous research mentioned above, that interpreters are keenly aware of threats to face and adopt politeness strategies (Brown and Levinson 1987) aimed at protecting their own or their addressee's face: downtoning or hedging (see Helen Tebble's analysis); introducing conventional apologies (see Mary Brennan's data, in which a sign meaning 'Again?' is interpreted as 'I'm sorry what do you mean?'). What these papers collectively show is that there is undoubtedly scope for a much more far-reaching investigation of the negotiation of face in interpreted encounters in relation to the variables of power and distance.

These then are some of the issues which surface in the studies brought together here and which suggest interesting directions that future research might take. In conclusion, let us note that all of these pointers lead away from concern with the measurement of 'interpreter error', 'correctness', 'equivalence', and so on and thus away from a narrow source-text/target-text comparison towards a more procedural account. Viewing the interpreter as a gatekeeper, coordinator and negotiator of meanings within a three-way interaction, descriptive studies have much to gain from linking observation of the process to pragmatic constraints such as power, distance and face-threat and to semiotic constraints such as genres and discourses as socio-textual practices (cf. Hatim and Mason 1997) of particular cultural communities.

IAN MASON
Centre for Translation and Interpreting Studies in Scotland, Heriot-Watt University, Edinburgh EH14 4AS, UK. I.Mason@hw.ac.uk

Notes

1.   This mode is new in the healthcare setting and is known as 'remote simultaneous'. That is, whereas the primary interlocutors (e.g. doctor and patient) remain face-to-face, the interpreter is at a separate location and relays each turn via headsets (Riddick 1998:45).
2.   Standards of Professional Conduct and Responsibilities for Members of the Judiciary Interpreters Association of Texas, cited in Berk-Seligson (1990:232).

References

Bell, A. (1984) 'Language Style as Audience Design', *Language in Society* 13: 145-204.
Brown, P. and S. Levinson (1987) *Politeness. Some Universals in Language Usage*, Cambridge: Cambridge University Press.
Goffman, Erving (1981) *Forms of Talk*. Philadelphia: University of Pennsylvania Press.
Hatim, Basil and Ian Mason (1997) *The Translator as Communicator*, London: Routledge.
Reddy, M. (1979) 'The Conduit Metaphor: A Case of Frame Conflict in our Language about Language', in A. Ortony (ed) *Metaphor and Thought*, Cambridge: Cambridge University Press, 284-324.
Riddick, S. (1998) 'Improving Access for Limited English-speaking Consumers: A Review of Strategies in Health Care Settings', *Journal of Health Care for the Poor and Underserved* 9 (supplemental): 40-61.
Simmel, G. (1964) *The Sociology of Georg Simmel* (transl. from German, ed. and with an introduction by K. H. Wolff), New York: Free Press.

For other references, see the Bibliography at the end of this volume.

The Translator. Volume 5, Number 2 (1999), 161-178   ISBN 1-900650-21-5

The Hospital Cleaner as Healthcare Interpreter
A Case Study

FRANZ PÖCHHACKER & MIRA KADRIC
Universität Wien, Austria

Abstract. *Against the background of current hospital interpreting practices in Vienna, the authors present a case study of an authentic therapeutic interaction in which a Serbian-speaking hospital cleaner serves as interpreter in a 47-minute voice therapy and briefing session. Communication between the two speech therapists and the ten-year-old voice patient and his parents from the former Yugoslavia (Bosnia) is described and analysed on the basis of twelve excerpts from the full transcript of the videotaped interaction. The findings show that the untrained ('natural') interpreter clearly fails to maintain a consistent focus on her translatorial role and task and introduces significant shifts in the form as well as the substance of communication. Unaware of the cleaner-interpreter's impact on the interaction, the therapists ultimately lose control over the quality and effectiveness of their professional work.*

Dialogue interpreting in healthcare settings has increasingly become a focus of attention as a significant speciality of translatorial practice. Despite a growing number of professionalization initiatives in Anglo-American as well as other countries however, the provision of interpreting services in healthcare settings remains characterized by *ad hoc* arrangements involving the use of untrained bilinguals, most commonly family members and hospital staff, as interpreters.

A recent survey carried out in a total of 71 departments of twelve hospitals in Vienna (Pöchhacker 1997) confirmed the present state of medical interpreter service delivery. Out of 464 doctors, nurses and therapists responding to the question of what kind of hospital staff served as interpreters, 61% indicated that it was frequently or nearly always "cleaning staff" – as opposed to nurses (44%) or doctors (10%). (Migrants from the former Yugoslavia represent the most numerous non-German language group in Vienna, and many women from this community have traditionally found employment as housekeeping staff.) Given their pivotal role in enabling communication between Austrian healthcare providers and non-German-speaking patients, Serbocroat-speaking hospital cleaners are a prime target group for any study of current healthcare interpreting practice in Austria.

While the use of untrained bilingual hospital staff, let alone cleaners, as interpreters may be flatly rejected by professional linguists (e.g. Scouller 1988: 66, Burley 1990:150), there are very few well-documented studies to date which investigate what actually transpires in an authentic provider-patient interaction involving "natural translation", i.e. "[t]he translating done in everyday circumstances by people who have had no special training for it" (Harris and Sherwood 1978:155)

Against this background of current interpreting practice in Austrian hospitals on the one hand and theoretical interest in the performance of 'natural interpreters' on the other, the present study investigates the translatorial behaviour of a hospital cleaner in a therapeutic setting. From a descriptive rather than a normative perspective, the nature of the interpreter's renditions as well as her behaviour in the role of interpreter will be analysed for their impact on the dynamics of the communicative exchange and on the functional quality of the professional interaction as a whole.

1. Material and method

The material analysed in this case study is derived from the Ear, Nose and Throat Department of a teaching hospital in Vienna, where speech therapists can and routinely do use a video camera to document patient encounters for subsequent reference and analysis. In the context of a survey project carried out by the first author, the head and staff of the department in question were requested – and agreed – to make recordings of sessions with non-German-speaking patients available for a study of translation practice. This arrangement obviated the need for participant observation and allowed for routine patient (parent) consent to the use of recordings for scientific purposes.

The recording used for this study was made in August 1995. It documents the initial voice therapy session of a ten-year-old boy of Bosnian descent and the subsequent briefing session with his parents. The session is conducted jointly by two (monolingual) speech therapists and a Serbian-speaking hospital cleaner who serves as interpreter.

The German-language portions of the interaction were transcribed by the first author and checked by the second author, who contributed the transcription of the Bosnian/Serbian utterances (which were in turn checked by a fellow sworn court interpreter for the respective languages). The working translations into English, which were made as readable as an interlinear approximation of the original would allow, are by the first author in cooperation with a native-Serbian professional interpreter in California.

The transcription system follows the basic approach of Ehlich and Rehbein (1976) and is largely congenial with Wadensjö (1992). The excerpts drawn from the full transcript of the interaction are referenced to the time on tape (from MIN.SEC to MIN.SEC), with the individual utterances numbered consecutively within each excerpt.

Given the explorative nature of this case study, which essentially aims at describing the behaviour of a hospital cleaner acting as interpreter, the analysis is focused neither on *a priori* categories or typologies nor on particular issues or problems. Rather than using isolated examples for illustration, the data are presented in such a way as to reflect the chronological development of the interaction (in so far as this is possible on the basis of a dozen excerpts). This descriptive approach is intended to provide the reader with a richly contextualized understanding of the interaction. In the discussion, these empirical data will then be summarized with regard to the interpreter's role and performance, ultimately leading to an assessment of the cleaner-interpreter's impact on the functional quality of the therapeutic interaction.

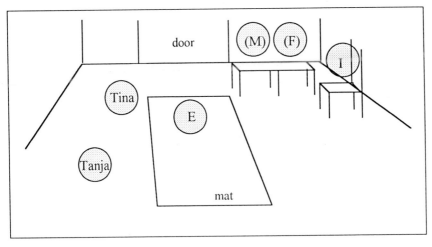

Figure 1: Constellation of Interactants

2. Setting the scene

The voice therapy session with ten-year-old Emir (approx. 39 minutes) is conducted jointly by two young speech therapists (under 30), Tanja and Tina. The latter does most of the actual 'hands-on' exercises while Tanja appears to act in a supervisory capacity and takes charge of the subsequent briefing with the boy's parents (approx. 8 minutes). The Interpreter is a middle-aged woman who speaks a Wallachian dialect of Serbian. The basic constellation of the interactants as seen through the camera is sketched in Figure 1. During most of the therapy session, Emir is lying on the mat, on his back with his head pointing to the door, while Tina is kneeling or sitting beside him. Tanja

mostly adopts a more distant position, closer to the camera. The Interpreter
(I) is sitting on a chair on the opposite side of the mat, often bending forward
towards Emir.

The content structure of the therapy session may be described as follows.
After several minutes of introductory exchanges and preparatory moves, such
as getting Emir to lie down on the mat, Tanja performs a relaxation massage
(approx. 5 minutes). Tina then takes over and guides the boy through a number
of exercises – awareness of breathing (2 minutes), exhaling (5 minutes), hum-
ming and voicing (8 minutes) – before concluding her physical work with a
demonstration of breathing movements and how to monitor them (3 minutes). The rest of the time is spent on preparing for the (breathing) exercises
at home.

When Tina brings Emir into the room, the interpreter is already sitting in
her chair. As is evident from Tanja's introduction (Excerpt 1:1), the woman
had been present in a previous encounter with the boy.

Excerpt 1 (00.06 – 00.15)

1	Tanja	Servus! Schau mal, kannst du dich an die Dame erinnern?
		Hello! Look, do you remember this lady?
2	I	(to Emir) Hallo.
		Hello.
3	Tanja	Die übersetzt ein bisschen, was wir machen mit dir heute, okay?
		She'll translate a little what we're doing with you today, okay?
4	Emir	(hoarse) Okay.

Paradoxically, Tanja addresses Emir in German, and the Interpreter provides
neither a translation nor an introduction of her own (2). While Emir's response by taking up the tag question (4) appears to signal understanding, his
insufficient command of German becomes evident a few seconds later (in
Excerpt 2).

Excerpt 2 (00.21 – 00.42)

1	Tina	Pass auf, heute werdn ma uns nicht hinsetzen, heute werdn ma uns hinlegen, so wie beim Schlafen.
		Now look, today we won't sit down, today we'll lie down, like in sleeping.
2	I	Tićeš ovde da legneš.
		You will lie down here.
3	Tina	Hm? ... . Macht dir das was aus?
		Hm? ... . Do you mind that?
4	Emir	(definite) Ja.
		Yes.
5	Tina	Mach ma das?
		Shall we do that?

6	Emir	JA.
		Yes.
7	Tina	JA, GUT. VERSTEHST DU MICH? (to I) SAGEN SIE IHM, ER SO/
		Yes, good. Do you understand me? *Tell him to/*
8	I	JE L' RAZUMEŠ? TETA KAŽE DA LEGNEŠ. TU DOLEĆEŠ DA LEGNEŠ, TU DOLE
		Do you understand? The lady says you should lie down. Down there you should lie down, down there.

In her first rendition (Excerpt 2:2) the interpreter addresses Emir using direct speech and reduces Tina's gentle instruction to a statement of what Emir will (have to) do. With his attention focused on Tina and his back turned on the interpreter, however, Emir does not react to either utterance and Tina soon realizes from his obliging affirmative answers that she needs to communicate through the interpreter. (Some 50 seconds later, a similar exchange prompts her to instruct the interpreter to "try and always translate right away" since she believes that Emir does not understand). Again, the interpreter renders the therapist's instruction in a much more command-like and rather insistent tone. In fact she cuts off Tina's utterance and produces her own as a mix of direct and reported speech.

3. Therapy session

Before Tina begins with her breathing and voice exercises, Tanja performs a relaxation massage, which she introduces as follows (Excerpt 3):

Excerpt 3 (04.45 – 05.05)

1	Tanja	SAGEN SIE IHM, DASS ICH SO EINE ART MASSAGE JETZT MACH, UND ER BRAUCHT GAR NIX TUN, ER KANN RUHIG DIE AUGEN ZUMACHEN,
		Tell him that I'll now do a kind of massage, and he doesn't need to do anything, he can close his eyes,
2	I	TETA KAŽE DA ĆE DA TE MALO MASIRA, TI SE OPUSTI, ZATVORI OČI. NEĆE TI NIŠTA BUDE, NEMOJ DA SE BOJIŠ, ZATVORI OČI, AKO HOĆEŠ, SKROZ ZATVORI.
		The lady says she will massage you a little, you relax, close your eyes. Nothing will happen to you, don't be afraid. Close your eyes, if you want, close them tight.
3	Tina	(Emir closes his eyes) ABER ER MUSS SIE NICHT ZUMACHEN, WENN ER NICHT WILL.
		But he doesn't have to close them, if he doesn't want to.
4	I	JA, ICH RED NUR WENN ER WILL.
		Yes, I says only if he wants.

The interpreter clearly expands on Tanja's explanation by explicitly telling

Emir to relax, close his eyes and, most strikingly, not to worry (Excerpt 3:2). When Tina notes Emir's obliging reaction and emphasizes that he does not have to close his eyes (3), the interpreter, changing her footing (cf. Wadensjö 1992:117f), replies that this is what she has said (which she did, but with considerably more illocutionary force), thus opting for a face-saving remark rather than a rendition of Tina's utterance for Emir.

Another case of face-work (cf. Wadensjö 1992:151) on the interpreter's part can be observed when Tanja has finished her massage (Excerpt 4):

Excerpt 4 (07.10 – 07.26)

1	Tanja	FRAGEN SIE IHN, OB DAS ANGENEHM WAR ODER UNANGENEHM.
		Ask him whether that was pleasant or unpleasant.
2	I	PITA TETA, JE L' TI BILO PRIJATNO IL TI NIJE BILO PRIJATNO, KAKO SE OSEĆAŠ. ... . KAD TE TAKO MASIRA. JEL' TI BILO LEPO?
		The lady asks if it was pleasant or not pleasant. How do you feel when she massages you like that? Was it nice?
3	Emir	LEPO.
		Nice.
4	I	ER SAGT ES/ ANGENEHM. (Tanja: MHM.) ES TUT IHM GUT.
		He says it/ Pleasant. It feels good for him.

As a result of the alternative phrasing in her rendition (2), the interpreter elicits an answer that does not quite fit the original question (3). As if to correct this mismatch, she drops her plan for a rendition in reported speech and gives the answer in terms of Tanja's question (4), subsequently adding another utterance, the nature of which (rendition or comment) remains unclear.

During the exercise which will ultimately become the focus of Emir's practice assignment, the translation is again worded in such a way as to elicit a verbal response (Excerpt 5).

Excerpt 5 (11.04 – 11.58)

1	Tina	GENAU. .. .. SEHR GUT. DER BAUCH WIRD GRÖSSER, UND WIEDER KLEINER. .. .. . (turns to I)
		Exactly. .. .. Very good. The belly gets bigger, and smaller again.
2	I	JE L' OSEĆAŠ KAKO STOMAK GORE-DOLE?
		Do you feel the belly go up-down?
3	Tanja	STE/ SAGEN SIE IHM, ER SOLL SICH VORSTELLEN, ER HAT EINEN LUFTBALLON IM BAUCH, UND WENN ER EINATMET, BLÄST SICH DER LUFTBALLON AUF.
		Ima/ Tell him to imagine that he has a balloon in his belly, and when he inhales, the balloon is inflated.
4	I	JA. TETA KAŽE DA ZAMISLIŠ DA IMAŠ BALON U STOMAKU I KAD TI DIŠEŠ ON VEĆI PA SE SMANJI, PA VEĆI PA SE SMANJI. MOŽE TO?

		Yes. The lady says, imagine that you have a balloon in your
		belly, and when you breathe it is bigger, then it gets smaller,
		and bigger and smaller. Can you?
5	Tanja	UND WENN ER AUSATMET, DANN GEHT DIE LUFT SO PFFFHHHHHH AUS
		DEM LUFTBALLON, =[UND DER BAUCH WIRD KLEIN.]=
		And when he exhales, the air goes like pffffhhhhhh out of the
		balloon, =[and the belly becomes small.]=
6	I	=[I KAD IZDAHNEŜÔ= ONDA VAZDUH IZADJE I
		STOMAK SE SMANJI, U{Z}DAHNEŠ – SVE VEĆI. MOŽE TO?
		=[And when you exhale]= the air comes out
		and the belly becomes smaller, inhale (sigh) – bigger again.
		Can you?
7	Emir	(nods, turns from I to Tina)
8	Tina	MHM. KANNST DU DAS SPÜREN. SEHR GUT.
		Mhm. So you can feel that. Very good.

Whereas the therapists merely provide descriptions to accompany and facilitate the exercises, the interpreter tends to use (tag) questions, implying the need for some response (Excerpts 5:2, 4, 6). While the therapist, unaware of the eliciting tags, appreciates Emir's affirmative response (7-8), the latter may in part be induced by the translation. The fact that the interpreter preempts the second part of Tanja's illustration (5) and incorporates it in her rendition of part one (3-4) is glossed over by a similar duplication in (6), and Tanja's simile arguably loses some of its clarity in the process.

The following excerpt marks the end of the exercises and introduces the next phase of the interaction (Excerpt 6:1):

Excerpt 6 (24.38 – 25.03)

1	Tanja	(to Tina) SOLL MA DEN ELTERN, DAS ZEIGN, DASS SIE DAS ZUHAUSE
		MIT IHM MACHEN ODER ERST / .. .. .. (to I) KANN SICH SCHON
		AUFSETZEN.
		Should we show the parents, show them that they do
		this with him at home or first / .. .. .. He can sit up now.
2	I	USTANI AKO HOĆEŠ.
		Stand up, if you want.
3	Tanja	.. .. . (to Tina) ABER S'HAT IHM EINDEUTIG GFALLN.
		But he clearly liked it.
4	I	(to Emir) JE L' TI BILO DOBRO?
		Was it good for you?
5	Emir	(smiles, nods, to I) JA.
		Yes.
6	I	(to Tanja, Tina) JA, ES HAT IHM GEFALLEN. (Tanja: MHM.) .. ..
		Yes, he liked it.
		(to Emir) TO SU SAMO VEŽBE BILE.
		That was just exercises.

As in many other instances throughout the session, the therapists, who are kneeling on the floor, talk to one another about how to proceed (Excerpt 6:1). When Tanja interrupts this consultational mode by suggesting that Emir sit (!) up, the interpreter takes her subsequent remark to Tina (3) as a prompt to formulate a direct question for feedback (4). Her rendition of Emir's affirmative response (5) – without a prior question by the therapists – is followed by a strikingly autonomous act of reassurance.

4. Homework preparations

Preparations for home exercises are initiated by Tina, who lies down on the mat herself to give a demonstration of diaphragmatic breathing, with Emir's hand on her belly.

Excerpt 7 (26.31 – 27.00)

1	Tina	GELL, DAS HAST DU VORHER AUCH BEI DEINEM BAUCH GESPÜRT. DER IS HINEINGEGANGEN UND WIEDER HINAUSGEGANGEN, HINEINGEGANGEN UND WIEDER HINAUSGEGANGEN DER BAUCH, GELL?
		This is what you also felt on your belly a little while ago, isn't it? It went in and out again, in and out again, your belly, right?
2	Tanja	FRAGEN SIE IHN, OB ER DAS AUCH GESPÜRT HAT.
		Ask him whether he felt this too.
3	I	JESI LI OSEĆ'O KOD TEBE ISTO TAKO KAO KOD TETE DA SE STOMAK DIZO GORE-DOLE?
		Did you feel this on your belly like on the lady, that the belly was moving up and down?
4	Emir	(shakes his head)
5	I	JESI OSEĆO? NISI? KAKO NISI KAD SI DRŽO RUKU. JESI OSEĆO KAKO SE STOMAK DIŽE, JESI?
		Did you feel it? No? Why not? But you did put your hand there. Did you feel how the belly was rising, did you?
6	Emir	JA.
		Yes.

As in a number of other passages, Tanja needs to prompt the interpreter for a rendition of Tina's question (Excerpt 7:1-2). When Emir shakes his head to signal a negative answer (4), the interpreter presses him to reconsider his reply with a series of direct follow-up questions and subsequently renders the boy's "yes" for the therapists. Similar 'questioning' by the interpreter occurs some three and again six minutes later. When Emir responds affirmatively to Tanja's question as to whether he has a room of his own, the interpreter probes further with "You sleep alone in the room? Neither, neither child, nor Mummy nor Daddy nor little brother?" (30.59 – 31.40) before rendering it into German for the therapists. Emir's preference for doing the exercises without his parents draws two follow-up questions from the interpreter ("You want to do it alone?" "And you'll be sure to do it?"), the latter preempting Tina's own words to that effect (32.37 – 33.22).

Another type of follow-up by the interpreter, with potential implications for therapeutic procedure, appears in Excerpt 8, when Tanja asks Emir about school:

Excerpt 8 (32.19 – 32.33)

1	Tanja	UND WAS MACHT ER AM LIEBSTEN IN DER SCHULE?
		And what does he most like to do at school?
2	I	ŠTA NAJVIŠE VOLIŠ DA RADIŠ U ŠKOLI? .... DA PIŠEŠ, DA ČITAŠ, FIZIČKO, ŠTA NAJVIŠE VOLIŠ, MUZIČKO, DA PEVAŠ, DA CRTAŠ? ŠTA NAJVIŠE VOLIŠ?
		What do you most like to do at school? .. .. Writing, reading, gym, what do you most like to do? Music, singing, drawing? What do you most like to do?
3	Emir	DA .. PISEM.
		.. Writing.

When Emir does not reply to the question regarding his favourite subject at school, the interpreter expands her rendition by suggesting a total of six options, whereupon Emir chooses the one first mentioned. Shortly after that, the therapists decide to make use of this preference for the procedure of documenting the home exercise: "If he likes writing, we can have him write a list for next time" (33.23). Tanja draws a grid on a sheet of paper and writes down the German name for every day of the week. As she is presenting the sheet to Emir, the interpreter volunteers an unprompted explanation, which immediately precedes – and preempts – an exchange between the therapists (Excerpt 9):

Excerpt 9 (37.28 – 38.26)

1	I	TU PIŠEŠ KAD SI RADIO VEŽBE.
		Here you write down when you have done the exercises.
2	Tina	.. .. .. UND WAS/ ER SOLL DIE ÜBUNGEN EINTRAGEN.
		.. .. .. And what/ He is supposed to fill in the exercises.
3	Tanja	NA, ER SOLL HINEINSCHREIBEN /
		No, he's supposed to write in /
4	Tina	WAS ER GEMACHT HAT.
		what he has done.
5	Tanja	(thinking) .. . NEIN, NUR DIE BAUCHATMUNG SOLL ER ÜBEN, JA?
		... No, only diaphragm breathing is what he should practice, right?
6	Tina	JA.
		Yes.
7	Tanja	(hesitating) .. OB ER /
		.. Whether he /

8   Tina   .. .. OB ER DRAN =[GEDACHT HAT.]=
            .. .. *Whether he =[remembered it.]=*
9   Tanja   =[Ob er dran]= gedacht hat, mhm. (to I) JA,
            ER SOLL, AH, HINEINSCHREIBEN, OB ER AH, AM ABEND ODER IN DER
            RÜH, JA, ODER UNTER/ UNTERTAGS EINMAL DARAN GEDACHT HAT, SICH
            HINZULEGEN, HAND AUF DEN BAUCH UND SO DIESE ATEMÜBUNG
            ZU MACHEN.
                            =[*Whether he*]= *remembered it, mhm. (to I) Yes,*
            he should, uhm, write in whether, uhm, in the evening or in the
            morning, right, or during/ some time during the day, he remem-
            bered to lie down, hand on his belly and do this breathing exercise.
10 I   ONA JE REKLA, SLUŠAJ, OVDE, OVDE, I TU UVEK DA NAPIŠEŠ KAD SI
            PRAVIO VEŽBE, UJUTRO - MORGEN, MITTAG ODER NACHMITTAG, TAKO
            ISTO SONNTAG, TAKO ISTO MONTAG SVE DO FREITAG DOK NE DODJEŠ
            OPET OVDE. JE L' ZNAŠ? JE L' ZNAŠ SINE? JESI RAZUMEO?
            She said, listen up, here, here you always write down when you
            have done the exercises, in the morning - morning, midday or
            afternoon, the same for Sunday, also Monday to Friday, until
            you come here again. Y'know? You know, my son? Did you
            understand?
11 Emir   Ja.
            Yes.

In formulating her own instruction (9:1), the interpreter uses a dialect form
of the temporal pronoun 'when', which could mean anything within the semantic range from 'when' to 'whether'. As it turns out, though, the therapists
are only beginning to work out what Emir is actually supposed to do (2-9).
When Tanja finally formulates the instruction to be passed on to Emir, the
interpreter not only repeats her non-standard usage of 'when' but also structures her rendition in such a way as to favour the temporal interpretation
('when') over the meaning intended by the therapists ('whether'; cf. the syntactic position of the German words for 'morning', 'midday' and 'afternoon').
Moreover, the interpreter expands on Tanja's instruction and seeks explicit
confirmation of Emir's understanding. Emir once again replies to a question
the therapist has not asked, and when Tanja does ask it a few seconds later, it
has become superfluous and is answered directly by the interpreter.

    When Tanja subsequently suggests that Emir may simply put a check
mark or an asterisk on the sheet, the boy's sense of understanding is clearly
shaken. His confusion about the instruction is not only reflected in subsequent
turns, when Tina reacts laughingly to Emir's uneasiness and hesitation, but
also becomes the subject of a lengthy exchange during the parents' briefing.

5. Parents' briefing

Emir's therapeutic regimen is explained to his parents as follows (Excerpt 10):

Excerpt 10 (41.32 – 42.27)

1	Tanja	Sagen sie, dass, ahm, wir Übungen gemacht haben, ah, für die Atmung, damit er nicht so verspannt ist, ja.

Say that, uhm, we have done exercises, uh, for his breathing, so that he isn't so tense, alright?

2	I	PRAVILI SMO OVDE VEŽBE DA ON DIŠE POLAKO, LAGANO, DA NIJE ONAKO NAŠPANOVAN, ONO ZNAŠ OVAKO, POLAAAKO, SVE POLAAKO, DA POLAKO DIŠE.

We have done exercises here, so that he breathes slowly, easily, so that he isn't so tense, you know like, slooowly, always slowly, so that he breathes slowly.

3	Tanja	UND DASS ER HALT JEDEN TAG ALLEINE VO/ DAS MACHEN SOLL, ... JA?

And well that every day he on his own, [bef]/ should do that, ... yes?

4	I	SVAKI DAN MORA MALO DA VEŽBA, KAD, KAD LEGNE , STAVI RUKU NA STOMAK.

Every day he has to practice a little, when he goes to bed, put his hand on his belly.

5	Tanja:	(to Tina) SOLLN IHN DIE ELTERN ERINNERN?

Should the parents remind him?

6	Tina	JA. JA, SCHON.

Yes, yes, they should.

7	Tanja	SIE KÖNNEN IHN SCHON ÄH ERINNERN, DASS SIE SAGEN: HAST DU HEUTE SCHON DIE ÜBUNG GEMACHT? DASS SIE IHN ERINNERN, JA?

You can, uh, remind him, that you say: Have you done the exercise today? that you remind him, alright?

8	I	DA GA PODSETITE, DA L' JE RADIO TE VEŽBE. UVEČE NAJBOLJE KAD LEGNE, KAD SE SMIRI, DA, NAJBOLJE.

That you remind him, if he has done these exercises. In the evening it's best, when he goes to bed, when he is already calmed down, yes, best.

At least two substantial shifts are introduced by the interpreter in this significant part of the briefing session. Whereas Tanja speaks about breathing exercises for relaxation (10:1) without further describing their nature (3), the interpreter puts the emphasis on "breathing slowly, easily" (2) and mentions not only what Emir is to do but also when he is to do it. One might speculate that Tanja was about to utter something like "before he goes to bed" (as Tina did, once, thirteen minutes earlier). Nevertheless, the fact that Tanja deliberately cuts herself short (3) is in accordance with her instruction (Excerpt 9:9) to do the exercise at any time during the day. In contrast, the interpreter not only introduces an explicit focus on bedtime (4) but also reaffirms it, even supplying her own rationale (8).

When someone at the door asks Tanja and Tina respectively to suggest a
date for an appointment and attend to a patient in another room, that interruption paves the way for a lively discussion between Emir, his parents and the
interpreter on how to use the exercise sheet. While both parents attempt to
address Emir's concerns about whether and what to write on the sheet, the
interpreter clearly serves as the main source of authoritative advice until the
therapists are ready to continue the briefing with further instructions on the
home exercise (Excerpt 11).

Excerpt 11 (43.44 – 43.57)

1	Tanja	WENN ER, WENN ER'S VERGESSEN HAT, IST ES OKAY, JA. ES IS NICHT SCHLIMM, =[WENN ER EINMAL VERGISST.]=
		If he, if he has forgotten it, it is okay, alright? It's no problem, =[if he happens to forget.]=
2	I	=[NICHT SCHLIMM, JA.]=
		=[No problem, yes.]=
3	Tanja	DANN SOLL ER HALT NICHTS HINMALEN.
		Then he just doesn't mark anything down.
4	I	(to parents) AKO ZABORAVI, DOBRO, ALI DA GLEDA DA SVAKI DAN UVEČE, NAJBOLJE UVEČE, NE?
		If he forgets it, okay, but he should try every day in the evening, best in the evening, right?
5	Father	MHM.

Rather than provide a rendition for the parents, the interpreter reacts to Tanja's
first utterance (11:1) by giving confirming feedback to her. When the interpreter does address the parents after Tanja's instruction (3), she relays only
the former statement and reaffirms her advice that the exercise be done at
bedtime (4).

When Tanja concludes the briefing by asking if there are any questions,
the father declines whereas the mother asks, via the interpreter, just what the
exercises are for. Given the scope of this incomprehension, Tanja launches
into an explanation of the relationship between breathing and the voice,
squarely addressing the interpreter rather than the parents.

Excerpt 12 (45.45 – 46.46)

1	Tanja	DIE ATMUNG, JA, DIE ATMUNG IST DIE, ÄH, EINE RICHTIGE ÄH BAUCHATMUNG /
		Breathing, yes, breathing is the, uh, correct uh diaphragm breathing /
2	Father	(questioningly to I) PRAVILNO DISANJE?
		Correct breathing?
3	I	PRAVILNO DISANJE.
		Correct breathing.

4	Tanja	IST DIE VORAUSSETZUNG, IST DIE VORAUSSETZUNG FÜR EINE GUTE STIMME, JA, UND ER IST SEHR =[VERKRAMPFT UND VERSPANNT, JA, AUCH WENN ER STEHT.]=

is the prerequisite, is the prerequisite for a good voice, you know, and he is very =[cramped and tense, you know, also when he stands.]=

5	Father	(questioningly) =[GLASNE ŽICE (XXX)

                                   =[*vocal cords (xxx)*

6	I	[XXX] ON STEGNE, PLASI SE.]=

                                (xxx) he tightens up, is afraid.]=

7	Tanja	AUCH WENN ER STEHT / SCHAUN SIE MAL, MAN SIEHT ER STEHT SO UND HAT DIE SCHULTERN IN DIE HÖHE GEZOGEN, JA, ER IST SEHR VERSPANNT.

*Also when he stands / Take a look, you see he stands like **that** and has his shoulders pulled up, right, he is very tense.*

8	Father	JA, NORMALNO, NORMALNO.

Yes, sure, sure.

9	I	ON JE STEGNUT, KO DA SE BOJI. TREBA DA SE OPUSTI (XXX).

He tightens up, as if he were afraid. He has to relax (xxx).

10	Tanja	MAN KANN ES, AUCH WENN MAN'S IHM SAGT, ER SPÜRT DAS NOCH NICHT SO SEHR, UND DESWEGEN MACHEN WIR DIE ATEMÜBUNG, DAS IST EINE ENTSPANNUNGSÜBUNG, UND AUCH GLEICHZEITIG ÄH FÜR DIE STIMME.

One cannot, even though one tells him, he does not yet feel that very well, and therefore we do the breathing exercise, that is a relaxation exercise, and also at the same time uh for the voice.

11	I	ON DA SE OPUSTI, DA PRAVILNO GLAS, MISLIM DA DIŠE PRAVILNO I DA LAKŠE GLAS DODJE, KAD PRIČA, DA NE GALAMI, DISANJE, KAŽE MNOGO STEGNE.

He is supposed to relax, so that the right voice, I mean that he breathes right, so that the voice comes easier, when he talks, that he does not shout, his breathing, she says, he tightens up very much.

12	Mother	(to Emir) JE L' SE BOJIŠ. BOJIŠ SE?

                         Are you frightened? Are you afraid?

13	I	NEMA ŠTA DA SE BOJIŠ. (to Mother) ONI SU SUPER OVDE S NJIM.

You don't need to be afraid.   *They are really great with him here.*

Trying to follow Tanja's explanation in German, the father seeks clarification from the interpreter for individual concepts he believes he has picked up (Excerpt 12:2, 5), which results in a considerable overlap of talk (4-6). Apart from confirming the father's guess at what Tanja is talking about (2-3), the interpreter limits her rendition of Tanja's explanation to an attempt at expressing the meaning of the technical keyword 'tense' (VERSPANNT). By

associating it twice with 'fear' (6, 9) rather than physical posture, the interpreter gives the briefing a final undetected twist. Tanja's effort to clarify the
relationship between posture, relaxation, breathing and voice (1, 4, 10) ends
up rather garbled in the Serbian version (11) and evidently fails to command
the attention of the mother, who had asked the question in the first place.
Following the interpreter's two reduced renditions (6, 9), the mother's concern shifts to her son's fear (12), whereupon the interpreter, who has introduced
that notion, moves to reassure both the boy and his mother (13). As Tanja
brings the briefing to a close, the therapists remain blissfully unaware of
both the preceding exchange about their patient's emotional state and the
mediator's flattering comment on their treatment of the boy.

6. Discussion

The 47-minute therapy and briefing session, documented above on the basis
of excerpts from the full transcript, represents a routine case of mediated
interaction with a patient of non-German-speaking background in a large
hospital in Vienna. From the therapists' point of view, nothing in the encounter was noticed as particularly problematic, either from immediate
recollection or upon subsequent reviewing of the videotape. Nevertheless,
close inspection from a translational perspective yields a number of striking
findings for the intermediary's behaviour in the role of interpreter and her
translational output as well as her impact on the dynamics of the communicative interaction.

6.1 Interpreter role

Since the ten-year-old patient's command of German is found to be all too
limited, the cleaning woman is explicitly assigned the role of interpreter (Excerpt 1:3). Despite the instruction to "always translate right away", the
interpreter often fails to provide a Serbian rendition of German utterances
unless requested to do so (e.g. Excerpt 7:1-3). Apart from numerous gaps
affecting the exchange in the boy's primary language (or some variant of it),
this passive attitude of the interpreter, which is also reflected in her physical
position on the sideline, as it were, of the therapeutic interaction, exacerbates
the indirectness of communication in both the verbal and the nonverbal dimension (i.e. Emir having to turn his head back and forth). In order to ensure
translation for the patient, the therapists need to preface their utterances by
an explicit request (ask him, tell him), which in turn leads the interpreter to
formulate her rendition in indirect speech (the lady asks, she says), as in
Excerpts 2 (7-8), 3 (1-2), 4 (1-2), 5 (3-4), etc.

   In many instances, the cleaner is thus less than actively fulfilling her role
as interpreter. At the same time, however, she is often prepared to go beyond

providing "renditions on request" and makes direct contributions to the communicative content of the interaction. In some instances, the two role orientations become manifest within a single turn, as in Excerpt 3 (2), when the interpreter combines her (indirect) rendition of Tanja's instruction with a reassuring comment of her own. Apart from taking the initiative to calm the boy down (cf. also Excerpt 13:5), the interpreter also assumes responsibility for the boy's answers and actions. In Excerpt 7 (5), she dismisses the boy's negative answer and prevails on him until he says 'yes', and in Excerpt 8 (2) she moves to elicit an answer by suggesting a number of alternatives. In other passages not documented in the excerpts, the interpreter even asks two consecutive follow-up questions before relaying the patient's utterance to the therapist.

The most consequential case of a substantive contribution by the interpreter is her specification that the exercises ought to be done at bedtime. Without any such indication on the part of the therapist in charge of the briefing, or even despite her deliberate move not to link the exercises to a particular time of day (Excerpt 10:3), the interpreter introduces her explicit preference in several of her mediating turns and even supplies her own reasoning and justification (Excerpt 10:4, 8; Excerpt 11:4). Other examples of the interpreter taking charge in a covertly co-therapeutic role include her preemptive explanations in Excerpt 5 (4) and Excerpt 9 (1) and her autonomous move to verify the therapists' impression that their patient had enjoyed the exercise (Excerpt 6:4). However, the interpreter's co-therapeutic attitude, which is never apparent to the therapists, is anything but consistent during the interaction. While her poorly phrased comment in Excerpt 6 (6) ('That was just exercises') may have been intended once again to reassure the boy, the interpreter actually sends the patient a message which strangely belittles the preceding 25 minutes of therapeutic work. Towards the end of the briefing, the interpreter again distances herself from the therapists with her comment on their treatment of the boy (Excerpt 12:13).

6.2 Translational output

As discussed above, the interpreter in many instances steps out of her role as an "honest spokesperson" (Harris 1990:118), either by not rendering utterances of the primary parties or by introducing substantive contributions of her own. In addition to such 'lack of rendition' and 'non-renditions', to use Wadensjö's (1992) terms, the interpreter's renditions as such also exhibit numerous deviations from the ideal of complete and accurate re-expression. Apart from 'reduced renditions', as exemplified in Excerpt 2 (2), some of the paraphrases making up the 'expanded renditions' of key technical terms introduce significant conceptual shifts, e.g. from 'not being tense' to 'breathing slowly' (Excerpt 10:1-2) and from being 'cramped and tense' to 'being afraid'

(Excerpt 12:6). A particularly salient and systematic shift results from the interpreter's dialectal Serbian usage of the pronoun 'when' (Excerpt 9:1, 10). The interpreter's fuzzy rendition, suggesting that the boy 'write down when' rather than 'mark down whether' he has done the exercise, creates considerable confusion about how the home exercise is to be recorded.

Apart from shifts in semantic content, the interpreter's renditions often alter the illocutionary force of the therapists' utterances. In Excerpt 5, several descriptive statements explaining what the patient is to become aware of are tagged with questions designed to elicit an affirmative response (1-2, 3-4, 5-6). Thus, whereas the therapists state *what* they want their patient to feel, the interpreter in addition asks *whether* he can feel it. To the therapist unaware of the interpreter's prompting, the boy's responsiveness understandably seems rather pleasing (8; cf. also Excerpt 9:10). In a similar vein, gently phrased indirect requests by the therapists are invested by the interpreter with considerably more directive force, as evident in Excerpts 2 (8), 3 (2) and 10 (8).

Given the interpreter's undeniable impact on the form as well as the content of the communicative interaction under study, it may well be asked whether she is more of a help or a hindrance in the therapists' professional interaction with their patient and his parents.

6.3 Interactional function

In all fairness, the cleaner-interpreter must be credited with enabling communication between providers and clients in a session lasting three quarters of an hour; without her help, the boy's voice problems could or would not have been attended to in this particular healthcare institution. From the professional point of view of the two speech therapists, the interpreter appears to have done her job well enough, and she is actually 'booked' again for Emir's appointment the following week. From the perspective of both the patient and the providers, then, the interpreting arrangement has fulfilled its purpose. Or has it?

As only a discourse-based translational analysis can bring to light, the interpreter in many ways leaves the clients with both much less and much more than the therapists intended them to understand. The boy's confusion about how to use the exercise sheet, which is cleared up only after a lengthy exchange among all the interacting parties, and the instruction to the parents that the exercise is to be done at bedtime, stand out as clear examples of the interpreter's undesired impact on the effectiveness of communication. Similarly, the fact that at the very end of the briefing neither parent is sure about the purpose of the exercise can be traced back to the interpreter's change of focus in expressing the patient's key physical symptom.

Following a review of the interaction on the basis of the transcript, the therapist in charge (Tanja) found the interpreter's initiatives to reassure, question and advise the client(s) totally unacceptable and was greatly disconcerted by the way in which the interpreter's renditions often blunted the points she had meant to bring across. From her informed professional perspective, the mediated interaction is judged as embarrasingly dysfunctional, even in the absence of an obvious breakdown of communication. With the cleaner-interpreter covertly shaping the content and form of their discourse, the therapists have in fact lost control of their professional (inter)action to such an extent that they can no longer ensure the quality and effectiveness of their work.

7. Conclusion

The mediated therapeutic interaction described and analysed in this authentic case study represents a routine and possibly typical example of current healthcare interpreting practices in Austria. Though unprecedented within its geographic and institutional context, the study corroborates many of the concerns voiced in the literature about the *ad hoc* use of bilingual staff for the function of interpreting. The untrained ('natural') interpreter clearly fails to maintain a consistent focus on her translatorial role and task and introduces significant shifts in the form and substance of communication. Naively unaware of the cleaner-interpreter's ignorance of translatorial standards of practice, the therapists, who are equally untrained as regards the management of non-German-speaking clients with the help of an interpreter, thus venture into an interaction, the professional quality of which they no longer control.

While the findings presented above are hardly controversial in highlighting the various inadequacies in the performance of a 'natural' interpreter, more far-reaching conclusions must be drawn for the mediated encounter as a whole. From a functional perspective, the case reported here ultimately bears not on the cleaner's lack of translation competence but on the failure of the healthcare institution and its staff to appreciate the complexities of mediated communication across cultures. It would be a great compliment to the emerging discipline of interpreting studies if case studies such as this one could help healthcare managers and providers recognize and remedy a serious gap in their quality assurance for professional services.

FRANZ PÖCHHACKER & MIRA KADRIC

Universität Wien, Institut für Übersetzen und Dolmetschen, Gymnasium-straße 50, A-1190 Wien, Austria. franz.poechhacker@univie.ac.at, miroslavka.kadric@univie.ac.at

References

Burley, Patrizia (1990) 'Community Interpreting in Australia', in D. Bowen and M. Bowen (eds) *Interpreting – Yesterday, Today, and Tomorrow* (ATA Scholarly Monograph Series IV), Binghamton NY: SUNY, 146-53.

Ehlich, Konrad and Jochen Rehbein (1976) 'Halbinterpretative Arbeitstranskriptionen (HIAT)', *Linguistische Berichte* 45: 21-45.

Harris, Brian (1990) 'Norms in Interpretation', *Target* 2(1): 115-19.

Harris, Brian and Bianca Sherwood (1978) 'Translating as an Innate Skill', in D. Gerver and H. W. Sinaiko (eds) *Language Interpretation and Communication* (NATO Conference Series III – 6), New York: Plenum, 155-70.

Pöchhacker, Franz (1997) *Kommunikation mit Nichtdeutschsprachigen in Wiener Gesundheits- und Sozialeinrichtungen* (Dokumentation 12/2), Wien: MA 15/ Dezernat für Gesundheitsplanung.

Scouller, Alastair M. (1988) 'The Training of Community Interpreters', in C. Picken (ed) *ITI Conference 2. Translators and Interpreters Mean Business*, London: Aslib, 66-70.

Wadensjö, Cecilia (1992) *Interpreting as Interaction. On dialogue Interpreting in Immigration Hearings and Medical Encounters*, Linköping: Linköping University, Department of Communication Studies.

The Translator. Volume 5, Number 2 (1999), 179-200   ISBN 1-900650-21-5

The Tenor of Consultant Physicians
Implications for Medical Interpreting

HELEN TEBBLE
Deakin University, Australia

Abstract. *Medical interpreting, like many other kinds of community interpreting, needs to have conveyed not only the content of
what speakers say but the way they say it. This paper outlines a
model, derived from empirical research, of the discourse structure
of the interpreted medical consultation. The generic structure of
interpreted physicians' consultations with non-English speaking
patients shows eleven stages, the climax being the exposition. It is
at this stage that the physician announces his/her findings of the
diagnoses and sets up a plan of action for the patient. The extent
to which the patient complies with the plan of action (e.g. change
of medication) does not depend just on the fact that an interpreter
interpreted the consultation, but substantially on the rapport and
impact that the physician had on the patient. So conveying accurately the interpersonal elements of what the physician and patient
say to each other is crucial. A theoretical framework for analyzing
the interpersonal metafunction is described and components of this
framework are applied to two case studies of the exposition, one
in nephrology and the other in hypertension. Enhancing medical
interpreters' understanding of how to 'read' the tenor of a physician's consulting style needs a theoretical basis. This paper offers
a contribution to the development of such a theory.*

Millions of immigrants, guest workers, refugees, tourists and indigenous people throughout the world, like the rest of us from time to time need medical
attention and perhaps even hospitalization. There are well over 31 million
such people in the USA alone (Hornberger *et al.* 1996). When patients and
their health care professionals do not speak the same language then both are
at a severe disadvantage. In such circumstances a medical interpreter is needed.
In several states of Australia non-English speaking immigrants are entitled
to an Interpreter Card. This card enables them to have access to a qualified
and accredited interpreter if they use the services provided by the state, for
example when attending a public hospital. State government departments
fund these interpreter services. Patients can of course also hire and pay for
the services of an interpreter but this seems not to be a common practice. If
patients and medical personnel do not use the services of trained, qualified

and accredited interpreters they run the risk of not having complete, accurate and confidential interpreting.

Medical interpreting is practised in many parts of the world with varying degrees of success depending on the competency of the interpreter, the interpreter's ethics, and the ability of the health care professional to make efficient use of the interpreter's services. Medical interpreters work in all branches of medicine, including emergency medicine, obstetrics, psychiatry and palliative care, and in a variety of locations such as hospital wards and clinics, consulting rooms, patients' homes and community health centres. They also interpret for patients and their ancillary health care workers such as nurses, physiotherapists and speech pathologists. Medical interpreters can expect to work in all areas of health care. The *practice* of medical interpreting is extensive; this is not to deny that even greater use could be made of the services of medical interpreters to improve the delivery of health care. However the *theory* of dialogue interpreting and medical interpreting in particular is significantly underdeveloped. This paper provides an overview of an emerging theory of medical interpreting being developed at the Centre for Research and Development in Interpreting and Translating at Deakin University, Melbourne, Australia.

The type of medical interpreting that is discussed here is the interpreting of the consultation between the English-speaking specialist or consultant physician and his or her non-English-speaking patient. The dialogue is normally conducted face-to-face between two participants who do not speak the same language well enough to be understood and need the presence of a third person, the medical interpreter. Given that the medical consultation is a type of discourse, that it is between two people and mediated by a third person, that the interpreter must listen, comprehend and relay what is said in the two languages, and that what is said occurs in a complex sociocultural context, it is proposed that the theory consist of four components:

1. a discourse component (discourse model)
2. an interpersonal component (interpersonal metafunction)
3. a psycholinguistic and neurolinguistic component
4. a sociocultural component.

The work to date addresses the first two components.

The development of a theory of medical interpreting can be regarded as an activity in applied linguistics, defined here as the application of insights from linguistics and other relevant disciplines to the solving of language-in-communication problems. The problem here is the need for an empirical description of the practice of medical interpreting. By understanding such a description, interpreters could then reflect on and account for their professional performance in an informed way; and initial and professional development courses could be devised for the training and education of medical interpreters (Tebble 1996). The work to date has taken an eclectic approach within linguistics but draws particularly upon systemic functional linguistics, which is a comprehensive theory of language in use. Other relevant disciplines whose insights have been used in the work described here include the cognate areas of discourse analysis, pragmatics, sociolinguistics, conversation analysis and ethnomethodology, social psychology and communication studies.

1. Discourse component

The discourse component provides the basis for the emerging theory of medical interpreting because descriptions of the various genres of medical interpreting will reveal the contexts and structures of these particular types of speech events. The generic structure of the various types of interpreted medical practices will provide the discourse models for medical interpreting. The discourse model discussed here is that of the interpreted specialist or consultant physician's consultation. (A different genre, the interpreted family meeting in palliative care, is currently being investigated as an extension of the research reported here).

1. The context

Since all discourses derive from particular social contexts, the configuration of the context of the genre of interpreted medical consultations can be identified. Hasan's (Halliday and Hasan 1985) approach to demonstrating the relationship of a discourse to its context is to delineate the three contextual variables of Field (subject matter), Tenor (roles and relationships of participants), and Mode (the role that language plays in constituting the event). The contextual configuration of an interpreted medical consultation involves the delineation of the Field, Tenor and Mode as shown in Figure 1. The medical consultation is an example of the discourse between a professional and a lay person. In this case the patient seeks the expert advice of a specialist or consultant physician, usually as a result of referral from another medical practitioner. Because the specialist and the patient do not share a common language they communicate via a medical interpreter. The patient may or may not know the nature of the problem. The role of the doctor is socially defined and bound by professional ethics. As the expert, he or she has the superordinate role while the patient who is seeking treatment has a subordinate role, not necessarily because of their social standing but because of the inequality of knowledge on how to treat the patient's medical condition. The relationship between the physician and the patient is thus hierarchical. The medical interpreter has an independent role since he or she is not an advocate for the patient but a professional interpreter who relays what is said by the physician to the patient and vice versa. The social distance between all participants is maximal compared to the minimal social distance of people who are intimate. The interpreted consultation is constituted by the use of two languages: that of the physician, usually the dominant language of the society, and the community language of the patient. The discourse is created through the talk of all three participants, which includes the spoken words, the paralinguistic features of their speech and their non-verbal communication. Written communication may also form part of the consultation as the physician for example records notes, writes a prescription, reads the label on a bottle of tablets and any other material such as the patient's medical history or laboratory reports. The channels of communication are therefore phonic and graphic (and signed for patients who communicate via sign language). The contextual configuration provides a summary of the variables which relate the discourse to the context.

> **FIELD**   Presenting with a problem that may need to be defined
>   and for which a solution is required.
> **TENOR**   *Role Relationship* – Hierarchical:
>   Professional: Superordinate
>   Client/Patient: Subordinate
>   Interpreter: Independent
>   *Social Distance* – Maximal
> **MODE**   Constituted by use of 2 languages.
>   Process of creating the discourse via:
>   • spoken medium
>   • written medium
>   • non-verbal communication
>   Channels of communication:
>   • phonic
>   • graphic
>   • signed

Figure 1. Contextual configuration of interpreted medical consultation

1.2 The data

The preliminary work for the discourse model entailed analyses of transcriptions of video-recorded, role-played medical consultations in the interpreting classes at Deakin University, observations of English-only medical and paramedical consultations, informal interviews with medical practitioners about the structure of their consultations, and a review of literature on doctor-patient communication. The main work for the model is drawn from empirical research into authentic interpreted medical consultations.

For the main research project, 13 authentic interpreted consultations, each of about 50 minutes' duration, were video-recorded using three synchronized cameras, one for the patient, one for the consultant or specialist physician, and one for the interpreter for each consultation. For each consultation the three separate videotapes were post-produced into one videotape that displayed the three pictures simultaneously, with time coding in microseconds. The language of the physicians was English. The patients spoke one of the following community languages: Greek, Italian, Serbian, Spanish, Cantonese, Mandarin and Vietnamese. The interpreters, accredited as NAATI[1] professional interpreters, spoke English and one of the community languages. The subjects were recruited at random. They included 13 patients (12 female and 1 male), 10 physicians (7 male and 3 female), and 10 interpreters (9 female and 1 male). The areas of medicine included oncology, nephrology, neurology, psychiatry, vascular medicine and hypertension. The consultations were transcribed, translated, back-translated and glossed in readiness for analysis. The method of transcription was a modified version of that used for conversation analysis and taken to the levels of the clause and tone unit.

The approach to the analysis of the discourse of these authentic (as distinct from role-played) interpreted medical consultations draws upon earlier work such as Tebble (1991a), which combined the bottom-up approach of Sinclair and Coulthard (1975) and the top-down approach of Hasan (e.g. 1978) to the analysis of discourse. The connection between these two approaches to discourse analysis is at the level of the genre element (Tebble 1991a, 1992). This combined approach provides a comprehensive analysis of the structure of the discourse. Every speech act is identified in every move a speaker makes. These moves are identified in each conversational exchange. One or a sequence of exchanges on one topic is identified as a transaction. One or more transactions on one topic are identified as a genre element, that is, a stage in the consultation. A sequence of genre elements, some obligatory and some elementary, makes up the genre, in this case, the interpreted medical consultation. The structural components can be ranked on a scale with each level incorporating the levels below it. Figure 2 shows the hierarchy of the linguistic structures that constitute the discourse of the professional consultation or interview. The structure of the discourse can be identified by analysing the transcriptions (each typically comprising more than 100 A4 pages) using the micro-analytic bottom-up approach of identifying speech acts, moves, exchanges, transactions and genre elements. The top-down approach can verify the genre elements which identify the stages of the consultation.

From the analysis of the discourse structures of the consultations eleven stages were identified in the interpreted medical consultation (Tebble 1993). They are listed in Figure 3. There are eight obligatory stages; the three optional stages are 'Diagnosing Facts', 'Decision by Client' and 'Contract'.

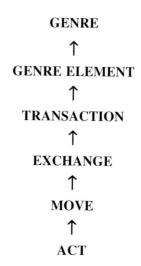

GENRE

↑

GENRE ELEMENT

↑

TRANSACTION

↑

EXCHANGE

↑

MOVE

↑

ACT

Figure 2. Hierarchy of discourse structures constituting the professional consultation or interview

The diagnosis will occur but may not be verbalized by the physician. The client's decision may be made but not verbalized or it may be made in another context. The contract is the stage when the interpreter declares his or her role before the consultation proper gets underway and assures the patient and physician of complete, accurate and impartial interpreting, and that what is said will be kept confidential. The occurrence of this stage will depend on the ethical requirements of the context and whether the interpreter has previously worked for both the physician and patient together, having already made such a contract. Some hospitals for example have interpreters as permanent members of their staff. They would be assumed to abide by the ethics of confidentiality of that hospital and would not necessarily utter the words of the contract. Freelance interpreters would however want to assure their clients, the patient and the physician, of their professional role, especially since not all patients and health care workers know how to make effective use of the services of professional medical interpreters (Tebble 1998). They would normally state the contract.[2] The stages listed in Figure 3 are more numerous than those identified in medical communication textbooks. From the medical educators' perspective the stages of a consultation are typically: 'Greetings or Introduction'; 'History Taking and Physical Examination'; 'Exposition and/or Conclusion'. The genre element 'Stating the Resolution' is equivalent to the 'Exposition' stage of Myerscough and Ford (1996). This obligatory stage of the consultation is now receiving further attention in the development of the theory of medical interpreting because of the importance of the interpersonal aspects of the consultation.

Greetings	=	G
Introductions	=	IN
(Contract)	=	CT
Stating/Eliciting Problem	=	EP
Ascertaining Facts ·	=	AF
(Diagnosing Facts)	=	DF
Stating Resolution/**Exposition**	=	SR/EX
(Decision by Client)	=	CD
Clarifying any Residual Matters	=	RM
Conclusion	=	C
Farewell	=	F

Figure 3. Basic stages of interpreted medical consultations

1.3 The exposition

The exposition is the climax of the consultation. It typically provides the answer to the problem posed in the earlier stage of the consultation – Stating or Eliciting the Problem. The exposition stage itself is problematic in two ways. Firstly, if interpreters do not have a schema in mind such as in Figure 3 they cannot predict what comes next, their energy may have been expended in the previous stages and their attention span diminished by the time this stage is reached. Such failures could result in the interpreter requesting the physician to repeat him or herself and lose the flow of what the physician has to say. This could be particularly irksome to the professional who is giving his or her professional opinion on the matters that brought about the medical consultation. So interpreters need to ensure that they do not experience fatigue at this stage and that they interpret accurately and completely as is expected at all other stages of the consultation. Secondly, the exposition is problematic in medicine. It is the time when the expertise of the physician is displayed through his or her description and explanation of the patient's medical condition. This is the stage when the physician announces his or her findings: announces the diagnosis, the prognosis and plans for treatment, and prescribes medication if appropriate. The information is usually imparted by telling, and checking that what has been told is understood. But this crucial stage is ultimately of little value if there is no patient compliance. Since most of the consultant physician's work is accomplished through talk, studies of doctor/patient compliance would do well to address the text of the talk rather than just the correlation between the medical record of the consultation and the patient's state of health, even if interpreters are used. Bad news can be delivered to patients and their relatives during the exposition. Particular communication skills and strategies are needed for this task. The outcomes of the consultation with all its attendant costs can depend considerably on the nature of the rapport that prevails between doctor and patient. So it is up to the medical interpreter to live up to the interpreters' code of ethics and convey what is said accurately.

Conveying what is said means not just conveying the content of the message but also the way the message is expressed. This means that the medical interpreter needs to relay the interpersonal features of each speaker's turn at talk. The main interpersonal issue concerning the exposition of interpreted medical consultations is how to deliver the findings (diagnosis, prognosis, prescription of medication and plan of treatment) in a way that will reassure the patient and also bring about patient compliance. A discourse analysis of the text of an interpreted medical consultation can reveal not only its linguistic structure, its cohesion and coherence, and the structure of the information as it is relayed, it can also reveal the nature of the interpersonal relationships of the participants. The contextual variable of tenor, which links the discourse and the participants in the interpreted medical consultation, is realized through what is called in systemic functional linguistics the 'interpersonal metafunction' (Eggins and Martin 1997).

2. The interpersonal metafunction

Following Halliday (e.g. Halliday and Hasan 1985), Eggins and Martin note that the interpersonal metafunction "is concerned with organizing the social reality of people we interact with (by making statements, asking questions, giving commands; saying how sure we are; saying how we feel about things)" (Eggins and Martin 1997:238-39). Martin (1998a, 1998b) provides a framework for the analysis of the interpersonal metafunction for any given register. He uses the terms 'power' (or status) to replace Hasan's use of 'role relations' and 'solidarity' (or contact) to replace her use of 'social distance' (as in Figure 1). For Martin (e.g. Martin 1998a, 1998b) power (status) and solidarity (contact) are the social indicators of tenor which have their linguistic realizations in the discourse semantics, lexicogrammar and phonology of the languages being used. Within discourse semantics Martin proposes three systems (see Table 1): negotiation (occurring in the speech function and the exchange), appraisal (such as affect, judgement and appreciation), and involvement (names and lexis that reflect, for example, formality, informality, distance and intimacy). Within the lexicogrammar, grammatical mood and tagging reflect negotiation. Speakers' power is shown in their lexicogrammar by their choice of modal verbs and modal adjuncts, polarity – choice between positive or negative (Halliday 1994), evaluative lexis, intensification, numeration, and logico-semantics. The solidarity of speakers is shown in the lexicogrammar by their choice of person, vocation (naming of people), specialized or technical lexis, slang and taboo lexis (after Martin 1992, 1998a, 1998b). At the phonological level of language, intonation conveys the speech function in the exchange, the loudness, change in pitch and voice quality convey the power of the speaker, while the solidarity of the speakers according to Martin (1998) can be conveyed through accent, whispering, acronyms and secret scripts. The ways in which the physician and patient negotiate their meanings, express their attitudes, judgements and appreciation, and build up a level of solidarity are all linguistic strategies that medical interpreters need to identify and relay if they are to meet the ethic of relaying what is said by each participant in the consultation.

REGISTER	DISCOURSE SEMANTICS	LEXICOGRAMMAR	PHONOLOGY
TENOR	**NEGOTIATION** • speech function • exchange **APPRAISAL**	• mood • tagging	• intonation
power (status)	• engagement • affect • judgement • appreciation • graduation	• 'evaluative'lexis • modal verbs • polarity • pre/numeration • intensification • repetition • logico-semantics	• loudness • pitch movement • voice quality
solidarity (contact)	**INVOLVEMENT** • naming • technicality • swearing	• vocation/names • technical lexis • specialized lexis • slang • taboo lexis	• 'accent' • whisper • acronyms • secret scripts

Table 1. Features of the interpersonal metafunction
(after Martin 1998a, 1998b)

The interpersonal metafunction permeates the total medical consultation (Tebble 1996) as both physician and patient move through the stages outlined in Figure 3. Typically the trust, respect and empathy that is built up during these stages needs to be maintained during the exposition stage so that what is advised, prescribed and decided upon is actually followed through by the patient. The issues for the physician in the exposition concern ways of delivering the findings (diagnosis, prognosis, prescribing medication and plan for treatment) in a way that will reassure the patient and bring about patient compliance. The interpersonal metafunction in the language of the physicians in the exposition stage of two interpreted medical consultations will now be discussed to show two different interpersonal styles. The medical interpreter needs to convey both what was said and the way it was said, remaining as close as possible to the physician's style.

3. The exposition in a nephrology consultation

The participants in this consultation are a Greek-speaking female patient in her sixties who had a serious kidney problem, a male consultant physician in nephrology, and a female interpreter who spoke Greek and English. The interpreter had interpreted for the the patient and consultant on previous occasions. This consultation was a review of the patient's condition in a programme of on-going treatment.

The genre element of the exposition in this nephrology consultation comprises two transactions. The first transaction has nine conversational exchanges. They are used by the physician to announce his findings, prescribe medication, propose a change to the dialysis treatment, express his medical opinion, and by the patient to seek clarification about procedures. The second transaction has eight conversational exchanges which are used by the physician to summarize, suggest a plan of action and give a medical opinion, and by the patient to reflect on her plight.

The status of the physician (D) is reflected in his professional role of having to announce his findings from his interpretations of the patient's medical history and his medical examination of the patient. The interpreter (I) relays these as follows:

D: there's + I suppose three things we have to fix up
I: έχει τρία πράγματα που θα πρέπει λέει να διορθώσουμε
      There are three things he says we must correct.
D: first of all we have to **wait** +
I: πρώτ' απ' όλα πρέπει να περιμένουμε
      First of all we must wait
D: to see what turns up + on the + tests about your tummy
I: τις αναλύσεις που έχουμε κάνει σχετικά με την κοιλιά σας να δούμε
     λέει το τι θα... λάβουμε
      the tests that we have done in relation to your tummy
      he says we see what will we get
D: we'll have to see the re**sults** of the fluid
     and the re**sults** of the **ul**trasound
I: θα πρέπει να δούμε τ' αποτελέσματα του υγρού που πήραμε
      We will have to see the results of the fluid that we took and the ultrasound

D: at this stage it's **har**:d to say
     I think it's probably more related to the old infection
I: τώρα αυτή τη στιγμή είναι πολύ δύσκολο λέει να πούμε κάτι αλλά
     εγώ νομίζω ότι μπορεί να έχει σχέση με τη μόλυνση την παλια
     Now at this moment he says it is very difficult to say something
     But I think that it may be related to the old infection   (N/E7:83-84)

. . .

D: the **oth**er thing is the **i**tch
I: το άλλο είναὶ η φ**ᾶ**γούρᾳ
     *The other is the **itch***
D: and we'll try this **dox**epin tablet first of all
I: και θα δοκιμάσουμε πρώτ' απ' όλα τα ντόξεφεν τα χάπια
     And we will try first of all the Doxepin the pills (N/E7: 84)

. . .

D: and the **oth**er thing in terms of the + **weigh**t or the amount of **flui**d they
     take off on the dialysis
     I'll **talk** to the dialysis girls about aiming a little bit lower
I: Και το άλλο είναι λέει η ποσότιτα του υγρού που θα πάρουνε στη
     διάλυση
     And the other is he says the amount that we take in the dialysis
I: θα μιλήσω εγώ λέει με τις κοπέλλες
     και ούτως ώστε λέει να πάρουνε λιγότερο υγρό
     he says he will speak to the girls
     so that they get less fluid   (N/E7:86)

The **status** of the consultant is maintained by there not being reciprocal use
of first names. He addresses the patient and interpreter by their first names
but they do not reciprocate. The patient does not use his name at all and the
interpreter addresses him once as 'you'. The status of the participants is unequal in Martin's (1992) terms because the relationships are hierarchical, at
least between the physician and the patient. The physician has the highest
status ascribed by his given social authority as a medical consultant; he is the
expert being consulted by the layperson, the patient. The patient has the subordinate role and the lowest status but has equal speaking rights, initiating as
many exchanges as the physician. The interpreter is independent of both the
doctor and the patient. The physician is in charge of the consultation and
uses framing moves as discourse management markers, for example *OK, all
right* and *well* to control the direction of the topics.

   The **contact** of the participants according to Martin's (1992) system of
contact is 'involved', 'at work' and occurs more 'regularly' than 'occasionally'. All three participants know each other to some extent in that the patient
is under the care of this consultant physician, the interpreter has interpreted
for them together on previous occasions, and the interpreter has interpreted
for the doctor on other occasions. The social distance is formal but friendly.

As noted, the doctor is on first name terms with the patient and the interpreter but this is not reciprocal.

In terms of **involvement**, and in particular **naming**, the appropriate way to use the services of a professional interpreter is to talk directly to one's interlocutor and not the interpreter. However, the physician does not consistently do this. He addresses the patient by her first name at the start of the exposition as he does at the start of the consultation, and he addresses her three times as *you*. But when he has something negative to report he distances himself from the patient by switching to the third person pronouns *she* and *her* and speaks to the interpreter instead of the patient. For example:

D: [1a]   she has + too much fluid   (N/E26)
    [1b]   she's lost some **bod**y weight   (N/E29)
    [1c]   she'll start getting short of breath again   (N/E41)
    [1d]   we **can't** + **do** a lot to treat her   (N/E59v)

It is then up to the interpreter to convey the 'bad' news in Greek as shown below:

I: [2a]   νομίζω έχετε πολύ+πολλά υγρά
           I think now you have much, a lot of fluid   (N,E/G7:87)
    [2b]   χάσατε βάρος από το σώμα σας
           you lost body weight   (N,E/G7:88)
    [2c]   θ' αρχίσετε πάλι να αισθάνεστε δυσκολίες με την αναπνοή
           σας
           you will start again to feel difficulties with your breathing
           (N,E/G7:89)
    [2d]   αυτό σημαίνει ότι δεν υπάρχει τίποτα που να μπορέσουμε
           να κάνουμε για να το βοηθήσουμε
           this means that there isn't anything that we can do to help it
           (N,E/G7:92)

The switch of pronouns and interlocutor by the physician allows him to keep his social distance and limits his involvement with the patient. The interpreter is obliged by the use of Greek syntax to address the patient and so uses the polite or formal morpheme ('you') in [2a], [2b] and [2c]. In [2d] the interpreter depersonalizes the physician's utterance by omitting reference to both the institutional *we* and the patient as *her/you*. When referring to himself the physician uses both first person pronouns *I* (7 times) and *we* (13 times). Most occurrences of *we* are inclusive, incorporating the physician, the patient and all of the various medical and nursing staff who participate in the on-going care of the patient.

The patient had previously experienced a very severe reaction to drugs associated with surgery, so when prescribing new medication this physician uses modulation and modalization to downtone any potential perceived threat to her well being:

D: it's a very it's a very low **dose** of the doxepin ...
    and it shouldn't have any other side effects at all   (N/E15)

The modulated repetition of the intensifier *very* to indicate that the dosage of the (then) new medication being prescribed is not high, together with the negated modal verb *shouldn't* and the emphatic expression *any ... at all* (meaning 'none') provide several ways of reassuring the patient about the medication. The back-translation from the Greek shows that no threat of further complications is conveyed, but whereas the physician refers neither to himself nor the patient, the interpreter expresses reassurance through the pronoun system (*naming*).

I: είναι λέει πολύ μικρή δόση αυτή που σας δίνουμε
    γι' αυτό λέει δεν περιμένω να σας
    επηρεάσει να σας κάνει καμμία αντίδραση

    it is a very small dose
    the one we are giving you, he says
    *that's why I do **not** expect that it will affect you*
    that it will give you a reaction   (N,E/G7:85)

The restart by the physician is not relayed but the intensifier *very* and the sense that it is a low ('small') dosage are conveyed. The name of the drug is substituted by a less specific referent, "the one we are giving you". The interpreter uses the equivalents of the institutional pronoun *we* and the singular first person pronoun *I*, and addresses the patient directly as *you*, attributing all this to the physician, "he says". In doing so the interpreter conveys the physician's reassurance by personalizing it. She removes the technical aspect of the physician's language: the name of the drug, the use of 'small' instead of 'low' for the dosage, and 'reaction' for 'side effects'. She thus conveys a stronger sense of solidarity than is arguably intended by the physician. This is nevertheless a means of helping convey a non-threatening message which the physician may be assumed to have intended.

In terms of **appraisal**, although the physician distances himself in the way he expresses negative information, he nevertheless does express what Halliday (1978:33) calls "a degree of emotional charge" or what Martin (1992:536) identifies as surge in the linguistic system of *affect*. His empathy towards the patient is expressed mainly through his auditor back-channel responses: *mm, yeah* and *sure* as the patient tells of her very serious state of health. His reassurance is expressed through various linguistic devices. One is *evaluation*; for example, rather than worry about the effects of the next type of treatment, the patient says that she would wait until she has the results of her tests. The physician replies, "I think that's wise, yes" (N/E51ii) and the interpreter conveys the reply as: νᾳι είνᾳι λογικό ᾳυτό (N/E52I). The back-translation from the Greek, "yes, it is logical" (N,E52ii) shows that the physician's judgement is conveyed but the interpersonal nuance of the evaluative lexis *wise* in English is lost. Although in this context *wise* and *logical* may be thought of as synonymous, the physician's strong regard for the patient's wise decision is downtoned to a depersonalized declaration of it being 'logical'.

In overall terms, the status of the physician is reflected through his management of the exposition, in his control of the topic flow, his use of discourse management markers, the announcement of his findings while the patient listens, the authority of his expressed opinion, "I think …", and his evaluation of the patient's perspective. The extent of solidarity between the physician and the patient is variable. This is shown particularly by the changeable use of pronouns for vocation/naming. The switch from the second to the third person singular pronoun (*you* to *she* and *her*) and the variable use of the first person plural pronoun *we* enables the physician to distance himself from the patient when delivering bad news and when distinguishing institutional roles from the patient. His use of technical terms is minimal but the patient seeks clarification of his colloquial expression, "I'll **talk** to the dialysis girls about aiming a little bit lower" (N/E21ii-22). There is however a certain amount of rapport conveyed by the physician through his voice quality when expressing auditor back-channel responses. He also downtones the potential perceived threat of the prescription of new medication by his repetition of an intensifier, modal verbs and an expression of reassurance.

It is difficult for the interpreter to interpret the physician's sympathetic auditor back-channel responses at the same time as relaying what the patient is saying to the physician. Nevertheless, finding the equivalent interpersonal expressions of the professional role as shown by markers of status, the discourse semantic, lexicogrammatical and phonological features is the responsibility of the medical interpreter who must convey the power, involvement and emotive states of the participants as they express them.

4. The exposition in a consultation for hypertension

The participants in the second consultation are a Serbian-speaking male patient in his seventies who knew some English and who was referred to the consultant because of his high blood pressure, a male consultant physician in vascular medicine and hypertension, and a female interpreter who spoke Serbian and English. This was the patient's first visit to this consultant. The patient and interpreter had not met previously but the physician and interpreter had worked together once before.

The genre element of the exposition in this consultation on hypertension comprises two transactions. The first transaction has six conversational exchanges. They are used to announce and reiterate the physician's findings, enable the patient to seek clarification and provide additional information about his medication, justify the recommended procedures, and provide reassurance to the patient. The second transaction has eight conversational exchanges. They are used by the physician to announce the precise tests he will order, provide information on procedures to be followed, comment on the patient's understanding, and invite the patient to ask questions.

The first part of the exposition serves an informing function as the physician announces his findings, namely that the patient's blood pressure is too high and that its cause needs investigating.

D: well Mr X
      hhh th the **find**ings er are con**firm**ed
      that your blood pressure is **high** at the moment
      I think the levels are + are somewhat **high**er
      than we'd **like**
      we need to work towards getting it down (VS/E38)

I: gospodine X
      u:m preged je potvrdio
      da **I**mate malo **pov**isen krvni pritisak
      i trebali smo nesto da nego
      sto bi triebalo da bude (trebali) smo da porazgovaramo o tome
      Mr X
      er the examination confirmed
      (draws breath) that you have a little raised blood pressure
      and we should [do] something
      then it should be
      we should talk about it   (S/EH3 EXP1)

  . . .

D: neverthe **nev**ertheless er at least er ++ er
      two doctors now (have) found your blood pressure
      + to be **high**er than we'd **like**
      and therefore I think we need to do some investigations
      find out if there is a **cause** for this blood pressure   (VS/E38-9)

I: (vec su) sad dva lekara sada vam pronasla
      da imate malo poviseni er krvni pritisak
      i i valjalo bi nesto ovaj preduzeti u vezi toga
      da vidimo + da li postoji neki uzrok tome
      i kako to moglo da sa leci
      already they have
      now two doctors have found
      now you have a little raised er blood pressure
      and something should be that is

(draws breath) undertaken in regards to that to see +
whether there is some reason for that
and how it can be treated   (S/EH3 EXP5)

The physician announces to the patient that his blood pressure is high, stressing *high*, noting that the levels are "somewhat **high**er than we'd **like**", and he reiterates this. In terms of appraisal the physician's judgement is categorical: the patient's high blood pressure needs to be reduced. The physician's choice of the graded quantifier *somewhat* does not specify how high the patient's blood pressure is, but it indicates that the blood pressure is to some extent above acceptable levels.

The interpreter's significant understatement, "a little **rais**ed blood pressure" (transliterated as "malo **po**visen krvni pritisak", using only the stressed adjective *povisen*, 'raised') downtones the seriousness of the patient's condition. That the patient's "blood pressure is **high**, … somewhat **high**er" even than two doctors believe is appropriate or would like for the patient, is omitted from the interpretation. The interpreter makes the content of the physician's message less threatening by diminishing its impact. In Martin's (1998a) terms of appraisal, the interpreter 'softens the focus'. After querying whether the patient felt anxious, the physician reiterates his findings (see S/EH3 EXP4). The back-translation of the interpreter's version of this restatement by the physician shows that the interpreter still understates the seriousness of the patient's high blood pressure by referring to it as "a little raised er blood pressure" (S/E3 EXP4-5).

The physician wants to do some investigations to find out if there is "a **cause** for this blood pressure". The back-translation of the interpreter's utterance shows an addition to what the physician said, namely "and how it can be treated" (S/E EXP5). It would generally be assumed that when the physician found the cause for the high blood pressure he would find a way to treat it, but this is not what he says here. The addition "and how it can be treated" shows that the interpreter adds to the content and tenor of the physician.

During the exposition the interpreter is consistent in playing down the main topic of the consultation, the patient's high blood pressure, by omitting reference to it, even though the physician does mention it. The interpreter implies that the patient has problems with hormones although the physician only suggests that there could be hormone excess causing the high blood pressure.

D: (draws breath) well
     before we adjust your therapy e- any any more
     I would like to do some investigation to see
     if perhaps there is er some underlying **kid**ney **prob**lem
     or some hormone excess that is **caus**ing your blood pressure (S/EH3EXP6)

I: pre nego sto nastavimo er
     pre nego sto er prepisimo er neku terapiju il' neko lecenje
     ja bih hteo da + da malo dalje **ispi**tamo da vidimo koji je to problem
     mozda imate (problema) sa **hor**monima
     before we continue er that is
     before we er prescribe er some therapy or treatment
     I would like to + examine further to see what the problem it is
     perhaps you have problems with hormones   (S/EH3EXP6-7)

There is an additional occasion where the interpreter avoids transmitting to the patient medical information that has a bearing on the seriousness of his medical condition. This concerns the omission of the reason for the physician wanting the patient to collect urine over a twenty-four hour period, "to measure the stress hormones" (S/EH3 EXP12). The back-translation of the interpreter's version in Serbian is "for examination for analysis of the urine" (S/EH3 EXP14). The non-specification by the interpreter of the reason for the analysis does not make clear to the patient the reasons for the mention of hormones.

The interpreter not only downtones content that can have a negative potential for the patient but also goes beyond what the physician actually says. For example:

D: I should check with Dr Y first and
     (draws breath) then then we could organize those tests at a later
     time (S/EH3EXP15)
I: ja cu prvo da proverim sa Doctorcom Y
     i ako sve bude u rede nema problema
     um um I would check first with Dr Y
     and if everything is alright
     no problems   (S/EH3EXP15)

In the physician's opinion the tests could be delayed. The physician does not declare at all that there are "no problems".

Although there is some careful transfer into Serbian of what the physician says, the interpreter adopts an attitude that downplays the seriousness of the patient's high blood pressure. It is as though the interpreter accommodates the physician's sense of solidarity and contact but mismatches them to the transmission of important medical information (the content), instead of the physician's attitude to the patient (the tenor).

Applied to the language of the exposition, Martin's features of the interpersonal metafunction (Martin 1998a, 1998b), summarized in Table 1, reveal the nature of the **status** and contact of the participants. The purpose of this consultation was for the patient to obtain a second opinion from the consultant physician. This physician's authority is shown by his taking the initiating move in the exchange structure to announce the findings of the physical examination. His medical authority is also reflected in the status of his opinion, "*I think* the levels are somewhat higher"; "*I think* we need to do some investigations". The physician uses fifteen direct speech acts to express his medical opinion and plan of action for the patient, for example, (apart from "I think"), "I'm going to order er er a kidney **scan test**" (S/EH3 EXP10). They are all conveyed by the interpreter except when the physician and interpreter on one occasion speak simultaneously and on the three occasions noted earlier when the interpreter downtones the physician's findings.

The physician's judgement is sought and given. He uses modulation to temper the announcement of his findings. His use (twice) of the modal verb of necessity *need*, namely "*need* to work towards getting it down" and "*need* to do some investigations", reinforces the medical finding – that something must be done to reduce the patient's high blood pressure. The euphemistic quality of the physician's repeated expression "somewhat higher than we'd like", expressed in the contracted form of the modal verb *would*, the positive lexical verb *like*, and the non-specific graded quantifier *somewhat* is not conveyed, as can be seen in the back-translation.

Although the findings are conveyed via the declarative mood, the physician wants to be sure that he is understood by the patient and switches to the interrogative mood to ask the patient if he has any questions or wants further information:

D: do you have any + **quest**ions
      you wanted to ask me
      or anything that I can ex**plain** to you (VS/E41)

Overall, this consultant physician's interpersonal style is more that of solidarity than a display of authority.

In terms of **contact**, the solidarity or degree of involvement by the participants with each other reflects a professional consultation that has maximal distance (see Figure 1), yet the physician attempts to establish rapport through the use of pronouns and a specific form of address. The exposition starts with the physician addressing the patient by name, which is typical of this genre. At the start of the consultation the interpreter introduces the patient to the physician and the physician introduces himself and the interpreter to ensure that the patient understands their respective roles. During the history-taking stage the physician addresses the patient as *Sir*, showing a significant attitude of deference towards him.

The use of the passive enables the physician to distance himself from being the one who discovered the bad news, "the **find**ings are confirmed" (S/EH3 EXP1). He continues to keep his distance from being the discoverer of the bad news by referring to himself in the collective expression "**two** doctors" (S/EH3 EXP4).

The first person pronoun *I* is used in the expression of the medical opinion. The institutional pronoun *we* is inclusive of the medical personnel and the patient. The first person singular pronoun *I* is also used by the physician to announce the procedures, for example:

D: I'll be contacting Dr Y (S/EH3 EXP12)
   I'm going to order er er a kidney **scan test** (S/EH3 EXP10)

When directly addressing the patient, the physician uses *you* and *your*. For example:

D: do you feel bit anxious   (S/EH3 EXP3)

Although the professional-lay role relationship between the doctor and the patient is hierarchical, the physician in other stages of the consultation shows deference to the patient by calling him *Sir*, acknowledging his age, his educational background and his youthful appearance.

Features of **affect** are significant in this physician's interpersonal style. Besides using euphemisms to downtone 'bad news', hesitation and repetition are characteristic of his interpersonal style. These have the effect of expressing sympathy and are not an aggravating type of repetition. There are five repetitions of words which are not self-corrections and thirteen occurrences of hesitations (*er, um, erm*). None of this repetition is interpreted. The physician also uses a formal expression of reassurance:

D: I can reassure you that + the heart and your lungs are fine
   that there is **no** er immediate **dang**er
   it's something that just needs attention (S/EH3 EXP7-9)

The sense of necessity rather than obligation, "needs attention", is less threatening and the modulation of "just" downtones any threat.

Even though the tenor of this consultant physician's style is friendly, he fulfills his role as a consultant physician by giving a second opinion, that the patient has high blood pressure. The tenor of the interpreter in the exposition however is to downtone even further the physician's message, especially when there is a serious matter about the patient's health to be conveyed to the patient.

5. Conclusion

This brief analysis of parts of the exposition of two interpreted medical consultations hints at the importance of conveying the style of the medical practitioner if the ethical requirement of conveying what is said is to be met. Understanding the discourse structure of medical consultations, knowing the types of medical conditions and their forms of treatment, and understanding the nature of the role relationships in these contexts for effecting patient compliance are all part of what the medical interpreter needs to know.

By identifying some of the discourse semantic, lexicogrammatical and phonological features of the tenor of consultant physicians' consultations, interpreters will attend not only to conveying the content of the message – particularly during the exposition stage of the consultation – but also the interpersonal aspects of what is said. When this happens the physician and patient will understand each other and the patient will be clear about what to do with the information being conveyed. Recent insights from work in systemic functional linguistics can be applied to the analysis of doctor-patient communication via the interpreter to enable trainee interpreters and practising medical interpreters to understand how better to relay what their clients say.

HELEN TEBBLE
School of Literary and Communication Studies, Deakin University, 221 Burwood Highway, Burwood, Victoria, Australia. htebble@deakin.edu.au

Notes & Acknowledgements

I acknowledge with sincere gratitude the patients, physicians and interpreters for their graciousness and generosity in allowing the video recording and analyses of their consultations, and the nursing staff for their support at the Monash Medical Centre. The work of four independent English/Serbian and English/Greek translators made the analyses possible. I also acknowledge Deakin University for the award of several research grants to undertake this project.

1. NAATI – National Accreditation Authority for Translators and Interpreters.
2. The Code of Practice of the Australian Institute of Interpreters and Translators Inc. (AUSIT) states that "Interpreters and translators shall explain their role to those unaccustomed to working with them." (AUSIT, 1996, *Code of Ethics for Interpreters and Translators*, Section 1: Professional Conduct, sub-section a) Standards of Conduct and Decorum, paragraph ii). This Code of Ethics was developed by the Australian Institute of Interpreters and Translators in consultation with the National Accreditation Authority for Translators and Interpreters in Australia.

References

Baker, G. (1998) 'Constructing Solidarity in the Educational Consultant-teacher Exchange'. Paper presented at the 10th Euro-International Systemic Functional Workshop, The University of Liverpool.
Eggins, S. and J. Martin (1997) 'Genres and Registers of Discourse', in T. A. van Dijk (ed) *Discourse as Structure and Process,* Discourse Studies: A Multidisciplinary Introduction, Vol.1, London: Sage.

Gentile, Adolfo, Uldis Ozolins and Mary Vasilakakos (with Leong Ko and Ton-That Quynh-Du) (1996) *Liaison Interpreting: A Handbook*, Melbourne: Melbourne University Press.

Halliday, M. A. K. (1994) *An Introduction to Functional Grammar*, London, Melbourne, Auckland: Edward Arnold, 2nd edition.

------ and R. Hasan (1985) *Language, Context, and Text: Aspects of Language in a Social-semiotic Perspective*, Geelong, Vic.: Deakin University.

Hasan, R. (1977) 'Text in the Systemic Functional Model', in W. U. Dressler (ed) *Current Trends in Textlinguistics*, Berlin: Walter de Gruyter.

Hornberger, J. C. et al. (1996) 'Eliminating Language Barriers for Non-English Speaking Patients', *Medical Care* 34(8): 845-46.

Martin, J. R. (1992) *English Text – System and Structure*, Philadelphia & Amsterdam: John Benjamins.

------ (1998a) 'Communities of Feeling: Positive Discourse Analysis'. Plenary paper presented at the 10th Euro-International Systemic Functional Workshop, The University of Liverpool.

------ (1998b) 'Evaluation: An Australian Stance'. Paper presented at the Australian Systemic Functional Linguistics Association Workshop, University of Sydney.

Myerscough, P. R. and M. Ford (1996) *Talking with Patients*, Oxford: Oxford University Press, 3rd edition.

Ozolins, U. (1998) *Interpreting and Translating in Australia: Current Issues and International Comparisons*, Melbourne: Language Australia.

Simon-Vandenbergen, A. M. (1998) 'Modality and Social Class: The Case of *I think*'. Paper presented at the 10th Euro-International Systemic Functional Workshop, The University of Liverpool.

Sinclair, John McH. and Malcolm Coulthard (1975) *Towards an Analysis of Discourse – The English Used by Teachers and Pupils*, London: Oxford University Press.

Taylor Torsello, Carol, Sandra Galina, Maria Sidiropolou, Christopher Taylor, Helen Tebble and A.R.Vuorikoski (1997) 'Linguistics, Discourse Analysis and Interpretation', in Yves Gambier, Daniel Gile and Christopher Taylor (eds) *Conference Interpreting: Current Trends in Research*, Amsterdam & Philadelphia: John Benjamins.

Tebble, Helen (1991a) *The Systems Analyst's Interview – A Linguistic Study of Spoken Discourse*. Unpublished Ph.D. Thesis, Monash University.

------ (1991b) 'Towards a Theory of Interpreting', in P. Hellander (ed) *Proceedings of the 13th Conference of the Interpreter and Translator Educators' Association of Australia*, Adelaide: South Australian College of Advanced Education.

------ (1992) 'The Genre Element in the Systems Analyst's Interview', *Australian Review of Applied Linguistics* 15(2): 120-36.

------ (1993) 'A Discourse Model for Dialogue Interpreting', in Australian Institute of Interpreters and Translators (AUSIT) *Proceedings of the First Practitioners' Seminar*, Canberra: National Accreditation Authority for Translators and Interpreters.

------ (1996) 'Research into Tenor in Medical Interpreting', *Interpreting Research* (Journal of the Interpreting Research Association of Japan) 6(1): 33-45.

------ (1998) *Medical Interpreting – Improving Communication with Your Patients*, Geelong, Vic.: Deakin University & Language Australia (book and videotape).

The Translator. Volume 5, Number 2 (1999), 201-219   ISBN 1-900650-21-5

Information Loss in Bilingual Medical Interviews through an Untrained Interpreter

JAN CAMBRIDGE
Wirral, Merseyside, UK

Abstract. *This paper presents research based on discourse analysis of seven extempore simulated consultations between practising General Medical Practitioners and non-English speaking volunteer patients, with language-switching provided by educated but professionally untrained native speakers of the foreign language. The research set out to examine how information is lost to both doctor and patient in the language-switching process. The results highlight the importance of appropriate interlocutor roles being occupied by all parties, as well as the dangers inherent in a lack of common ground within the transaction. The language pair used in the data is English-Spanish, but the results are discussed as applicable by extrapolation to any language pair. The findings highlight the risks to all parties of dysfunctional communications across language and culture. Cross-language communication is shown to be complex, and highly trained doctors' skills blunted by malfunctions in language-switching. Information is lost in such malfunctioning encounters, to the detriment of effective medical practice.*

The purpose of this study was to look not simply at medical encounters but in particular at the effects on medical encounters across language and culture of using untrained language switchers. A medical interview is a very specific type of encounter, with constraints of time and many other factors placed upon it. The patient may well present symptoms unrelated to the real problems, and the diagnostic skill of the doctor relies heavily on skilful questioning. Where doctor and patient do not have an adequate command of a shared language, someone must act as a language switcher. This may be an untrained mediator. I use the term 'mediator' to indicate the difference between a trained interpreter and an untrained language switcher, after the work of Knapp and Knapp-Potthoff (1987). I will not address the many reasons for avoiding the use of family members or children in this situation, but will look instead at the use of bilinguals who are unknown to the patient, who appear to the other participants in the encounter to have a good command of both languages, but who have no relevant professional training.

ISSN 1355-6509

1. The type of encounter

Interactions have many governing factors, which determine how they are carried out. They are influenced by goals, by the sex and status of the speakers, the existence or not of common ground between the speakers, the social distance between them, and their role within the conversation.

Cheepen and Monaghan (1990) borrow the terms 'transactional' and 'interactional' from Brown and Yule (1983:1-3). I shall be using Cheepen and Monaghan's definition of the terms, in which there are three principal features of a transaction. The first feature is asymmetry of power. One interlocutor has knowledge or some other commodity in his or her gift, which puts the other in a position of relative powerlessness. Solidarity, unity of interests or sympathies among members of any social group, is a function of power and social distance. In transaction there is asymmetry of power and there is social distance, even though there may be no social distance between the two individuals when they meet in other spheres. Maximum solidarity is the point at which there is minimum social distance and minimum asymmetry of power, as shown in Figure 1.

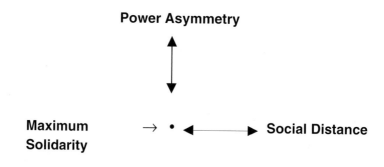

Figure 1   Power, Distance and Solidarity

The second feature, particularly in an institutional context, is an external goal. The goal of the encounter, such as the exchange of goods or services for money, is external to the encounter itself. The third feature is a sequence of topics, determined by the goals; and that one person has control of turn-taking. The person in 'client' role will often guide the conversation by asking for a sequential set of information regarding the goods and culminating with an offer of payment. The doctor-patient transaction, however, is supplier-(i.e. doctor-) led. In other words transactional roles that apply in most settings are changed in the doctor-patient setting. Instead of the service provider (doctor) waiting to be asked for information in an ordered sequence of utterances controlled by the client (patient), the doctor's expert knowledge leads him or her to take charge and control the flow of information. In a medical interview, it is the doctor who knows what the probabilities are, the various permutations of symptoms, possible treatments and likely side effects. The goal, external to the encounter itself, is the enhanced wellbeing of the patient who has requested an appointment. In interpreted medical encounters, the interpreter is "implicitly co-ordinating the conversation as a common activity simply by providing renditions" (Wadensjö 1992:73).

For my purposes, this transaction has the added factor that the patient does not necessarily know the 'rules'. Topic change and turn taking are governed by the doctor. However, there are occasions when the doctor appears to assign power to control both these elements to the patient within certain parameters. For example probing or open questions like "what do you think these symptoms mean?" or "is there anything you would like to ask me?" seem to invite the patient to take control briefly and offer an opinion. The doctor is in fact still in charge of both elements, since it is he or she who decides when this part of the transaction will take place, how long it will last, and what sort of contributions are admissible. A patient from another cultural and linguistic background may not be competent to pick such signals up or confident enough to offer any contribution anyway.

1.1 Face, equity and politeness

When a third party to an encounter is used to perform language-switching functions, potential loss of face becomes an issue if this person perceives him/herself as being personally accountable for the words being uttered by others, or as identified with the ideas expressed by them (Knapp *et al* 1987: 184-85). Brown and Levinson (1987) define positive and negative types of both face and politeness and discuss the severity of Face Threatening Acts (FTAs). Face is defined as the public self-image that everyone wants to preserve for themselves. The term has two related aspects. One is negative face, which is the basic right to freedom of action and freedom from imposition. The second is positive face, which is essentially self-esteem and the positive regard of others. The question of face, and identifying with one or other of the parties, is particularly relevant in a clinical setting, where the danger is that an untrained linguistic mediator may 'filter out' utterances seen as showing the ethnic minority group in a bad light. Western medicine, for example, is distanced from traditional forms of healing in other cultures such as curanderismo, voodoo, or shamanism. If a patient were to refer to having consulted a shaman before visiting the doctor, a mediator who is identifying strongly with his or her home culture and feeling protective of it may not relay this information. Such filtering may protect the bilingual intermediary from the fear of ridicule, but it also deprives the clinician of potentially vital information. Apart from the loss of clues to the patient's perceptions of illness, 'wellness' and healthcare, it is quite possible that a doctor may pursue a diagnostic course or system of treatment while completely unaware that the patient has been, or is still, taking some preparation recommended by the traditional practitioner, and which has a pharmacological effect.

People engaged in talk change their footing within the encounter constantly. That is to say that there is an altered relationship between the interlocutors, in terms of the presentation and reception of utterances (Goffman 1979:5). Wadensjö (1992:118) describes this framework as accounting for "speakers' distribution of responsibility for the spoken words". These shifts are subtle and often paralinguistic, and are designed to preserve equity and face. The maintenance of equity within an encounter demands that speech acts which threaten the hearer's face be mitigated by some threat-reducing strategy. This includes negative politeness and positive politeness. Negative politeness uses strategies such as indirectness, questions and hedges, impersonal and passive constructions, among many others, all designed to acknowledge the hearer's wants. Essentially it is "respect behaviour ... [and] performs the function of minimizing the particular imposition that the FTA unavoidably effects" (Brown and Levinson 1987:134). Positive politeness offers redress in a wider sense, acknowledging the other's wants, asserting reciprocity of wants, offering gifts (of praise, or help, etc.) and is typified by joking or familiar behaviour. Both seek to soften the impact of an FTA such as criticism or complaint.

It is expected of the parties to an encounter not only that each will display self-respect but also that they will respect the other parties' own face. When this is not adhered to, the dominant party is thought to be behaving 'unfeelingly' or 'rudely'. This happens in clinical settings where the clinician fails to attend to patients' views of themselves and, for example, uses euphemism inappropriately, either thoughtlessly or in order to serve his or her own needs in preference to the patient's. Where the glib use of 'baby talk' is a superficial gesture towards establishing solidarity, as in "slip your pants off dear and pop onto the couch", the patient will lose face and feel belittled. Where a doctor feels unequal to delivering bad news, a euphemism can sound unfeeling. 'Cyst' as a substitute for 'tumour' or a phrase such as "try not to mope" following a terminal diagnosis may serve a need and save face for the doctor but does not preserve equity or face for the patient. Brown and Levinson (cited in Clark 1996:295) consider that politeness strategies for maintaining and restoring equity are universal, or almost so, across the world's languages. Nevertheless, the actual practicalities of those strategies are culturally bound and therefore an issue in establishing cross-cultural common ground as the basis for joint action.

1.2 Common ground

Clark (1996:12) defines common ground as "a great mass of knowledge, beliefs, and suppositions [people] believe they share". There is common ground that the cultural group shares: that the earth is round, that 707s are capable of flight, that the potato is edible. This is communal common ground. Personal common ground draws on mutual experience, either perceptual or linguistic. This means that two people can have communal common ground in that they belong to the same theatre club, for instance, but no personal common ground when they meet for the first time. If they then both attend the same performance of a play, they have personal, perceptual common ground. If only one of them sees the show but afterwards describes it to the other, they have linguistic common ground based on reporting an experience. The concept of communal common ground, as opposed to personal common ground, is reflected in the lexicon that identifies a speech community. Words which appear in the lexicon of one group may have another meaning for a different group. In common parlance the word *contagious* is used loosely to mean that an illness is easily caught from other people, making it synonymous in that lexicon with the words *infectious* and *catching*. Doctors, on the other hand, use it to mean that the disease is transferred from one person to another by physical contact. Successful communication between doctor and patient will rely on first establishing which lexicon is being drawn on.

Where no communal common ground exists, patients can be alienated and even disempowered by the inappropriate use of a lexicon which belongs to a particular speech community. What Holmes (1992:276) has described as 'occupational style' is often experienced by the patient as impenetrable jargon and is caused by the doctor's mistaken assumption that there is communal common ground, which causes him or her to use an inappropriate lexicon. Where the hearer is not empowered, as in a medical interview, this can be intimidating. West (1984:112) remarks: "Patients do not like medical jargon, and physicians do not know what constitutes it".

When an interpreter is added to the encounter the situation is even more open to complications. The interpreter may share communal common ground with the doctor, for example an understanding of how such interviews are conducted in this culture; but he or she may not share the medical lexicon, may not understand a medical concept or the purpose behind a particular line or form of questioning. Questions which may pose a threat to face are unlikely to be answered truthfully, and are therefore often prefaced with some kind of hedge or non-judgemental statement like "Would you mind telling me your age?" or "It's common for people to find themselves comfort-eating when they're very stressed. Do you think that might be happening to you?". An interpreter who is unaware of the strategy involved in this may put the questions baldly: "How old are you?", or "Are you overeating?".

1.3 Interlocutor roles

Clark (1996:20) draws on Goffman's (1981) model of interlocutor roles and describes speaking as being composed of three levels of action: meaning, formulating and vocalizing.[1] The Vocalizer utters the sounds which represent a message. This message may have been composed by another person, the 'Formulator', who actually scripted the content of the message. The 'Principal', on the other hand, is the agent who means what is contained in the message. In extempore face-to-face conversation a speaker will usually fill all three roles. A police officer reading a person their rights prior to arrest is vocalizing a message, but will not have formulated what he or she is saying. When a lawyer reads a statement on behalf of a client, the lawyer is vocalizing a message, but it is the client's meaning that is represented and quite possibly a clerk who formulated it.

At the same time there are Listener roles: Attender, Identifier and Respondent. When speaking to the class, a lecturer may ask a question of the listeners. They may or may not be attending to what is said. If they are attending they will be identifying words and phrases, and then perhaps responding. In this framework (Clark 1996:20-21), the Attender pays attention, the Identifier identifies the words and the Respondent understands what is meant by them and answers the question. The two activities which most actively engage the personality and judgmental faculties of an individual are those of Principal and Respondent. It is the Respondent who glosses the content of a message in terms of an individual's own life experience, opinions and beliefs; and the Principal inserts meaning, on the same basis, into a message that the Vocalizer sends. In a monolingual encounter between doctor and patient, one speaks and conveys information and the other responds. The first speaker is therefore able to assess whether or not the message he or she sent was accurately received. If it was not, then they can take immediate corrective action.

This is the basis of the diagnostic skill involved in medical interviewing. Underlying symptoms are rarely offered directly by the patient. A doctor in general practice in England told me that when a patient comes to consult her "the presenting sign may be false, so it must be checked out, which involves probing by questioning" (Dr C. Brace, personal communication, September 1997). This probing by questioning is skilful and relies as much on unconscious clues in the patient's replies as it does on the phrasing of the questions themselves. In a monolingual encounter each interlocutor is able to operate all three of the functions involved in each activity for themselves and exercise their own judgement and choices. When an interpreter is interposed between the primary interlocutors, that feedback is broken. The patient speaks, but the next turn goes to the interpreter, so the patient cannot know if his or her intentions were properly recognized. The doctor meanwhile has been attending, but unable to identify or respond. He or she must wait until the interpreter takes a turn, and will then attribute the meaning of what the interpreter says to the patient. The doctor has no choice in this, since he or she has no way to check. If the interpreter should change the content of the message during this process, and act in the role of Principal, creating his or her own message, it will be four 'turns' before the patient can take corrective action, if the doctor's reply should seem not to match expectations. When Pablo, speaking Spanish, describes his headaches through an interpreter, Dr Jones may attend to Pablo's utterances without identifying or understanding them. Although she attends to, identifies and understands the interpreter's English, she attributes to Pablo the meaning expressed. This decoupling can be seen in the data transcripts discussed later in this paper and is the cause of some misunderstandings.

The fundamental problem of communicating through an interpreter is that, in Clark's model, it is not a joint action between interpreter and interlocutor or between two interlocutors directly. As can be seen in the data, both listener and speaker roles are decoupled in an interpreted encounter. The interpreter is both Vocalizer and Formulator in the sense that he or she composes the actual words, though not the meaning, of the message. The interpreter also delivers the message. When he or she identifies too strongly with one party or the other, the tendency is for the interpreter to take over the role of Principal as well, which creates the potential for misunderstanding, since listener roles have also become decoupled. When the interpreter adopts the role of Principal, it is his or her meaning that is being relayed and not the original speaker's. Wadensjö (1992:118) points out that "if someone speaks/ is heard as speaking as if not referring to anyone else as "principal" of her utterance, this would imply that she takes a personal stand and is responsible for what she says herself". Because the interpreter tends to take over the role of Principal covertly – and probably inadvertently – either doctor or patient remains in the roles of Attender and Identifier but will attribute the role of Principal inappropriately. Thus Pablo may remark that his headaches cause him to vomit and suffer visual disturbance, in that he sees rainbows round lights. An interpreter who is listening in all the listener roles may make the judgement that the final part of the message is fanciful, therefore irrelevant, and relay only the first two symptoms. He or she therefore responds to the doctor in Principal role and says that Pablo suffers from vomiting and loss of sight, omitting the rainbows. The doctor attributes this meaning to Pablo, treats him for migraine and thus fails to check for acute glaucoma.

2. Collecting the data

The data consist of seven extempore conversations between practising GPs (General Practitioners) and non-English speaking 'patients', using volunteer interpreters. These conversations were unscripted role-plays; the scenarios were provided by the doctors. None of the doctors was aware however of what the 'patient' would present with since each prepared a scenario for one of the others. The filming was done at the training suite of the Robert Darbyshire Medical Practice in Rusholme, Manchester. This is part of the Faculty of Medicine's Department of General Practice and is a training practice, operating as a normal city health centre in a multi-ethnic area, serving a multilingual population. The practice as a whole is experiencing communications problems. The training suite offers a mocked-up consulting room with video link to an adjacent room, so that participants were able to carry out their conversations in conditions as close to reality as possible.

The doctors concerned gave up time during their normal surgery hours to hold a consultation with the volunteers. All the doctors were well used to working in this way and were perfectly comfortable with the video camera. Four doctors did seven consultations with four patients, using two interpreters. The interpreters were both women, which reflects the fact that the majority of people working in the field of public service interpreting are women. For this reason, I will refer to mediators and interpreters in general as 'she' throughout. Both were in their thirties and married. Interpreter A was Mexican, and had lived in England for 15 years. She had some teacher training, but did not practice. She was married to an English nurse and had in the past been called on to interpret for patients at hospitals near to her home. Interpreter B, who came from the north of Spain, had lived in England for 10 years and was married to an Englishman. Both she and her husband were teachers of Spanish. The two women had quite different styles as interpreters but neither had any relevant formal training. Interpreter B doubled as a 'patient' in the final interview, as the other volunteer 'patients' were all men. There were three volunteer 'patients'. Patient C came from the Canary Islands and was studying music at the Royal Northern College of Music. He was in his early twenties. Patient D and Patient E were from Alicante, both in their mid-twenties, had university degrees – one in law and the other in economics – and were in England to improve their English. They were working in a hotel in an English tourist resort, and had been in the country for about three months. Of the doctors, one said that she was accustomed to working with non-English speakers, without the benefit of interpreters, having spent some time in Australia working with Aboriginal people. Another said that at the age of 16 he had spent about three months in Colombia. He could not speak Spanish, he said, but could understand it.

3. Discussion

It should be remembered that there are particular constraints on interpreters, some of which are specific to public service interpreters. Common to all types of interpreting are the problems of speed; lack of access to, or time to use reference materials during the assignment; accent; jargon; and the likelihood that no advance briefing has been given. Specific to the difficulties facing public service interpreters are poor acoustics (especially in Britain's older hospitals), loud background noise and surrounding conversations, the possibility that extra time will not have been allowed for an interpreted interview, and the five features described by Nathan Garber (1998), which distinguish public-service from other groups of interpreter:

- The setting involves an interview between a service provider and someone who needs or wants the services (a 'client').
- The interview arises out of some sort of crisis in the life of the client.
- There is a significant level of risk inherent in the situation.
- Cultural differences between provider (doctor) and client increase the risk.
- There is a power imbalance between provider (doctor) and client.

These factors do not affect the work of conference or diplomatic interpreters, nor those working in industry. Furthermore the public service interpreter may not offer one language as active and another as passive. She must work both into and out of all her languages.

By far the commonest cause of miscommunication is the mediator's occupying inappropriate interlocutor roles. There are three main types of malfunction attributed to inappropriate interlocutor role: loss of content, addition to content, and alteration of meaning. These will be discussed below. There are also two less frequent but more obvious malfunctions which demand repetition of the original message, namely failure to identify a word or phrase, and failure to attend adequately, which results in getting the time wrong or forgetting a list.

On many occasions information is lost due to the Attender role failing. Either the mediator (M) has simply forgotten the content of a long preceding utterance, since she took no notes, or else she has judged some part of the utterance to be irrelevant and omitted it, as in the following extract. The patient (P) complains of diarrhoea and the doctor (D) has asked if he knows of anyone else with the same symptoms.

Extract 1

P   Pues la verdad que no caigo ahora. Hombre hay alguien que me ha dicho alguna vez ¿no? Porque comemos todos en el mismo sitio, que está un poquito mal de estómago o algo así pero [no realme/ No, no]
Well, at the moment I can't think ... Oh there is someone who told me once, you know? Because we all eat in the same place, that they had a bit of an upset stomach or something but not really. No, no.

M   [No significa] No, he has heard of some other people that have had the same upset but he's not sure that it's the same thing. The same condition.
It doesn't mean .. No, he has heard, ...

The mediator appears to be going to say something of her own in response but stops herself. The fact that all the students eat in the same place is not relayed, with obvious public health measures therefore ruled out as an option open to the doctor. During consultations in which the doctor could understand some Spanish, he corrected these omissions once or twice. Ironically though, a little knowledge of the other language involved can cause its own problems: the mediator actually failed to correct a misinterpretation by the doctor in one interview.

On other occasions the mediator is speaking in Principal role, relaying her own meaning and giving information that is additional to the primary interlocutor's meaning:

Extract 2
D   Okay (.) Um, I think it might be helpful if I had a look at you to check for any physical reason for the weight loss, but it sounds most likely that it's related to the worry. Change. Coming here. Um, and I would like to look at, look at you and, and then we can talk again.

M →   Sí, va a examinarte un poco para ver si va a encontrar una causa física con presión de la sangre para examinarte de manera que se asegure de que no hay nada específico fisicamente que te está afectando. El piensa

→   que fácilmente sea el cambio de, estar viviendo en un entorno diferente,

→   el cambio de alimentación y las preocupaciones, exámenes, familia, lo normal. Pero va de todas maneras a examinarte.

Yes, he's going to examine you a bit to see if he can find a physical cause with blood pressure to examine you so as to be sure there's nothing specific, physical that's affecting you. He thinks it could easily be the change of, living in a different environment, the change of food and the worries, exams, family, the usual. But he's going to examine you anyway.

Alternatively, still in Principal role, she subtly alters the primary interlocutor's meaning in potentially very dangerous ways, as in Extract 3 below.

Extract 3
D   So, you said about exams soon
M   ¿Tienes exámenes ahora?
           Do you have exams now?
P   Yeah. Uhuh.
M   ¿Ahora, en junio?
           Now, in June?
P   Yeah.
M   Now, in June, so they're about to happen.
D   Quite soon? Okay. How do you think you will feel after the exams?
M   ¿Cómo crees que vas a encontrarte después de los exámenes?
           How do you think you'll feel after the exams?

P   Pues eso (.) Si las apruebo, bien.
           Oh, that. If I pass, fine.
M   ¿Y si no, será una desgracia? (laughs)
           And if not, will it be a disgrace?
P   Bueno, si no, ya veré
           Well, if not, I'll find out
M   Uh, he thinks he's going to feel much better if he pass exams of course.
           Otherwise he will have to reorganize his life and think over what he is
           going to do.
D   I feel that you are quite worried, but I don't sense that you're unhappy
           or depressed. Do you, d'you feel like crying?
M   Em, eh, entiende, cree que estás preocupado pero mmm, de momento
           no ve que estás infeliz o que estás deprimido, que mm si a veces lloras o
           que haya una sensación en ti mismo de angustia o depresión. ¿Tú crees,
           eso te pasa?
           *Um, er, he understands, he thinks you're worried, but mmm, at the
           moment he doesn't see you as unhappy or depressed, mmm do you cry
           sometimes or do you feel inside yourself that you're anxious or depressed.
           Do you think that happens?*
P   Que me/ mmn hombre de eso me dan gana ¿no? Porque lo típico de eso
           es saber ¿por qué me tiene que pasar a mí?
           *I Mm, oh I do feel like it, you know? Because the thing is I think why
           does this have to happen to me?*
M →   He sometimes, he doesn't reckon it's too serious, he feels depressed
           because he feels how, why this has to happen to me? And when things
           are difficult around and when it's a bad moment to be suffering ehhm,
           but/
D   Right.
M →   Only occasionally. He is not unhappy continuously.

I interviewed the doctor who appears in this part of the film. I offered him
the transcript of his consultation to read. We discussed the exchange about
depression, and I asked him if he would have proceeded otherwise, had the
patient's full, actual replies been clear to him at the time. He replied that the
mediator "may have understated" the severity of the problem:

> If I had felt the severity of the mood disorder was consistent I might
> have talked about anti-depressive drugs or recalled him after the ex-
> ams or probed a bit further ... I might have agreed to sleeping pills,
> but I would have explored his feelings about anti-depressive drugs.
> So I might possibly have missed a more serious depression because I
> thought it was not a persistent mood disorder. (Dr Perry, personal
> communication, August 1997)

The transcript shows that the mediator adds two statements of her own opinion to the patient's replies, i.e. "he doesn't reckon it's too serious" and "Only

occasionally. He is not unhappy continuously". If the patient had really been suffering from depression, all the parties would have been at risk.

Finally, subtle linguistic changes, such as reversing the polarity of a question, as in Extract 4 below, may alter meaning in a potentially significant way.

Extract 4
D   Okay. Does he vomit with the headache?
M   ¿No tienes vómitos?
         You don't vomit?
P   No.
         No.

The mediator's negative question in Spanish prompts for a negative reply, in contrast to the doctor's phrasing, which allows for a positive or a negative response (Cruttenden 1986:97).

3.1 Distance

It is noticeable throughout the data that the mediators both use the third person style of interpreting. No discussion had taken place beforehand about how they would proceed, and so this was a free choice. It may have been influenced by the doctors' use of the third person. Only one of the doctors makes any attempt to address the patient directly, using the second person. This does not seem to have any effect on the malfunction figures, which may be due to the fact that the mediator does not use the second person when relaying from patient to doctor. Both mediators tend to use the second person when relaying from doctor to patient, though, which continually changes the focus regarding 'principal addressee', and keeps the mediator firmly in Principal role throughout. On several occasions, the doctors speak to the mediator as though she were the responsible adult in charge of the patient:

Extract 5
D   Is he tending to eat regular meals? Because as a waiter or working in a
         restaurant it is often difficult to eat regularly, is he eating properly,
         looking after himself?

and

D   Ask her to tell me again where the pain is.

Another aspect of the distancing effect of the third person style is that the doctor's supportive comments tend not to be relayed. It is not apparent whether this is because the mediator thinks them irrelevant, or whether she thinks they were addressed to her and not to the patient, or why they are left out. However, the following examples illustrate the point.

Extract 6

D In the meantime I'm also going to give him some tablets to try and help
→ this pain get better quickly so that hopefully he will not miss time off
→ work because I hear what he's saying about not wanting to lose his job.
M Ahora, para que no pierdas tus horas de trabajo te va a dar por lo mientras unas tabletas para que te alivien un poco el dolor para que puedas seguir trabajando, solamente mientras esperas el análisis de sangre.
Now, so you don't lose your hours of work she's going to give you some tablets in the meantime to relieve the pain a bit so you can go on working, just while you wait for the blood tests.

The doctor has offered the information that she has taken note of the patient's concern about losing his job and is trying to help him, specifically, to address that. The phrase "I hear what he's saying" is omitted in the mediator's version, and the result could be taken to mean that the treatment is to prevent idleness.

To the suggestion that he may be suffering from headaches as a reaction to the stress of moving to live overseas, the patient replies:

Extract 7

P No creo. Yo estoy acostumbrado a viajar. Estoy acostumbrado a salir.
I don't think so. I'm used to travelling. I'm used to being abroad.
M He is/ he doesn't think so because he is used to travel around and go out and about.
D That's fine. Well that's something for him to think about, because he's in a strange country. Students sometimes have work problems or money problems, so just for something for him to think about. What I would like to do is to arrange to meet him again in a couple of months time just to see his progress and to see how he's getting on ...
M Would you be able to come back in a couple of months time/ eh, podrás venir dentro de dos meses a, para revisar la situación o/ sí
Would you be able to come back in a couple of months time, eh, could you come in a couple of months to review the situation or, yes
P Sí
Yes

The offer of understanding and support implied in the doctor's remarks about possible work or money problems is not relayed, nor is the suggestion of a friendly visit being made to "see how he's getting on", and the patient is left with the idea that his headaches are being attributed to stress caused by not being used to being away from home and that he is being offered a further, purely clinical, check-up in the future.

The doctor's continuous use of the third person, which identifies the mediator rather than the patient as principal addressee, causes both patient and mediator to take responsive action. The patient, where he has enough English to recognize what is happening, responds on his own behalf and puts in a few English words. The mediator, where she is being treated as responsible adult, i.e. in charge of the patient – *in loco parentis*, as it were – responds by changing her transactional role altogether and replying to questions on the patient's behalf without relaying them first. The fact that the mediators are in Principal role throughout leads them to build up a solidary relationship with the patients on the basis of common ground (common language and cultural background) and of a symmetrical power and social distance structure. This causes the mediator to step out of role completely and offer advice and personal opinions. In extract 8 below, the structural change has not been signalled in any way and the covert nature of the mediator's interventions is the cause of a misunderstanding about 'vitamins' (and the reason for the problem with the 'depression' conversation in extract 3 above).

All the above types of malfunction are hidden from the primary interlocutors, whose Attender may be working perfectly but who are denied the use of their Identifier or Respondent by the nature of the encounter. They will therefore attribute the meaning they hear from the mediator to the wrong interlocutor (i.e. to the other primary interlocutor instead of to the mediator). This is very clearly seen in the depression interview (Extract 3), quoted above. The doctor suspects that the patient's mood swings may indicate a serious depression. The mediator puts words into the patient's mouth, which the doctor naturally responds to as though they were genuinely the patient's, having no danger signal to guide him. There are occasions when the mediator steps out of the mediation role altogether, becoming a primary interlocutor in her own right, and sending messages entirely of her own. Extract 8 provides a good illustration of this.

Extract 8

D   In someone of yo/ a young person with the change that you've described, it's very likely to be related to worry, the weight loss. I wonder if we should check your weight again, and talk again, after the exams ... How does that sound?

M   El mm piensa que sería bien pasar los exámenes porque a esta edad con la presión de los exámenes, el trabajo y presiones exteriores y personales, puede ser un síntoma todo ese peso, perder. Entonces le gustaría volverte a ver una vez que se relajen ciertas partes de las preocupaciones, y volver a ver el tema. ¿Bien?

He mm thinks that it would be good to finish the exams because at your age with the pressure of exams, the work and outside and personal pressures, all that weight that you lost could be a symptom. Then he

would like to see you once some of your worries are over, and look at
the matter again. Alright?*
D   If that sounds alright to you?
M → ¿Qué te parece? ¿Quieres hacer algo más, o (.) esperar un poco mas
→   hasta que pase la situación. Quieres algún tipo de vitamina quieres/
      How does it seem to you? Do you want to do something more, or (.)
      wait a bit until the situation's over. Do you want some kind of vitamin,
      do you want/
P   Yo creo, no sé. Si él ve que, que está bien, que, que no hay ningún
      problema pues de acuerdo. Si me manda algún vitamina y funciona pues
      no sé ... se lo agradezco.
      I think, I don't know. If he thinks that, that it's okay, that, that there's
      no problem, well I agree. If he orders some vitamin and it works well I
      don't know ... I'll be grateful.
M   He thinks what you decide is right unless you want to give him some
      vitamins or something you reckon is going to help, he will be happy to
      wait for a while and come back to you.
D   Right. I don't think vitamins will help. I think that there are some simple
      things you could do about the sleep at night that might help.

We can see here that the issue of vitamins has come directly from the mediator, who appears to be acting in Principal role, as the student's mentor and protector. This is a hidden role change as far as the other two interlocutors are concerned. Inadvertently, she poses a real threat to the patient's face, since he would not have risked rejection by the doctor's refusal had it not been for the mediator. These incidents show the mediator's failure to realize that she holds a very specific and specialized place within this transaction, and that the other participants cannot know that she has changed her status within it, unless she herself is aware of it and signals the change clearly.

3.2 Word order and structure

The next largest reason for the common ground problem is that the mediator does not understand the reason for a particular question being framed in the specific way the doctor has asked it. For instance, in Extract 9, the doctor prefaces his potentially face-threatening enquiry with a carefully phrased acceptance of the use of alcohol as a soporific.

Extract 9
D   Right, yes. Sometimes when we don't sleep, sometimes when people
      don't sleep very well they tend to drink more. I just wondered, d'you,
      are you having any more alcohol?
M   Eh, el/ eh, tienes un/ ¿Bebes más de lo normal? porque a veces cuando
      se está un poco desequilibrado para coger más fuerzas o ánimos eh, la
      gente bebe más de lo normal. ¿Crees que estas tomando más alcohol del
      que deberías?

> *Er, he/ er, do you have a/ Do you drink more than usual because*
> *sometimes when one's a little off balance people drink more than usual*
> *to give them more courage or strength ... Do you think you're drinking*
> *more alcohol than you should?*

The mediator fails to realize that there is a purpose behind this preamble and turns the utterance round. Her re-phrasing and omissions mean that the doctor's attempts to probe for underlying psychosocial influences are potentially frustrated.

There are many instances of the mediator taking on a full interlocutor role. In Extract 10, she does this, unsignalled, of her own accord (as mentioned above) and replies to a question from the doctor without reference to the patient.

Extract 10

D   She said she wasn't sleeping well. I wondered why that was? Is it the stomach or something else?

M   No, it's not the pain that wakes her up.

At other points, she puts words into the patient's mouth, asks a question of her own or offers an opinion of her own. But both doctor and patient occasionally change the transactional structure themselves. The patient, because he understands some English, replies directly to the doctor but does so in a mixture of Spanish and English, partly usurping the mediator's role.

Extract 11

D   Two years. And did he have problems with headaches when he was living in Spain at all?

P   Pues no, no he tenido problema. Posiblemente, yo creo que puede ser influencia de tiempo. Weather influence.
      No, I haven't had a problem. Possibly, I think it could be the influence of the weather. Weather influence.

3.3 Face threats

The doctors who took part in the study appear to be well aware of both face threats and gender issues, and very practised at minimizing or avoiding them. The patient seems to feel that he is not free from imposition, since he understands some English and needs to assert himself, as for example in the "weather influence" quote (Extract 11). In Extract 12, the sequence shows him to be unwilling to admit that he may have self-prescribed.

Extract 12

M   ¿Tomas pastillas o algo?
      Do you take pills or anything?

P   No, es la primera vez, que consulto al médico
        No, this is the first time I've been to the doctor
M   ¿O sea que no has tomado aspirina o una cosa así por ejemplo, em, por
        tu cuenta?
        *I mean have you taken aspirin or something like that for example, um,
        off your own bat?*
P   Paracetamoles.
        Paracetamol.

Later in the interview, his face is threatened by the suggestion that he may be under stress simply by being away from home. The repeat of the question may be attributable to other causes, of course, such as a belief that *pastillas* referred to medication available over the counter as distinct from prescribed medicines. On the other hand, in Spain, the home country of this patient, antibiotics, including those for intravenous administration, are still available over the counter on a self-prescribed basis. The most outstanding examples are the face-threats offered by taboo words. In Extract 13, the patient describes his problem thus:

Extract 13
P   Cuando me levanto por las mañanas, la primera orinar, normalmente
        suele ser (.) fuerte y me escuece, ¿se dice escuece?
        *When I get up in the mornings, the first time I urinate, is usually ...
        strong and it stings me, do you say stings?*
M   Sí.
        Yes
P   Me escuece orinar, se escuece el pene al orinar.
        It stings me to urinate, my penis stings when I urinate.
M   He has got a problem. When, the first time he goes to the toilet in the
        morning he usually feels some pain and, and it um, and um, it's hard to
        pass the water. So
(...)
D   He doesn't, no. Okay. Has he noticed er anything else such as a discharge
        from, from the penis, when he's not passing urine?
M   ¿Has notado, em, has sentido algún otro síntoma en, en el pene cuando
        no estás orinando, no sé, que puede (haber) algo?
        *Have you noticed, um, have you felt any other symptom in, in your penis
        when you're not urinating, I don't know, there could be something there?*
P   ¿Como cuál?
        Like what?
M   No sé, algún tipo de/
        I don't know, some kind of /
P   No
        No
M   No, he doesn't have any symptoms, really.

It is the mediator's face that is threatened by the use of taboo words, and probably also by the personal nature of the information. If she were not 'owning' all the words she is relaying but had closed off her Principal and Respondent roles, the words *penis* and *discharge* would not be so embarrassing. If she were to relay directly, the position of the patient as Principal would be maintained. In fact she fails to find a word for *discharge* and so asks rather vaguely about other symptoms, leaving the doctor with the false impression that his question was asked and answered.

4. Conclusion

Miscommunication occurs throughout the data for a variety of reasons. To a certain extent this is due to a lack of awareness in the doctors, in that their use of the third person style of address has a distancing effect and tends to sideline the patient, and cause all the participants to change role within some encounters. The majority of miscommunications are initiated by the untrained mediators and are due to several causes. Unfamiliarity with the routines and procedures of medical consultations leads to uncomfortable moments. Insufficient command of the appropriate lexicon leads to difficulty in describing pain, and confusion in the use of technical terms. Occupying an inappropriate interlocutor role causes the mediator to over-identify with one party to the encounter (in this case the patient), which lays her open to threats to her own face. This use of inappropriate interlocutor roles also causes relay of meaning to suffer from omission, addition and alteration. Among the additions are the mediator's own, unsignalled, opinions and advice.

Overall, what is lost is an element of available diagnostic resources, and the doctor's skill in developing a satisfactory relationship with the patient. So, while a mismatch of messages may be occurring in a discursive sense, 'data bits' of hard information are also being lost – usually to the physician – and it is precisely this loss which most damages the patient's interests.

This piece of research suffered from several drawbacks. The interviews were simulated, and no post-simulation interviews were done. The data produced, however, are rich and have only been 'unpacked' here to a limited extent. Interesting further work could be done on studying the output of untrained interpreters, who are the principal linguistic resource in most healthcare settings (see Pöchhacker and Kadric, this volume). This may shed light on training issues. Changes to clinical practice, however, are unlikely to result from anything less than a comparative study under clinical conditions.

JAN CAMBRIDGE
'Dinorben', Park West, Heswall, Wirral, Merseyside, L60 9JE, UK.
jan@spanish.demon.co.uk

Notes

1. Clark uses the terms 'Vocalizer' and 'Formulator' to replace Goffman's 'animator' and 'author'.

References

Brown, P. and S. C. Levinson (1987) *Politeness: Some Universals in Language Usage*, Cambridge: Cambridge University Press.

Brown, G. and G. Yule (1983) *Discourse Analysis*, Cambridge: Cambridge University Press.

Clark, H. H. (1996) *Using Language*, Cambridge: Cambridge University Press.

Cheepen, C. and J. Monaghan (1990) *Spoken English: A Practical Guide*, London: Pinter.

Cruttenden, A. (1986) *Intonation*, Cambridge: Cambridge University Press.

Garber, Nathan (1998) 'Community Interpretation: Another View', Paper Presented at *Critical Link 2: Interpreters in the Community,* Vancouver, Canada, May 1998.

Goffman, E. (1979) 'Footing', *Semiotica* 25:1-29.

------ (1981) *Forms of Talk*, Philadelphia: University of Pennsylvania Press.

Holmes, Janet (1992) *An Introduction to Sociolinguistics*, London: Longman.

Knapp, K., W. Enninger and A. Knapp-Potthoff (1987) *Analysing Intercultural Communication*, Amsterdam: Mouton de Gruyter.

Wadensjö, Cecilia (1992) *Interpreting as Interaction: On Dialogue Interpreting in Immigration Hearings*, Linköping: Linköping University, Department of Communication Studies.

West, Candace (1984) *Routine Complications: Troubles with Talk between Doctors and Patients*, Bloomington: Indiana University Press.

The Translator. Volume 5, Number 2 (1999), 221-246   ISBN 1-900650-21-5

Signs of Injustice

MARY BRENNAN
University of Edinburgh, UK

Abstract. *Recent research on court interpreting has demonstrated that interpreters themselves often intrude upon proceedings more than they or other participants realize. Moreover, as in any inter-preting, there is always some tension between the nature of the source and target language output. When interpreting occurs not just between two languages, but between two languages with dif-ferent modalities – spoken and signed – the relationship between source and target texts can be even more complex. This article discusses some of the issues which arise in part because of differ-ences in modality. Special attention is given to the notion of visual encoding in British Sign Language (BSL) whereby BSL incorpo-rates information about the physical world in a more regular way than is typical of spoken languages. This results in dilemmas for the interpreter and potential problems of access to justice for the Deaf person.*

This article explores some of the particular interpreting dilemmas that occur when the interpreting involves not just two languages, but two languages with different primary modalities. British Sign Language (BSL) is a visual-gestural language, exploiting movements of the hands, face and body in its production and requiring visual access in its reception. BSL is used by a minority language group of approximately 60,000 'core' members of the Deaf[1] community in Britain. However, knowledge and use of the language is somewhat wider than this, given that hearing family members and an increasing number of both hearing and deaf people may also acquire or actively learn BSL. BSL has no written form. In contrast, English is an oral-aural language, exploiting sounds created by the human speech mechanisms in its production and requiring access through human hearing. English has a written form and, as is well known, is used by many millions of people throughout the world. It may be a first language, one of the official languages of a specific society or one of several used by individuals or groups. The world language status of English contrasts sharply with the minority status of BSL and this has a range of socio-linguistic consequences. In order to understand the complexities of bimodal court interpreting, it will first be necessary to explore further the nature of signed language generally and BSL in particular.

ISSN 1355-6509   © *St Jerome Publishing, Manchester*

1. Characteristics of British Sign Language

Early accounts of sign languages generally (Stokoe 1960, Brennan *et al.* 1980) tended to focus on the manual elements of the language. Indeed, prior to the development of linguistic analyses of these languages, the term 'manual communication' was often used to describe the communication used by Deaf people: the focus was on the shape and movements of the hands. Later accounts of sign languages (Kyle and Woll 1985, Baker-Shenk 1983, Brennan 1992) additionally recognized the importance of non-manual features: movements of the mouth, eyes, eyebrows, facial muscles, head, shoulders and trunk. These non-manual features are seen to operate at every level of the language, but play a particularly important part within syntax. They express, at least in part, negation, questions and topic-comment focus. However, they also operate at the lexical level and as morphological adverbial and adjectival markers.

Much of the 'lexical weight' of BSL is carried by manual signs. These may be of different types: one-handed; two-handed symmetrical signs, with both hands exploiting the same handshape and complementary movements; two-handed asymmetrical signs, with both handshapes and movements different for each hand. Additionally there are 'multi-channel' signs: these make use of both manual and non-manual elements. Thus the sign glossed as 'exists' or 'there exists in this place' and typically translated by forms of the verb 'to be' involves a one-handed manual element (closed fist with thumb extended) performing a very short twisting action in front of the body) and a non-manual element (the lips pushed forward as if producing the sound 'sh').

While the grammatical structure of BSL, like other sign languages, does indeed bear direct comparison with spoken languages in that we can describe levels which are the equivalent of phonological, morphological, syntactic, semantic and discourse structure, there are several key differences which are crucial to our understanding of the dynamics of bilingual, bimodal interpreting.

At surface structure level, patterning in English is essentially linear and sequential: we can legitimately describe ordering of phonemes, morphemes, words and clauses. Linearity does occur in BSL: we can recognize ordering of elements within key structures. However, cutting across this linearity are two other forms of patterning: simultaneity and spatiality. The characteristics of human gesture are such that we can do several things at once very easily. We have two hands, each of which can represent two lexical meanings simultaneously; we have a face with several potential articulators – two eyes, two eyebrows, two cheeks, a mouth, a nose; we have a head which can tilt in different directions, nod, move in a single or repeated action; we have shoulders which can be brought forward or back, hunch or droop – all such actions can be, and are, made use of in BSL grammar. Thus the signer can produce a subject sign with one hand, an object sign with another, use the mouth to show intensity and a headshake to express negation. Such simultaneity is further enriched by the second feature, spatiality. The signer uses the space in front of the body to set out participants within the discourse. If several people are mentioned it is likely that they will be given differentiated locations within the signing space. The signer will refer back to these locations as the discourse continues, through such devices as use of eye-gaze and pronominal pointing, and will, for example, direct certain inflected verb forms towards or away from these locations. Such spatiality plays a key role in the expression of the phenomenon of visual encoding.

1.1 Visual Encoding

In earlier accounts of the structure of individual sign languages, there was a tendency to stress that signs were created from arbitrary, conventional components and that sign languages, like other languages, were essentially arbitrary in nature. In the late 1970s, Klima and Bellugi spoke of the 'two faces of the sign – the arbitrary and the iconic' – with iconicity often lying dormant in the signs but with the capacity to be awoken for the creation of new signs (Klima and Bellugi 1979). In more recent years, there has been an increasing recognition of the extent to which iconicity pervades sign language structure, although the nature and extent of iconicity remains controversial. The view presented here, and argued for in a number of publications (Brennan 1990, 1992, 1997a, 1997b), is that iconicity does indeed pervade all levels of the language. As several researchers have noted (Johnston 1996, Brennan 1997a, 1997b), our experience of the world is more visual and spatial than aural:

> Although oral-aural language is suited to iconically encoded sounds, the fact that our experience as a whole is visual, temporal and spatial, means that a language that has visual and spatial resources for representation has greater means for mapping onto those very visual and spatial qualities. (Johnston 1996:65)

I have argued elsewhere (Brennan 1997b) that BSL exhibits a creative tension between visual encoding and arbitrariness. The language clearly exploits a limited set of conventional symbols, yet the norm is to encode real-world visual information as a matter of course. Such encoding has a major impact on the nature of the evidence considered in courts of law. The kind of iconicity that has long been recognized in BSL and other sign languages is lexical iconicity. Many, indeed most, signs denoting objects show direct visual links between the form of the sign and its meaning. Typically the form of the sign represents some aspect of the size and shape of an object or, alternatively, how people interact with that object – most often how they get hold of the object. The signer can refer to objects in a number of different ways, by focusing on different salient features, although a specific sign will probably have emerged as the standard sign for that meaning. Thus a signer may focus on the salient features of an elephant, such as its trunk, its large floppy ears, its huge legs or its overall bulk, but the standard sign focuses on the trunk. What is suggested here is that it would be very odd indeed to find a sign in any sign language meaning 'elephant' which did not in some way focus on its physical features.

Morphologically, it has been possible to establish a set of morphemes, known as classifiers, which primarily fall into the categories of size and shape specifiers (SASes) and handling classifiers (Supalla 1986, Brennan 1992). These are expressed in BSL through specific handshapes. By exploiting these classifier handshapes along with other morphemes in the language, the signer can create 'new' lexical items as required. In this respect, they are compara-ble to the derivational morphemes of a language such as English. In practical terms, the existence of these resources not only permits but in a sense en-courages the signer to be more specific about the size, shape and handling of objects than one would expect in a language such as English. This may mean that in recounting an incident – often a key element in court proceedings – a witness may provide quite specific information relating to objects in the en-vironment. In English a statement such as "I arrived home, opened the front door and went through into the kitchen" gives no particular information about the entrance to the home, the way in which the door opened or the location of the kitchen with respect to the front door, whereas all such information could typically be gleaned from the equivalent BSL statement.

Both at the lexical and morphological levels, iconicity goes well beyond the encoding of physical features. It has been suggested (Brennan 1990, 1997a, 1997b, Wilcox 1993) that BSL and other sign languages make use of a range of visual metaphors to express more abstract meanings. Just as metaphors have been found to be an inherent part of everyday spoken language (Lakoff 1987, Lakoff and Johnson 1980, Sweetser 1990), so sign languages make frequent use of metaphor. However, in the case of sign languages, the meta-phors are themselves expressed iconically. The following expressions may all be viewed in English as metaphorical: "I think I've grasped what you mean"; "Her news hit me hard"; "I don't follow your line of thought". These are everyday expressions, but as Lakoff and colleagues have shown all too clearly they express not just single metaphors but sets of metaphors. BSL happens to use some of the same metaphors; the difference is that the notion of grasping is actually expressed by a grasping action of the hand; 'hit hard' is expressed by a sign meaning 'hit' which involves a punching action; 'lines of thought' are expressed by the spread fingers of the hand held at the head. It has been suggested that some of these metaphorical expressions link to wider gestural expressions of abstract meanings, which may even be univer-sal. Thus in BSL, 'doubt' is expressed by several signs making use of side to side or up/down alternating movements: similar signs are found in many of the world's sign languages and similar gestures are often used in co-verbal gesture.

The combination of the exploitation of spatial locations in BSL syntax, metaphoric use of space and signs and the pervasiveness of iconicity all provide sign languages in general, and BSL in particular, with an enormous potential for encoding both real world visual information and metaphoric meaning. The claim here is that sign languages typically exploit this potential and this fact raises very particular issues for the signed/spoken language interpreter.

1.2 The use of English by Deaf people

English plays an important part in the lives of many Deaf people. Indeed in recent years, that role has increased with the advent of sub-titled television, text telephones, fax machines and email. However, there is considerable variation in the nature and use of English by Deaf people and indeed in their attitudes towards it. Some may be fully bilingual; others may have quite low-level literacy skills and hence their access to the written word will be limited. Conrad (1979) reported that the reading age of a large cohort of deaf school-leavers in the mid-1970s was just over 8 years. A recent review of the literature by Gregory, Powers and Thoutenhoofd (1998) has suggested that deaf school leavers today may not fare much better. It must also be recognized that for many Deaf people, access to English has been primarily through visual means – the written language and the spoken language accessed visually through lip-reading. Again, Conrad's findings with respect to lip-reading were rather surprising: he found that deaf school-leavers were no better than hearing school-leavers at lip-reading. Of course, the findings are not so surprising when we realize that deaf pupils often have limited and distorted access to spoken language. It is therefore much harder for them to make sense of the lip patterns they observe. There is also considerable variation in the use of speech by Deaf people. So, those who are bilingual in terms of their command of BSL and written English may nevertheless make no use of speech whatsoever. Some have made a personal, or even political, decision that speech is not their way of communication. A number of Deaf people have described how their assumption while at school that their speech was intelligible proved unfounded once they left the familiarity of their own classrooms and schools. In recent years, the increase in the number of deaf pupils educated in mainstream settings means that there is more likelihood that they will have used speech as a means of communication, either mainly or partially. However, the intelligibility of their speech and their own perception of its appropriateness will vary considerably across the deaf population. Some Deaf people may use some lip-patterns, but without any vocalization. Some may use a considerable amount of vocalization.

1.3 The relationship between English and BSL

BSL has borrowed and continues to borrow from English. It does this primarily through the use of fingerspelled forms and English-based lip-patterns.
Fingerspelling is a way of representing written English words by means of a
manual alphabet, with each letter of the English alphabet having a manual
representation. Some people outside of the Deaf community falsely assume
that fingerspelling and sign language are one and the same. Many have learnt
fingerspelling at some point in their lives and thus imagine that Deaf people
communicate by spelling out English words. Part of this assumption is that
Deaf people will 'know' English. While there have been periods in the history of Deaf education when fingerspelling has been used as the primary
means of communication (for example, in some Scottish schools at the beginning of the 20th century), this is currently not the case. Despite this, BSL
continues to make use of fingerspelled forms of English words. However,
these forms are frequently adapted away from their original letter by letter
manual formats, so that they look and act more like BSL signs (Colville 1979,
Sutton-Spence 1994). Fingerspelling within BSL is often accompanied by
an English-based lip pattern, although usually without any vocalization of
the English word.
      Lip-pattern may also accompany other parts of the signed message. Thus
we can have English information on the lips, whilst the rest of the message is
exploiting BSL grammar. If there is continuous English lip-pattern, then certain features of BSL grammar may be lost, including those normally expressed
by BSL mouthshapes. Nevertheless, some English lip-pattern is typical of
BSL usage. Such patterning can be seen as comparable to fingerspelling and
indeed may often co-occur with fingerspelling. However, the fact that we
can sign some English-linked forms 'on the lips' at the same time as using a
primarily gestural language system does create a highly complex linguistic
situation. This complexity may also be confusing for the uninformed observer whose primary language is English, since the observer may give sole
attention to the lip pattern and (usually mistakenly) assume that he or she has
understood the content of the message.

1.4 Sign variation

BSL, like other languages, exhibits variation linked to such factors as social
grouping, gender, age and status. However, several other factors also influence variation amongst Deaf users. These may include age of acquisition of
or access to BSL; the language of one's parents; and the language(s) used
within schooling. Deaf people also live in a wider hearing society, and in
order to communicate with members of that society contact varieties have
also developed, sometimes referred to as 'pidgin' varieties. These contact

forms exhibit some of the features of pidgins in that they have variable rules, differ both within and across speakers and exploit elements of both the spoken language and BSL in a wide variety of combinations. For most Deaf people in the UK, the spoken language concerned will be English, although for some it may be other spoken languages such as Scots Gaelic, Hindi, Punjabi, Bengali or Welsh. Deaf people may use contact varieties not only with hearing people, but with d/Deaf people who have a different linguistic background to their own. In some varieties, the spoken language features will be dominant, in others BSL elements.

2. The 'Access to Justice for Deaf People' project

The research reported here relates to BSL/English interpreting in legal settings, particularly in courtrooms. This research derives from the 'Access to Justice for Deaf People in the Bilingual, Bimodal Courtroom' project, funded by the Leverhulme Trust and carried out by a team of Deaf and hearing researchers at the Deaf Studies Research Unit, University of Durham, UK (Brennan and Brown 1997). The project had several key components:

- *Observations of trials in England and Wales.* The project team undertook close observations of several major trials and a number of other cases in which Deaf defendants and/or Deaf witnesses were involved and during which BSL/English interpreters were employed.

- *Observation and videotaping of trials in Scotland.* Members of the project team observed a considerable number of court proceedings in Scotland, most of which were within the Sheriff courts, with some also in the District courts. The team were able to obtain permission to videotape proceedings in a Sheriff Court. This videotaped material provides unique data.

- *Interviews with Deaf people concerning their experiences of the criminal justice process.* Interviews were held with Deaf people who had been involved in the legal system, for example as victims of crime, witnesses to crime, individuals charged with crime but found not guilty and individuals in prison at the time of the interview.

- *In-depth interviews with BSL/English interpreters.* Interviews were undertaken with 57 people working as BSL/English interpreters. Almost all of the interviews were tape-recorded and they provide a rich set of qualitative data which include many important insights into the demands made on interpreters by the courtroom situation.

- *Questionnaires.* Two questionnaires were circulated to interpreters and trainee interpreters.

3. The demands of bimodal legal interpreting

The project team had predicted that bimodal interpreting would create specific issues for interpreting and legal personnel and for those Deaf people involved in the justice system. The observations and findings from interviews suggest that there are indeed major problems in ensuring that Deaf people have full access to legal processes. A major finding from this research is that legal personnel are often completely unaware of what is happening before their very eyes. They are not aware of changes in message from source to target language; they are not always aware of interpreter intrusion; and they are often unaware of interactions taking place between defendants, witnesses and members of the general public, even where – as the research team observed – these actually take place within the courtroom.

3.1 Court dynamics

Descriptions of interpreters and interpreting, including those found in many professional codes of practice, often suggest that the interpreter will be an almost invisible presence. However, research into spoken language courtroom interpreting (Morris 1995, Berk-Seligson 1990) has provided evidence that the mere presence of an interpreter or interpreters can have a considerable impact on the nature of the courtroom interaction: "The court interpreter is a new variable in the ecology of the courtroom. She is an intrusive element, far from being the unobtrusive figure whom judges and attorneys would like her to be" (Berk-Seligson 1990:6).

The intrusiveness of the interpreter is even more obvious within a bimodal courtroom. Signed/spoken language interpreters almost always use simultaneous interpreting. The Deaf participant has to look at the interpreter throughout. This can be very disconcerting to the legal personnel, especially to a lawyer engaged in cross-examination. Direct interaction involving eyegaze is lost. The fact that Deaf participants have to focus their attention on the interpreter to access the proceedings may also mean that they themselves miss key information. The gestural activity of the legal personnel, for example, a shrug of the shoulders, a look of amazement, raised eyebrows, pointing towards evidence, may all have an impact on the rest of the court, but not on the Deaf person.

Although the interpreting is technically 'simultaneous', this label ignores the time-lag that is typical of such interpreting. Thus the Deaf person will have a 'delayed' response to aspects of the discourse and may appear, therefore, to respond inappropriately. The team observed a Deaf person smiling at a previous reference, while the lawyer was presenting rather distressing evidence. The jury and others in court may well judge such reactions negatively. Legal personnel may make other assumptions about the Deaf person, based either on the actions of the interpreter (see further below under 'Register') or on misconstruals of the Deaf person's behaviour. Some Deaf people may use unintelligible speech for example, or vocalizations which are unclear or viewed as 'off-putting' by the non-Deaf participants. Ironically, reasonably intelligible speech may lead the listeners to assume – possibly falsely – that the Deaf person can easily engage in spoken interaction. Other participants may also be unaware of the negative impact of 'visual noise' on the Deaf person; whilst the court may require silence, except for the formal interactions which are occurring, a considerable amount of visual movement may be regarded as acceptable. This is particularly true in the lower courts.

Simultaneous interpreting can also make the interpreter exposed and vulnerable if he or she is aware that others in the court are bilingual in BSL and English, since there can be a continuous evaluation of the interpreter's performance. BSL/English interpreters do not work only or primarily into their first or native language, which tends to be the practice amongst spoken language conference interpreters. Like other dialogue interpreters, they typically work into both languages. Some interpreters may have developed BSL as their first language or in parallel with English. These are hearing people who have Deaf parents and who typically have grown up at least partially in a Deaf cultural environment. However, many, probably most, hearing interpreters have learned BSL as adults. Deaf native users of BSL cannot work directly between spoken English and BSL, precisely because they cannot access spoken English. However, in recent years, some Deaf people have worked as 'relay interpreters': the source message is accessed by a hearing interpreter who conveys the meaning to the Deaf person via a contact variety of signing – the Deaf person then adapts this into a full BSL output. The reasoning behind this approach is that very few hearing non-native signers will be able to reach the peak of idiomatic fluency achievable by native Deaf users. Of course, such a system involves additional costs in terms of both personnel and money. So far, relay interpreting has been used to a very limited extent in courts, and the Durham project team were unable to observe any relay interpreting within court cases. Thus all of the BSL interpreting we observed was produced by hearing signers, a small proportion of whom had Deaf parents.

3.2 Interruptions

One of the ways in which the interpreter and the interpreting become obtrusive is through interpreter interruptions. Interruptions to the interaction within the court can in theory come from any of the personnel involved. In practice, within interpreted proceedings, the key interrupters are the interpreters themselves and the lawyers. The interpreter may interrupt in order to make sure that he or she has understood the message. These interruptions may be explicitly made known to the court, as in the following examples from our data: "I'm sorry I'm not picking this up"; "I'm just clarifying". However, on many more occasions within our videorecorded data we noted the interpreter seeking direct clarification from the Deaf person, without spelling out to the court what was going on. Sometimes this involved the interpreter asking clarifying questions in BSL which were not spoken aloud for the court, for example "Who kept the log book?"; "Were you sitting down?". These examples reveal how the interpreter can actually alter the dynamics of the discourse, without the court being aware of what is happening. Rather surprisingly, although the interpreter's actions in signing directly to the Deaf person must be visible to the court personnel, the interpreters are rarely asked about their behaviour.

One phenomenon noted during the research, which does not involve interrupting as such but does involve a checking process, is the tendency of some interpreters to add signs to their spoken English interpretation of the Deaf person's BSL. Such signing occurs relatively frequently within the videotaped data. On some occasions the interpreter is also looking at the Deaf witness with non-manual features of raised eyebrows and head tilt: it is as if the interpreter is using the signing as a way of demonstrating to the Deaf person the nature of the English interpretation he or she is proffering and asking, in effect, 'Have I understood you correctly?'. In other instances, the interpreter is looking towards other court participants, but again it is almost as if the interpreter expects these participants to receive a fuller version of the meaning because he or she both speaks and signs. Such bimodal communication is not all that unusual in the spoken language communication of hearing people who work with Deaf people. However, it is worth considering the functions of such bi-modality within the court. Given that the BSL signs will usually not be directly accessible to other hearing people in the court, they may serve to give the interpreter a false sense that he or she is communicating the message fully, even though this may not be the case.

It is also worth noting here that interruptions by the lawyers often appeared to be more disruptive than we might otherwise expect. This is because they are often interruptions of the spoken interpretation, which take no account of where the Deaf person is in their own signed text. Such interruptions were quite common in the videotaped samples. Here are some examples:

> Can I stop you there please? Yes I have stopped you there because we have to go a little more slowly.
> Yes can I stop you please before we get to that?
> Can I stop you there please?

It is likely that the most efficient recounting of an event or incident will be one in which the Deaf person is able to use the full resources of spatial syntax. The signer will be able to establish participants within the signing space and show relationships. However, the signer was rarely able to enter into such an extended discourse of even a few sentences. This made it considerably more difficult for the interpreter to capture the full intent of the signer. Because the lawyers are typically unaware of how BSL works, this problem will not be apparent.

3.3 Role dilemma

Given the evidence from other research and practice, it is not particularly surprising that the BSL/English interpreter faces a dilemma in terms of role. BSL/English interpreting is a new and evolving profession. It is not many decades since interpreting would have been undertaken by a 'missioner for the deaf': usually a hearing person, often a religious minister, who saw their role as helping and supporting the Deaf person. The missioner would not just interpret at a job interview, but may have set up the interview or intervened with employers on behalf of the Deaf person. In the 1960s and 1970s social workers gradually took on interpreting tasks, but this dual function often led to confusion and dissatisfaction. In the 1980s, attempts were made to separate out the roles of social worker and interpreter, so that Deaf people could have access to an independent and disinterested interpreting service. However, it is clear from this and other research (Collins, 1994) that these roles often remain confused.

Within the research interviews, individuals described being required to interpret both in court and within police stations as part of their employment as social workers. In some cases, the individuals concerned did not have an interpreting qualification and some had not even achieved higher level BSL skills qualifications. Their competence to interpret in court was thus highly questionable. Collins (1994) also reports that many Deaf women choose not to make use of the services of a professional interpreter in medical contexts, including consultations with their doctor. Thus there remains ambivalence on the part of Deaf people themselves and others in relation to the role of interpreters.

Observations in legal contexts reveal that participants have internalized different models of the interpreter and the interpreting process. The predominant view of interpreters themselves, at least from those who have gone through interpreter training relatively recently, is that they are essentially linguistic and cultural mediators. It appears that legal personnel typically espouse the machine or conduit model, while Deaf people very often expect the interpreter to be an ally or advocate. Legal personnel often appear to have a mixed perception of the interpreter: within court the interpreter is expected to supply 'a literal interpretation'; however, outside of the court the interpreter may be expected to take on a range of duties which belie their professional status.

Even while espousing a notion of linguistic and cultural mediation, the interpreter may be pulled in different directions. It may be that by sticking to some preconceived notion of 'professionalism' they see themselves as letting the Deaf person down. One interpreter described the situation in a civil case where the Deaf person's partner had died in prison. The interpreter was asked by the court to interpret, but only when the Deaf person gave evidence. This meant that for the rest of the Inquiry, the Deaf partner was denied information about her partner. The interpreter had been employed for one specific purpose by the court, yet she felt the Deaf person had a right to know what was happening. The interpreter was therefore faced with several possibilities: she could put the case for further interpreting to the court; she could provide interpreting herself free of charge if the court would allow it; she could contact an appropriate Deaf organization and ask them to make representations or she could put in for her fee and ignore the Deaf person's situation. The very fact that interpreters worry about such matters, whether or not they always act in relation to them, demonstrates the nature of the problem.

Typically interpreters find themselves trying to deal with the cultural and information gap between the courts and Deaf people. As one interpreter commented, "Every time I go to court, I present a Deaf Awareness course".

The impact of this more general role dilemma can be seen even within the actual process of interpreting from one language to another in the courtroom. The findings of the Durham project reveal that interpreters often modify the source message in such a way that there are key differences in propositional content and/or pragmatic effect. It is suggested here that there are several different types of motivation for such modifications:

- processing errors;
- changes linked to inherent differences in the modalities and structures of the two languages;
- changes linked to the interpreter's internalization of role.

It is fully accepted that interpreters will make errors because of tiredness, lack of preparation, even inadequate levels of competence. The research team observed individuals working as interpreters who did not have appropriate qualifications. In most cases, these people were unable to work adequately between the two languages and the standards of interpreting were unacceptably poor. However, this account does not focus on such interpreters, but rather on interpreters who do have an interpreting, although not a legal interpreting, qualification. Even these interpreters, like spoken language interpreters, will almost certainly make processing errors. Often they are unaware that they have done so; in other cases, they may be aware of the error and try to rectify it.

The particular focus of the discussion below is on dilemmas which will inevitably arise for all signed/spoken language interpreters because of the inherent differences between signed and spoken language. An additional dimension will be the claim that perceptions of role may influence performance. In order to explore these claims further, some specific examples of interpreter modification are presented below. Most of these are taken from video-recorded proceedings, and it has therefore been possible to make careful comparison between source and target message.

4. Interpreter modifications to the source language output

4.1 Lexical issues

There are numerous examples throughout the videotaped samples, as well as the observed court proceedings, of apparent mismatches between BSL signs and English words. It goes without saying that the lexical composition of the two languages is different. We cannot expect one-to-one correspondences. However, even where there might appear to be fairly clear correspondences, the interpreter sometimes makes surprising choices.

In some cases, the source word may have more than one meaning and the interpreter chooses the wrong meaning in context. These are examples of what are known sometimes as 'false friends'. The interpreter who uses a sign meaning 'concerned/worried/anxious' when interpreting the English phrase *concerned with*, has at some level been misled by the different English meanings of the English word *concerned*. Similarly an interpreter's choice of an inflected form of the BSL sign LEARN,[2] meaning in use 'go on learning', when interpreting the phrase *my learned friend*, is similarly misguided. In the latter case, a modification of the sign KNOW as in *knowledgeable* would have been more apt. Of course, this is also an example of a polite form of address which has no direct equivalent in BSL usage. While 'false friends' may be construed as simple processing errors and may be caused by tiredness or a lapse in concentration, they may also mark an interpreter's over-dependence upon English. Many interpreters appear to 'stick close' to the English as if it provides a safety mechanism. In fact, the opposite may be the case.

An ongoing problem for interpreters is that the speaker often uses an English generic term for which BSL has no direct equivalent: the opposite problem is that BSL is frequently much more specific than English. Some examples of generic English terms occur again and again in the data. These include: *touch, hit, murder, assault, hold*. While the English word *hit* does not specify **how** someone was hit (for example with the flat hand, the fist, the back of the hand, etc.) or **where** someone was hit (on the face, head, legs, back, etc.), a signed version of *hit* would typically be quite specific in relation to how and where. The problem for the interpreter is to decide which one of these to use. Even signs meaning 'murder' derive from particular ways of killing someone. Thus several different signs co-exist in the language, one deriving from stabbing, another from strangling, another from slitting the neck. and so on.

In one murder case, the defence team wished to argue that the victim had been accidentally stabbed. In order to make the case, they needed to be quite specific about the way in which the defendant had held a knife. The difficulty for the interpreter was that every time some version of *hold the knife* was expressed, she had to choose a specific version of a holding classifier. There was no obviously neutral version. This dilemma remained and was almost more acute when the focus was not on how the knife was held:

> Were you holding the knife when X came into the room?
> When did you first notice that Y was holding a knife?

One mechanism in such cases is for the interpreter to use a more English structure at such points. Thus the typical pattern in BSL would be to use a holding handshape (classifier) appropriate to the object. Instead, the interpreter may use the fully open 5 handshape closing to a fist, which may be construed as generic. This would then be followed by the separate sign KNIFE, even though normally in BSL this would not need to be signed separately.

In all of these cases, the interpreter has a dilemma: whatever choice is made could be questioned and could cause confusion and inaccuracy. This does not mean that there are no ways around the problems, especially if all concerned are aware of the issues involved. Thus one of the most common signs meaning 'murder' derives from the stabbing action. However, the sign itself is already partially neutralized in that the stabbing action of the dominant hand (a closed fist) is made against the flat non-dominant hand, rather than a specific part of the body. For many Deaf people this sign has become a neutral sign meaning 'murder': they ignore the embedded meaning of 'stab' just as the origins of the word *murder* are ignored in English. A number of BSL signs are going through such a process of standardization and to some extent neutralization: of course, the process takes time.

In a number of cases, the interpreter uses what might be called simplifications, which do not express the full complexity of the original message. English words such as *effects, implications, assumptions, presume* and *incident* are often given simplified translations, or even omitted. The team collected many examples of *assume* and *presume* either being ignored or translated as THINK or SAY. A typical example of oversimplification can be seen in the following example. A lawyer's question "Have there been any long-term effects?" was interpreted as "Have you had any problems?". Although the context would lead us to expect negative effects, the word *effect* in English is neutral. Therefore the propositional content of the two messages is different. In many such examples, the interpreter also uses a 'simpler' English word on the lips. We noted one interpreter translating the English word *incident* by a sign often glossed as TROUBLE. However, on several occasions the same interpreter used a different sign which could be glossed as INCIDENT, but continued to use the mouth-pattern "trouble". The motivation for this type of change appears to relate to preconceptions about the individual Deaf person or, more usually, Deaf people generally. Interpreters often told us that a given English word was "not a Deaf word". When pressed to clarify what this meant, two different explanations were given: Deaf people would not use this word; Deaf people would not understand this word. Of course, if we were interpreting from French into English, we would not balk at using the appropriate English word because our client could not understand the source French word. The irony is that interpreters sometimes appear reluctant to use specific BSL signs because they deem their translations to be too difficult for the Deaf person.

4.2 Focus on the interaction

The way in which interpreting can alter the dynamics of the court and the nature of the messages being transferred can be revealed by looking closely at a short stretch of court interaction. The following extract is taken from the proceedings of a trial within a Sheriff Court in Scotland. The case, which was videotaped by the research team, involved two deaf accused (defendants) and one hearing accused. There were both deaf and hearing witnesses. Three interpreters were involved throughout. In the period represented by the section below, one interpreter is working between the deaf witness (W) and the lawyers (L). This interpreter is thus using both English and BSL. Additionally, two interpreters are working to each of the accused, i.e. one interpreter per accused. These two interpreters are using BSL only. Thus when the Deaf witness signs, this is interpreted into spoken English (for the hearing members of the court) by Interpreter 1 and then that spoken message is used as the source by Interpreters 2 and 3. Interestingly, the accused can if they wish watch the signing of the Deaf witness and even, as they often do, move between looking at the signer directly and watching the interpreters. In other court cases observed by the team, the accused simply watched the Deaf witnesses directly, rather than having an interpreter re-sign the message. In this case, however, there were three signed versions of the same message.

The section is presented in the form of a written transcript of the spoken utterances heard in court, including the interpreted utterances which are themselves based on signed utterances. The complex relationship between signed and spoken versions is discussed with reference to particular parts of the text.

Transcript

521 L Did he actually see any hands being laid on his wife? Or simply assume that she had been pushed because of the way she came in backwards?

522 W I just saw my wife falling back and Alex Mackay coming past her at the same time as she was falling back.

523 L So he did not actually see Alex Mackay putting hands on his wife?

524 W No. No it was just that these things happened at the same time.

525 L These things happened at the same time. So for all you know she might have stumbled?

526 W No. No. I saw her falling back and luckily something was behind her and broke her fall.

527 L But what he saw Alex Mackay doing was walk past her?

528 W When I was sitting down what I saw was my wife stagger back and Alex Mackay came in at exactly the same time that she was staggering back. I saw that.

529 L I understand that. But if I am to understand your evidence correctly, it's at that point you say you were struck?

530 W Yes, as my wife was falling back, I was punched at the same time.

531 L At the same time?

532 W Well, you know, I'm saying the same time but as she was staggering back then I was punched.

533 L And I noted in your evidence this morning you said "I twisted round and tried to save my face". Is that correct?

534 W Yes.

535 L And I think you've told the court that you put both hands up to your face?

536 W Yes I did that.

537 L Could you show us that again please?

538 W That's what I did.

539 L And did you put your face down towards the carpet?

540 W When I was punched, I turned away and then fell on the floor…

541 L Yes…

                                    .....

551 L Mr X will you please be careful when you're answering questions that I ask. You have to tell the whole truth.

552 W Yes, yes.

553 L You told me a moment ago, you were turned towards a chair.

554 W Yes that's right.

555 L Were your knees on the chair?

556 W No, my knees were on the floor.

557 L You were on the floor.

558 W Yes, my head was over the chair.

559 L You were crouched over the chair.

560 W I was crouched on the seat.

561   L   Was your head on the seat of the chair?
562   W   Yes. Yes.
563   L   Was your face into the seat of the chair?

This section (turns 521-563) begins with the following question:

521   L   Did he actually see any hands being laid on his wife? Or simply
             assume that she had been pushed because of the way she came in
             backwards?

The interpreter renders this in the following way:

> Interpreter   [MEAN REALLY IMPORTANT WHAT YOU REALLY SAW]
>   It's really important to say what you really saw.

The interpreter has, it seems, decided what the pragmatic intent of this utterance is and completely changed the propositional content. She omits the actual question, in part because the witness begins to sign before she has completed the signing: it would be necessary at this point either to stop the witness signing or to sign what the lawyer is presenting. She chooses to do the latter. Note that it is the interpreter who has decided to tell the witness that this is 'really important': the lawyer has made no such comment.

   So we here have a situation where the question asked by the lawyer has been totally omitted, but the lawyer has seen the interpreter sign towards the witness and therefore may well have assumed that the question has been asked.

   The early part of the transcript shows the lawyer using the third person form: not "did you see any hands laid upon your wife?", but "did he see any hands laid upon his wife". It is perhaps not altogether surprising that at times the interpreter appears to take on the role of answering for the Deaf person, when the lawyer is placing the interpreter in that very position. As is typical of many such interactions, the lawyer is not consistent, but moves between third and first person.

   An ongoing problem within this sequence involves the exact meaning of the classifier forms used by the witness. Thus he produces a classifier form in which each hand is a Person Classifier. The following is a literal version of the signer's first production of this:

> Two persons move towards each other (movement towards the signer);
> the one on the right bends back; the one on the left separates and
> moves to the left (towards the signer – as if going behind the signer)

Prior to the production of the classifier form, the witness signs

JUST SAW WIFE

He then produces the classifier form and vocalizes the name as he produces the final part of the classifier form. The resultant text is translated by the interpreter as:

> I just saw my wife falling back and Alex Mackay coming past her at the same time as she was falling back.

As the interpreter speaks this, she also produces a version of the classifier form herself while looking at the witness, as if to confirm with him that her understanding is correct. The lawyer then asks:

> So he did not actually see Alex Mackay putting hands on his wife?

The witness responds by using a complex classifier form again. The two single person classifier forms are brought together and then move apart. It is also worth noting that the witness has actually changed the direction of the movements of both hands so that the hands move away from rather than towards the body. This either means he has changed the perspective from which he is viewing the action or he has made an error. This is exactly the type of example which a Deaf lawyer or a lawyer who understands BSL would wish to investigate further. A possible translation would be "They came towards each other as they moved away from me and then separated". The interpreter produces the following spoken version of this:

> No. No it was just that these things happened at the same time.

This response appears to express a meaning inferred by the interpreter from what the witness has signed: it cannot be said to represent an accurate translation of what has actually been signed. It is as if at this point the interpreter has moved into the role of answering for the Deaf person. However, there is no overt marking of this shift and it would be impossible for the lawyers to detect this without knowing BSL. It is also highly unlikely that the interpreter is even aware of having operated in this way. Once again she reproduces the classifier form used by the witness at the same time as she speaks the response.

The importance of the interpreter's version can be seen in the way that the lawyer immediately picks up on the notion of these things happening at the same time:

> These things happened at the same time. So for all you know she might have stumbled?

In responding to this, the Deaf witness again uses a classifier form showing two persons coming together and separating; then both hands move forward and then move back (towards the signer) and to the right to show the action of 'falling back'. Although both hands are used at this stage, given the vocalization 'wife', we can assume the witness is referring only to his wife. Again someone recognizing the ambiguity here would have sought clarification. The interpreter translates the response as:

> No. No. I saw her falling back and luckily something was behind her and broke her fall.

The solicitor continues: "But what he saw Alex Mackay doing was walk past her?". Here the witness responds 'Yes', but then produces a complex classifier form, again using two person classifiers. This time the hands come together so that one hand is behind the other, but then does not move beyond the other hand. This could be translated as "one person came up to the other" or "one person came up behind the other". The interpreter voices 'Yes', but then seeks clarification from the witness by signing:

> Do you mean Alex Mackay came up behind your wife or went past her?

At this point the lawyer has started the next question, "Now your evidence is ...", but the witness signs "NO, NO WAIT ..." and the interpreter says "I want to clarify". Again, one might expect the lawyer to be aware that the interpreter is signing a question which he himself has not asked. The interpreter is after all signing at a point when we would expect her to be speaking. However, the lawyer takes no action. It is also worth saying that throughout this session – and indeed for much of the case – the Procurator Fiscal's depute, i.e. the person who is prosecuting the case on behalf of the Crown, is actually sitting with his back to both the witness and Interpreter One. In other words, he takes no direct visual notice of the way in which the witness gives evidence or of the actions of the interpreter: he is reliant completely on the spoken utterances. The other solicitors, acting for the other accused in the case, are sitting in positions which would allow them to watch what is happening, but one does so rarely. It is as if the whole activity (signing and interpreting) is simply a closed book to the lawyers. It would indeed be impossible for them to comprehend fully what is happening, unless they knew BSL, and there is a very real danger of them misinterpreting gestural activity. Nevertheless if they had some general awareness of the processes involved, one might expect them at the very least to question what is happening when the interpreter signs to the witness without the lawyer having asked a question.

At this stage the Deaf witness goes on to explain further what happened. This is interpreted into English by the interpreter as follows:

> When I was sitting down what I saw was my wife stagger back and
> Alex Mackay came in at exactly the same time that she was stagger-
> ing back. I saw that.

The interpreter omits the final part of the signing in which the witness indicates that as his wife is staggering back, he himself is punched on the brow
by Alex Mackay. In fact, the lawyer picks up this point in the very next
question. Since the signed version of 'he punched me on the brow' is in part
an approximation to such an action, it may be that the lawyer has actually
understood the signing at that point, even though the meaning is not
interpreted.

We can see then that within a very short stretch of courtroom interaction,
several key differences between source and target message, both from and to
English and BSL, can be observed. Almost inadvertently the interpreter has
taken control of the discourse, yet at the same time one might argue it is out
of control since none of the participants in the interaction has full access to
what each is expressing.

While some of the differences between source and target message may be
seen as avoidable errors, other derive directly from differences between the
two languages. Again and again the interpreter has to deal with the dilemmas
of visual encoding. In the following sequence, the interpreter has to present
in a gestural language the action of putting both hands up to the face:

> And I think you've told the court that you put both hands up to your
> face?

In signing this question to the witness, the interpreter chooses to use the open
handshape B for both hands, i.e. the hands are held so that all of the fingers
are together and there is slight bending at the major knuckles: the hands are
held at either side of the face. The Deaf witness then re-enacts what he did,
and the interpreter speaks: "Yes I did that". When the witness responds, he
produces a very similar version to the interpreter, except that his hands are
clenched into fists. The interpreter then copies the witness. In response to the
next question from the solicitor, "Could you show us that again please?", the
Deaf witness repeats the action with closed fists; the interpreter also reproduces the same action while saying: "That's what I did". Note that the
interpreter had to choose a way of signing a gestural action without having
full information. There is no way of signing 'put one's hands up to one's
face' without choosing a shape for the hands. It might be assumed that once
the information has been supplied by the witness, there is no further problem. However, such detail may be a matter of contention, in which case the
interpreter would be placed in an impossible position.

In a number of examples the interpreter produces a form which omits the
specificity expressed in the source language. Thus when the lawyer asks "And

did you put your face down towards the carpet?", the interpreter signs this as

[FACE HEAD DOWN SAME TIME HEAD DOWN]
Did you put your head down at the same time?

The interpreter does not sign CARPET, so the specificity of the question is lost. A similar example occurs when the solicitor comments: "You told me a moment ago, you were turned towards a chair". The interpreter signs this as

[CROUCH OVER/HANDS AT FACE/HEAD DOWN]
You were crouched over with your clenched fists protecting your face and your head downwards.

Again there is no specific mention of 'chair' by the interpreter. Note that the response of the witness (as spoken by the interpreter), "Yes, that's right", is therefore a response to a different question than that asked by the lawyer. This exchange occurs immediately after the witness has been warned by the solicitor to tell the truth:

Mr X, will you please be careful when you're answering questions that I ask. You have to tell the whole truth.

The problem for the Deaf witness is that he is not always accessing the questions which the lawyer is asking. Therefore he may be answering completely different questions – truthfully or not.

The fact that the interpreter feels under pressure in expressing some of this complex visual-spatial information can be shown in the following sequence:

"Were your knees on the chair?"

Rather than using a BSL sign meaning 'chair', the interpreter actually bends down towards a chair which happens to be at her side and indicates this – after having produced a classifier compound meaning 'kneeling on a flat surface'. There is no particular reason why she should do this at this point. There are several signs meaning 'chair' in BSL. However, the fact that she has not set up a particular spatial location for 'chair' – indeed has not established a 'scene' as such – is clearly causing difficulty.

4.3 Register and style

Evidence from the Durham research reveals that BSL/English interpreters often change the register of the source message. The types of change involved are partially but not wholly comparable to those noted by Hale (1997) with respect to interpreting between English and Spanish in courtroom settings.

Hale found that interpreters tended to raise the level of formality when working into English and lower it when interpreting into Spanish. There are frequent examples in our data of the tendency to raise the level of formality of the English interpretation. Within the videorecorded data, one Deaf witness stood throughout much of the questioning with one hand resting on the rail of the witness box. This meant that he signed mainly with one hand – even where signs would normally be made with two hands. He also often produced the signs loosely in terms of the handshape – the handshapes were often articulated some distance from the target location, and often also responded with one-sign utterances or very short signed responses. Overall the signing could most appropriately be characterized as casual: it was certainly not formal. In contrast, the spoken language version came across as formal.

Hale quotes examples of interpreters expanding syntactic structures and adding linguistic items in order to raise the level of formality (1997:48ff). Comparable additions can be noted in the BSL/English data, for example:

> Witness: BEFORE?
> Interpreter: Do you mean at the time of the incident or before?
>
> Witness: AGAIN
> Interpreter: I'm sorry what do you mean

In raising the level of formality, the interpreter may also distort the intention of the signer. In the second example, the signer has simply produced the sign AGAIN and appears to be asking the interpreter to repeat the signing of the question. What actually happens is that the lawyer completely rephrases the question and so does not allow the Deaf witness to see the same question asked again. How do we decide what would be appropriate in such contexts? If the interpreter had said "Could you sign that again?" or "Could you repeat the question?" it would have accorded more to the original request, but placed it within a register appropriate to the court. Some degree of cultural media-tion would have taken place. It is perfectly polite in BSL discourse to use this one word request, with appropriate non-manual markers. The signer could have added further politeness, for example the sign PLEASE, but the signer chose not to do this. The interpreter did not use this politeness marker, but instead chose an apologetic opening – 'I'm sorry'. There is little indication that the signer intended such an apologetic opening. We can see how even such an apparently trivial example can give a different image of the witness: to BSL users the witness may seem assertive at this point, to English users unnecessarily apologetic.

The approach to register within English to BSL does not accord wholly with Hale's findings. There appears to be a general tendency amongst inter-preters to use a more English-influenced variety of BSL. Such a variety was traditionally seen as appropriate to more formal contexts, such as church services or committee meetings. While it is still often used in religious contexts, newer, less English-influenced formal varieties of BSL have developed more recently. These can be seen on television, in presentations and lectures and in the formal proceedings of Deaf organizations such as the British Deaf Association. The analysis of some of the signing within court suggests that some of it is barely grammatical or comprehensible, since it has been so stripped of the requisite BSL grammar. However, the signing often appears impressive to those who do not know the language.

Within the specific court case discussed earlier, where three interpreters were working simultaneously, it is possible to note variation in usage between these three interpreters. The most important point to stress here is that major differences can be noted between the interpreter working between witness and lawyer and the other two interpreters. The witness-lawyer interpreter uses the resources of BSL more fully, including non-manual elements, referencing and some, though limited, spatial grammar. She is clearly influenced at times by the witness's own usage – picking up signs and signed expressions from him. It appears that the demands of ensuring that the witness has fully understood the question make themselves felt in the interpreter's signing. For the other two interpreters there is no such immediacy: they do not expect their interpreting to be interrupted by the accused, or indeed the lawyers. They tend to use much more English-based structure, fingerspelling and mouth pattern, with very little use of non-manual components. This suggests that the interpreter's usage is not influenced simply by the nature of the language, but also by the nature of the client demands. The interpreter for the witness appears to use whatever is available to ensure that the witness has understood the message; the others may see themselves as serving a wider role in the court – ensuring that signing is seen in a positive light, perhaps. Certainly this whole area deserves fuller elaboration.

5. Conclusion

Hatim and Mason (1990) have suggested that "translating involves a conflict of interests, it is all a question of where one's priorities lie" (Hatim and Mason 1990:17). They go on to discuss the different orientations of the translator: author-centred translation, text-centred translation and reader-centred translation. The court interpreter is similarly faced with comparable conflicts of interest. The interpreter has to try to be accurate in terms of transmitting the original message; ensure that the resulting text works as an example of BSL or English text; and ensure that the watcher or listener is able to access the message fully. However, cutting across this central dilemma are the power differences within the court. The interpreter is almost inevitably pulled in the direction of supporting the Deaf person, simply because the Deaf person is typically so disempowered in the courtroom setting.

Few of the participants have any real understanding of the language and cultural background of Deaf participants. The research reveals that they are the least likely to be consulted about their interpreting or other requirements: instead decisions are made for them. The interpreters are expected by court officials to act as go-betweens, not only within the context of linguistic interpretation, but also outside of the courtroom. The interpreter is the one who is seen by the court 'to know about Deaf people' and is also the one who is seen by the Deaf person as 'knowing about the court'. Almost without realizing it, many interpreters seem to take these burdens of responsibility into the actual interpreting context. It is clear that interpreters themselves need to have much more opportunity to examine what they themselves do in court and court officials need to develop a much richer understanding of the complex linguistic demands of bimodal interpreting. Until this begins to happen, Deaf people will not have full access to the justice system.

MARY BRENNAN
Moray House Institute of Education, University of Edinburgh, Charteris Land, Holyrood Road, Edinburgh, EH8 8AQ, UK. maryb@mhie.ac.uk

Notes

The research discussed here was funded by the Leverhulme Trust. Members of the research team were Mary Brennan, Richard Brown, Brenda Mackay, Maureen Reed, Caroline Taylor and Graham Turner.

1.   The term 'deaf' with lower case 'd' is used to refer to people who have a hearing loss, but who do not necessarily see themselves as part of a linguistic minority group; the term 'Deaf' with upper case 'D' is used to refer to those people, usually also 'deaf', who identify themselves as belonging to a distinct linguistic minority group with its own culture and heritage.
2.   Glosses of signs are shown in capitals: whole utterances are shown as glosses in square brackets. Such representation does not show the complexity of BSL grammar.

References

Baker-Shenk, C. (1983) *A Micro-Analysis of the Non-Manual Components of Questions in American Sign Language,* PhD Thesis, Berkeley: University of California.
Berk-Seligson, Susan (1990) *The Bilingual Courtroom: Courtroom Interpreters in the Judicial Process,* Chicago: Chicago University Press.
Brennan, Mary (1990) *Word-Formation in British Sign Language*, Stockholm: Stockhom University Press.

------ (1992) 'The Visual World of British Sign Language: An Introduction', in David Brien (ed) *Dictionary of British Sign Language/English,* London: Faber & Faber.

------ (1997a) 'In Sight – in Mind: Visual Encoding in Signed Language', in C. Loades (ed) *Proceedings of the Australian and New Zealand Conference for Educators of the Deaf,* Adelaide: ANZCED.

------ (1997b) 'Seeing the Difference: Translation Across Modalities', in Karl Simms (ed) *Translating Sensitive Texts: Linguistic Aspects,* Amsterdam & Atlanta: Rodopi.

------, M. D. Colville and L. K. Lawson (1980*) Words in Hand: A Structural Analysis of the Signs of British Sign Language,* Edinburgh: BSL Project.

------, M. D. Colville, L. K. Lawson and G. Hughes (1984) *Words in Hand: A Structural Analysis of the Signs of British Sign Language,* Carlisle: British Deaf Association and Edinburgh: BSL Project (Second Edition).

------ and R. K. Brown (1997) *Equality before the Law: Deaf People's Access to Justice,* Durham: Deaf Studies Research Unit.

Brien, David (ed) (1992) *Dictionary of British Sign Language/English,* London: Faber & Faber.

Collins, J. M (1994) 'Who Needs Medical Interpreters?'. Paper presented at the first *Issues in Interpreting* conference, Durham: Deaf Studies Research Unit.

Colville, M. D. (1979) 'Loan Signs from Fingerspelled Words'. Paper presented at the *NATO Conference on Sign Language Research,* Copenhagen.

------ (1984) 'Patterns of Fingerspelling'. Paper presented at the *Sign '84* conference, Edinburgh.

Conrad, R. (1979) *The Deaf School Child,* London: Harper Row.

Ebbinghaus, H. and J. Hessmann (1996) 'Signs and Words: Accounting for Spoken Elements in German Sign Language', in W. H. Edmondson and R. B. Wilbur (eds) *International Review of Sign Linguistics* 1: 23-56.

Gregory, S., S. Powers and E. Thoutenhoofd (1998) *The Educational Attainments of Deaf Children: A Literature Review,* London: DfEE.

Hale, Sandra (1997) 'The Treatment of Register Variation in Court Interpreting', *The Translator* 3(1): 39-54.

Hatim, Basil and Ian Mason (1990) *Discourse and the Translator,* London & New York: Longman.

Johnston, T. (1996) 'Function and Medium in the Forms of Linguistic Expression Found in a Sign Language', *International Review of Sign Linguistics* 1(1): 57-94.

Klima, E. S. and U. Bellugi (1979) *The Signs of Language,* Cambridge, Mass.: Harvard University Press.

Kyle, J. G. and B. Woll (1985) *Sign Language: The Study of Deaf People and Their Language,* Cambridge: Cambridge University Press.

Lakoff, G. (1987) *Women, Fire and Dangerous Things: What Categories Reveal about Thought,* Chicago & London: University of Chicago Press.

------ and M. Johnson (1980) *Metaphors We Live By,* Chicago & London: University of Chicago Press.

Morris, Ruth (1995) 'The Moral Dilemmas of Court Interpreting', *The Translator* 1(1): 25-46.

Schermer, T. M. (1990) *In Search of a Language: Influences from Spoken Dutch on the Sign Language of the Netherlands*, Rotterdam: Eburon Delft.

Stokoe, W. C. (1960) 'Sign Language Structure: An Outline of the Visual Communication System of the American Deaf', *Studies in Linguistics, Occasional Papers 8*, Buffalo: University of Buffalo.

Supalla, T. (1986) 'The Classifier System in American Sign Language', in C. Craig (ed) *Noun Classes and Categorisation*, Philadelphia: John Benjamins.

Sutton-Spence, R. (1994) *The Role of the Manual Alphabet and Fingerspelling in British Sign Language*, PhD Thesis, Bristol: University of Bristol.

Sweetser, E. E. (1990) *From Etymology to Pragmatics*, Cambridge: Cambridge University Press.

Wilcox, P. (1993) *Metaphorical Mappings in American Sign Language*, PhD Thesis, Albuquerque: University of New Mexico.

The Translator. Volume 5, Number 2 (1999), 247-264   ISBN 1-900650-21-5

Telephone Interpreting & the Synchronization of Talk in Social Interaction

CECILIA WADENSJÖ
University of Linköping, Sweden

Abstract. *The present paper compares telephone interpreting and on-site interpreting in order to investigate the ways in which social interaction in these different interpreting situations is influenced by the setting. Two real-life encounters recorded at a police station are used to illustrate and explore differences in the participants' – including the interpreter's – conversational behaviour. The encounters involved the same participants and concerned the same case. In one encounter, the interpreter communicated by telephone, in the other she was present on site. The on-site exchange was strikingly more fluent, compared to the telephone-interpreted one. The difference is made manifest discursively, for instance in the average length of the participants' turns at talk and in the patterns of overlapping speech. It would appears that a significant difference between the two types of interpreter-mediated encounters lies in the possibilities they provide for the participants to coordinate and to synchronize their collective activity, or interaction.*

This paper links theoretically and methodologically to studies of situated social interaction, such as Duranti and Goodwin (1992), Drew and Heritage (1992), and to earlier studies of interpreter-mediated interaction carried out at the Department of Communication Studies, Linköping University (e.g. Wadensjö 1997, 1998, Linell 1997). Above all, the paper applies a dialogical view of language and mind, inspired by the work of Bakhtin (1979/1986) and some of his followers.

In research on interpreting, a monological, essentially textual view of language is frequently adopted. People's talk (as well as the interpreter's task) is explored as *text,* or *production of texts*. Investigations normally reveal facts about the relationship between a given 'text' and established standards in a given, linguistically and grammatically defined language. An alternative way to explore talk is as *activity*, or rather activities (other than text production), such as explaining, complying, and so forth. This is an essentially different point of departure, which draws on sociolinguistics and social psychology. However, neither approach excludes the other. They correspond to different levels of abstraction. I have found it useful to combine the two when exploring the dynamics of interpreter-mediated interaction. In this approach, the

ISSN 1355-6509

main unit of exploration is not a language, nor is it the interpreter or any other participant involved in interaction. It is the three-party conversation as a situated system of activity (see Linell 1998 and Wadensjö 1998, Chapter 2, on the difference between monologism and dialogism).

1. Telephone interpreting vs. on-site interpreting

Telephone interpreting is a fairly common phenomenon in many countries today. A recent report by Pointon, Ozolins and Doucouliagos (1998) catalogues and analyses mainly financial aspects of telephone interpreting services organized by some telephone companies in Europe, Australia and the USA.[1] Leaving aside the matter of cost, an obvious advantage of telephone interpreting – compared to on-site, face-to-face interpreting – from the point of view of clients, care providers, police officers and others who occasionally need the service of interpreters is the relatively greater accessibility of interpreters. If a need arises too far away, too late at night or at too short a notice for an interpreter to meet it in person, the problem can in principle be solved if there are a competent interpreter, a shared willingness between the primary parties to communicate by phone, and suitable telephone equipment at both ends.

Telephone interpreting may save time, money and – in cases if urgency – human suffering. Nevertheless, people may prefer either telephone or on-site interpreting for a range of reasons. To judge from interviews I have conducted within various research projects, people seem to prefer the type of interpreting they are used to. By no means all informants, however, express an opinion – positive or negative – about the one or the other type. People may lack enough experience, or may simply not see that the mode of interpreting in itself would make any significant difference.

As a point of departure, I assume that the interpreter's being there or being on the phone is not necessarily decisive for the quality of performance, in terms of adequacy or exactness of translation. Neither type of interpreting seems, in and by itself, to guarantee better quality. Irrespective of working mode, interpreters' performance is dependent on their knowledge of the working languages and of the subject matter, their skill, experience and current form. Moreover, as is evident from empirical studies (e.g. Wadensjö 1998), the outcome of interpreters' work is dependent on the primary participants, on their mutual relations, on how they relate to the interpreter and on their communicative style.

Nevertheless, I take it that telephone interpreting and on-site interpreting differ in nature as communicative situations. Contrasting two encounters organized in these different ways, I will investigate possible differences between the conditions in which each of them takes place. In particular, the analysis will focus on what they imply for an injured party's telling of her story about an event under investigation. Numerous studies of narratives as social activities have emphasized storytellers' need for an attentive audience (e.g. Goodwin 1984, Polanyi 1985, Duranti and Brenneis 1986, Aronsson and Cederborg 1994, Ochs and Capps 1996). How can this need be satisfied in an on-site and a telephone-interpreted situation respectively? Before focusing on this question at a 'local' turn-by-turn level of interaction, I will discuss some general aspects of telephone interpreting which are more 'global' in character and not necessarily visible in discourse data. They relate to the physical setting, observable prior to any investigation of what goes on in the exchange, and to participants' ideas of telephone interpreting, as they are expressed, for instance, in my interviews.

Basically, there are three aspects mentioned by people in practice when telephone interpreting is touched upon as an issue, namely confidentiality, feelings of being marginalized (or the opposite, of being involved in a shared event), and non-verbal communication.

1.1 Confidentiality and involvement

As a rule, the *Official Secrets Act* which normally applies to public service officials is also valid for interpreters. Interpreters are obliged to observe strict confidentiality and not disclose any information about their clients to anyone. Telephone interpreting can be perceived both as an advantage and a disadvantage in this connection. A young suspect in the Linköping data said he preferred telephone interpreting because it protected him from being recognized by the interpreter outside of the encounter. This young man lived in a small town, where his language was spoken by relatively few people. A psychiatric nurse interviewed for another project communicated a similar idea, claiming that some patients, in particular young people, are less embarrassed when the interpreters cannot see them.

In contrast, some clients may feel that the 'invisible' interpreter might be able to identify them, while they, in turn, cannot identify the interpreter. Seeing the interpreter can apparently sometimes prevent primary parties from feeling insecure about the interpreter's reliability, while sometimes quite the opposite may occur. In the present telephone-interpreted encounter there is evidence of the interpreter (Irina) being sensitive to the issue of confidentiality. A police officer (Peggy) conducts a hearing with a woman who has accused her husband of assault. They sit opposite one another, behind and in front of a big desk in an office at the police station. The police officer has called the interpreter on the phone. Irina works from her home via the telephone and is present at the office only as a voice in a loud-speaking telephone apparatus placed on the desk. At one point when Irina interprets for Peggy she specifies the 'participation framework' (Goffman 1981, Wadensjö 1998:86-94).

Excerpt 1 (P3:2)

	69	Peggy	jag gör anteckningar under tiden som ska ligga till grund
			I take notes meanwhile which will be the basis
	70		för ett målsägarförhör,[2]
			of a [written record from this] hearing of the injured party,
→	71	Irina	я записываю пока говорит полицейская и эти
			I'll take notes meanwhile says the police officer. and these
	72		записи будут лешать в осзнове допроса исца.
			notes will form the basis of the hearing of the injured party.

Irina can anticipate possible misunderstanding and adds "says the police of-ficer" (1:71), thus preventing the client from thinking that she (the interpreter) is talking about herself when she says "I'll take notes" (1:71). In the Swedish context, interpreters are normally trained to destroy any notes they have taken in front of a client, and to dispose of them in the room where the encounter took place, all to avoid making clients feel that the principle of secrecy may be endangered.

When they are present on site too, however, interpreters sometimes talk explicitly about the current 'participation framework', both in order to com-municate a separation between the speaking *I* and the meaning other, as in the example above, and in order to clarify who is talking to whom, and who is selected as next speaker. This tends to happen when face-threatening mat-ters are brought into the discussion and when one of the primary interlocutors is a child (see Wadensjö 1998, Chapter 9 and 7).

The issue of feeling marginalized in telephone-interpreted encounters was raised, for instance, in an interview with an interpreter working for providers of psychiatric care and traumatized refugees. She categorically refused to work on the phone in these encounters, referring to her own well-being as a professional interpreter. In her opinion, telephone interpreting in these situa-tions could imply an increased risk of burn-out. Being left alone, after having put down the receiver, she had felt it hard to avoid taking patients' traumatic stories to heart. Being on site and sharing the event more concretely with the professional care provider made her own feelings of sadness and desolation easier to understand and handle. Being physically there, she argued, means that interpreters can exchange a few words with the therapist after the ses-sion if they need to.

Being on site does not guarantee that interpreters will not feel marginalized, however. Several interpreters in my interview data provided stories about feeling completely ignored – in particular by the professional party – in a way which affected them quite negatively.

1.2 Non-verbal communication

In some of my interviews, interpreters commented on one obvious disadvantage of being on the phone and the corresponding advantage of being on site, namely that the telephone line might aggravate the problem of grasping what people say when they speak in a low voice, or with an unfamiliar accent. Naturally, interpreters working with spoken languages are always dependent on the acoustic environment. If people speak inarticulately and interpreters cannot see their movements, gestures and facial expressions, they can mishear, or not hear at all. They can be forced to ask for repetition, and thus momentarily lose their concentration on the current flow of talk. In contrast, a simultaneous visual impression of the speaker can help interpreters to stay on track when the pronunciation of a word or two is unclear.

In the telephone interpreted encounter in question here, the flow of talk was clearly interrupted on several occasions, when the telephone interpreter was unable to grasp what the client was saying, or whether she had more to say. In other words, these occasions involved for the interpreter both a problem of translating the message and a problem of coordinating the interaction. For instance, the police officer asked the client (Katya) what her husband had done with the knife after he cut himself. The interpreter translated, and the client answered, at first in a low voice.

Excerpt 2 (P3:3)

	152	Irina	а что он сделал потом с ножом после того как
			and what did he do with the knife after he had
	153	Irina	он порезался?
			cut himself?
	154	Katya	°потом он его положил,°
			°*then he put it [down],*°
			(1)
→	155	Katya	efter eh::: потом он его положил.
			after er::: then he put it [down].
	156	Irina	så la han den. åt sidan.
			then he put it. aside.

Katya, the client, waits for a while (a second). Then she tries to address the police officer directly, in Swedish. She stops at *after er:::* (2:155), however, and goes back to the established interaction order, repeating, in Russian this time, what she just said in a louder voice, in the direction of the telephone apparatus, and the interpreter then translates her message (2:156).

Another example: later in the telephone-interpreted encounter the officer asks Katya whether her husband had threatened her on other occasions, apart from the night described in the police report. The interpreter translates the question and the client answers, at first in a voice which is apparently a bit unclear:

Excerpt 3 (P3:7)

381	Katya	○ уграⱬал,○ (hawks)
		been threatening,
		(1)
→ 382	Katya	уграⱬал,
		been threatening,
		(0.5)
→ 383	Katya	да.
		yes.
384	Irina	ja. han har hotat mig.
		yeah. he has been threatening me.

After a long pause (again about one second in duration), having heard no translation of her reply, the client repeats it in a louder voice (3:382). The silence that follows is shorter (half a second), but Katya again interprets it as an indication that her answer is not clear. She then says "yes" in a distinct voice (3:383). Only after this third attempt on the part of Katya does the interpreter hear what she has said *and* establish that she has finished talking: that Katya wants her to take over the turn at talk. It is worth noting that Katya, when saying "yes." (3:383), not only spoke louder but also with more 'termination intonation', while both times when she said "been threatening," (3:381, 382) the tone of her voice had been rising. With no non-verbal cues at hand to guide the interpreter, the speaker's intonation may have become all the more decisive.

On the other hand, a watchful interlocutor can partly compensate for some of the telephone interpreter's disadvantages in being out of sight. For example, the police officer in the current telephone mediation informed the interpreter when significant non-verbal communication occurred in the office, which the interpreter (Irina) could not see. The following excerpt involves two such instances. It starts at the point when the police officer (Peggy) asks the woman (Katya) who accused her husband of assault where she was when he, as she claimed, had threatened to kill her or himself with a knife. Peggy asks Katya to use her hands to demonstrate where she and her husband were in relation to each other.

Excerpt 4. (P3:4)

164	Katya	вот так. (xx)
		like this. (xx)
165	Irina	på det viset.
		in that way.
→ 166	Peggy	ja, hon visar mig nu.
		yeah she shows me now.
	Katya	här- här Björn, här ja.
		here – here Björn, here I.

	167	Peggy	där var du. och där var Björn. ungefär en meter
			there were you. and there was Björn. roughly one meter
	168	Peggy	och rakt framför.
			and straight ahead of [you].
	169	Irina	так значит приблизительно метра от Бёрна и
			so that is roughly a meter from Björn and
	170	Irina	прямо перед ним.
			straight in front of him.
	171	Katya	да.
			yes.
	172	Peggy	mm
	173	Irina	ja.
			yes.
			(4)
→	174	Peggy	nu skriver jag lite så det blir tyst ett tag.
			now I write a little so it'll be silent for some time.
	175	Irina	jaha.
			aha.

The stretches highlighted with an arrow (4:166 and 4:174) show that the police officer, Peggy, was aware of the interpreter's need to be informed about ongoing non-verbal communication. In the first case (4:166), Peggy refers to Katya's ongoing demonstration in the room, performed with gestures and words. Katya at the same time says in Swedish: "here – here Björn, here I" (4:166).

The second case (4:174), shows that the police officer was alert to the fact that Irina could misinterpret a long stretch of silence. Peggy's comment assures the interpreter that the telephone connection is working, even if she (Irina) cannot hear the other participants for a while. Communicating via the phone means that interpreters have to wait for spoken confirmation to establish that they have been heard.

Somewhat later in the telephone mediation another silence (2.5 seconds) apparently made the interpreter unsure on this very point. The police officer asks the client how she knew that her husband used drugs.

Excerpt 5 (P3:6)

	302	Peggy	hur vet du det?
			how do you know that?
	303	Irina	а как вы знаете это?
			and how do you know that?
			(2.5)
→	304	Irina	алло. откуда вы это знаете?
			hello. from where do you know this?

305   Katya   потому что я же живу с ним.
                because I live with him, don't I.

Here the interpreter apparently feels the need to ensure that the lines of communication are still open. So she calls out "hello" and provides a new translation of the officer's question (5:304).

For the interpreter, then, there is an obvious disadvantage in being on the phone compared to being on site when it comes to capturing the communicative cues provided by interlocutors' gestures, posture, mimics, and other non-verbal behaviour, all of which have a role in guiding the interpretation. As we saw in Excerpt 4 above, an experienced user of interpreters can compensate for some of the difficulties that may occur due to the lack of access to non-verbal information. Nevertheless, the more inarticulately primary interlocutors speak, and the poorer the quality of the audio equipment they use, the greater the interpreter's disadvantage in terms of not having access to non-verbal features accompanying talk in interaction. At times, these restrictions can affect interpretation quality in adverse ways, in terms of adequacy of translation and in terms of confusion of the order of interaction, i.e. the turn-by-turn organization of talk. The other two aspects discussed above, confidentiality and involvement, do not seem automatically to constitute a difference between on-site and telephone-interpreted encounters.

2. Telling one's story through an interpreter

I will now go on to explore in more detail the local turn-by-turn organization of the already quoted telephone-interpreted encounter and compare it to the local organization of an on-site encounter. But first some background information on the case to which both encounters relate. A woman had accused her husband of assault and battery. She was heard twice regarding this same issue, by the same police officer, assisted by the same interpreter. The woman spoke Russian and the officer spoke Swedish. In the first encounter, the interpreter was connected through a loud-speaking telephone. The second time, a month later, she was present at the office.

After the first encounter, the Russian-speaking woman told me she found it very difficult to talk when the interpreter was on the phone. She could not explain why she did not like that situation. It was just a feeling. She actually did not want to complain, she said. She definitely had preferred this interpreter (Irina) to the one who had assisted on site at the social welfare office some time ago. After the second encounter, where the interpreter (again Irina) was present, the client repeated that she had very much appreciated the interpretation, and that she preferred it when the interpreter was present face-to-face.

In both encounters, the client Katya talked about the night her husband battered her. This was not the first time it happened, but the first time the Police had come to their apartment. At the same time an ambulance had come to pick up the husband who was badly injured, cut with a knife. In both hearings, the officer asked for details about the cutting event, and Katya told Peggy her story. In the telephone encounter she started quite insecurely. At first she just answered the officer's questions very briefly. After some thirteen minutes she started to talk in longer sequences, and she recalled how her husband was injured and how, prior to this, he had beaten her up, as he had done on several occasions before. In the on-site encounter, her storytelling started after just four minutes. It was rather more detailed in terms of what her husband had said, and what she had said to him when he aimed the knife at her.

In trying to identify discourse features that distinguished the two encounters, I started from my intuitive impression that people talked 'more' when on site than when using the phone. Counting the words spoken in each encounter, I found that the telephone-interpreted talk consisted of 4856 and the on-site one of 4277 words. The telephone-interpreted encounter took all in all 38 minutes and the on-site encounter lasted for 25 minutes. Hence, the on-site encounter involved saying more, counted in words spoken per minute (more precisely, it had an average of 43 words more/minute), and it involved – one might guess – speaking faster.

2.1 Tempo

Estimating the client's talking tempo in the two encounters, I found that she spoke slightly faster when the interpreter was on site. Counted roughly, her average speed was 2.4 words/second, compared to 2.3 words/second in the telephone mediation. It was clearly easier for the client to find her words and to speak in the second encounter. A simple reason for this might be that she was more used to the situation and to the people involved. Having been through a similar encounter once, it was less of a problem to confide her story to the officer (and the interpreter), since she had done so already. Moreover, the story was already formulated. In a sense, the second version was a more rehearsed one. Only a couple of details had to be added.

From the client's point of view, however, these details constituted crucial information. The second time she told her story Katya 'confessed' that she had said "Do it!" when her husband had threatened her, and that she thought this made it partly her fault that her husband cut himself with the knife. But now she was less inclined to take guilt upon herself, which may be partly why she felt more at ease when talking about the event. Another reason that may have facilitated the client's storytelling during the on-site encounter was that she was less depressed then, compared to when she first met Peggy, the police officer. In the second meeting, the sound of her voice and her whole appearance was more secure and stable.

Yet, the fact that people talked more in the on-site encounter cannot be explained only by Katya's somewhat faster tempo. Roughly estimated, the interpreter's average speed was 2.1 words/second on both occasions, and the police officer in both encounters spoke at an average speed of 2.7 words/ second. The three participants thus spoke each at their average pace, which was more or less constant from one exchange to the other.

In estimating participants' talking tempo I counted only the time when speech was heard. Pauses were not included. Moreover, looking at the frequency of longer pauses (significant silences) in the encounters, I found that they were quite equally distributed between the two exchanges. Neither did the proportion of each participant's talk in relation to the talk of others vary much from one exchange to the other.

2.2 Distribution of turns at talk

In both encounters, the police officer contributed somewhat less than a third of the words spoken, the client spoke about a fifth of them, and – perhaps not surprisingly – the interpreter's share in both cases amounted to approximately half the total number of words. Still, when I listened to the two encounters and compared them, the on-site one struck me as more fluent. Then, comparing the length of turns at talk in both encounters, I found the following variation:

Tele. encounter	Police officer	Client	Interpreter
Turns (434)	112	131	191
Average length	≈14 words	≈7 words	≈12 words

On-site encounter	Police officer	Client	Interpreter
Turns (557)	177	126	254
Average length	≈8 words	≈6 words	≈8 words

The above comparison shows that there were fewer turns at talk (all in all 434) in the telephone mediation than in the on-site encounter. In the latter case, which was 13 minutes shorter, 557 turns at talk were exchanged between the officer, the client and the interpreter. Estimating each participant's average length of turns in terms of number of words, I found an interesting difference between the two encounters. In the telephone-interpreted one, the average turn at talk of the police officer and the interpreter was relatively longer (14 and 12 words per turn respectively) than that of the client (7 words/ turn).[3] In the on-site encounter, the pattern had changed (8, 8 and 6 words/ turn). In the on-site encounter, the interpreter thus took longer turns relative to the police officer and client, which meant that the time slots made available for the primary participants' contributions became relatively shorter. How could this promote a more fluent conversation? Discussion of other features such as feedback and overlapping talk may help us to answer this question.

2.3 Feedback

A couple of empirical studies of interpreter-mediated institutional encounters indicate that these generally involve fewer verbal feedback tokens (for instance, *mm*) compared to direct, one-language institutional talk (Jönsson 1990, Linell *et al.* 1992, Englund-Dimitrova 1997). The feedback tokens actually heard in this kind of encounter tend to appear – for obvious reasons – between the turns of the interpreter and the person she or he is currently addressing. The interpreter can use *mm* explicitly as a tool for encouraging talk from an interlocutor currently holding the turn; as Englund-Dimitrova puts it, "the interpreter can work as a kind of deputy listener" (Englund-Dimitrova 1997:163).

In interpreter-mediated interaction, the ordinary function of feedback, that of facilitating participants' orientation and coordination between themselves, is partly lost due to the regular suspension of the primary interlocutors' contributions. They may be able to anticipate signs from each other showing who is selected as next speaker, but they normally have to await a sign from the interpreter before taking the turn. Taking every second turn at talk, interpreters perform both tasks of translation and coordination of others' utterances (Wadensjö 1998).

In ordinary conversation, listeners' feedback often overlaps with speakers' talk. Tannen (1981) has noted that talking in overlap may be one way in which an interlocutor can communicate positive involvement; she refers to this as "cooperative overlap" (Tannen 1981:146). She further argues that the meaning attributed to simultaneous talk is culture specific. If overlap in some contexts counts as polite, in others it can be seen as pushy and aggressive. Tannen puts this down to ethnic and cultural conventions. In the case of interpreter-mediated events, I would rather see the difference as mainly an outcome of the communicative situation, and interlocutors' familiarity with it. My own analyses of the Linköping data suggest that individuals who are used to expressing themselves via an interpreter have a tendency to talk partly in parallel with the interpreter, in other words to engage in 'cooperative overlap'. The interpreter's overlap sometimes seems to encourage participants to provide more talk, in the sense that they seem to read it as a sign of the interpreter's active listening. It may take some time, however, for participants to adapt to a conversational style involving frequent parallel talk.

In the on-site encounter under discussion, the interpreter's overlap was, at least to start with, a little disturbing for the primary interlocutors. The police officer at one point lost her thread.

Excerpt 6 (P4:1)

    14 ⎡ Peggy   och eh::: (reads) han påstår här i eh:::
       │   *and er:::*   *he claims here in er:::*
       │ Irina   он утверждает здесь.
       ⎣   *he claims here.*
                  (.)
    15   Peggy   han påstår nu då att eh::: i förhöret här säger han att,
                  he claims now then that er::: in the protocol he says that,
    16 ⎡ Peggy   kniven har du-
       │   *the knife it was you-*
       ⎣ Irina   и в допросе он говорит,
                  and in the protocol he says,
-> 17   Peggy   vad sa du?
                  what did you say?
    18   Irina   ä ja fortsätt (light laughter)
                  no yeah go on
    19   Peggy   jaa.
                  yes.
-> 20 ⎡ Irina   °jag tolkar.°
       │   *°I'm interpreting.°*
       ⎣ Peggy   kniven har **du** hållit i.
                  *the knife **you** were holding.*
    21   Irina   что вы держали в руках нож.
                  that you held. the knife in your hands.
    22   Peggy   mm

After the above exchange and Peggy's question (6:17), which occurs at the
very beginning of the on-site encounter, Peggy does not allow herself to be
interrupted in mid-sentence by simultaneous talk from the interpreter. By the
time Irina has answered Peggy's off-the-record question (6:20) the latter seems
to have adapted to the mode of communication introduced by the interpreter.
So, it seems, has the client, encouraged by the officer. At one point, also
fairly close to the start of the encounter, Katya must have been visibly hesi-
tating when the interpreter came in while she was talking.

Excerpt 7 (P4:3)

    132 ⎡ Katya   это невозможно. у нас очень маленькая кухня.
        │   *this is impossible. we have a very little kitchen.*
        ⎣ Irina   det var- det är en
                                it was- it is an
        ⎡ Katya   чтобы драться.
        │   *to have a fight*
    133 │ Irina   omöjlighet. vi har ett litet kök det finns inte plats att eh::
        │   *impossibility. we have a little kitchen there is no space to*
        ⎣   *er:::*

→	Peggy	mm. ja prata på du.	
		mm. yes do keep talking.	
	Katya	очень маленькая.	
		very little.	
134	Irina	för slagsmål där. det är så pass lite.	
		to fight there. it is so little.	
	Peggy	mm	aa
		mm	*yeah*
135	Irina	utrymme där.	
		room there.	

The police officer urges her Russian-speaking visitor to go on talking, and to do so in overlap with the interpreter, saying (in Swedish) "mm. yes do keep talking." (7:133). With these encouraging words Peggy simultaneously demonstrates her own willingness to communicate, and her involvement in interaction also during the interpreter's turns at talk; she asserts her position as a person ultimately 'in charge' of the encounter, as it were.

The participants' mutual involvement in conversation is probably quite decisive for achieving fluency in the turn-by-turn organization of interaction (Wadensjö 1998:266-67). Probably no less decisive is their relatively greater possibility to synchronize talk, thanks to the immediately visible 'contextualization cues' (Gumperz 1982) in terms of gestures, facial expressions, handling of artefacts, and so forth. As the on-site encounter continues, the exchange gains in fluency and the frequent overlap seems not to be disturbing at all, rather the opposite.

2.4 Overlapping talk

In interpreter-mediated interaction, it seems, the interpreter's sense of timing and interlocutors' tolerance of talk in overlap play a role in shaping the process of storytelling (Wadensjö 1998:252-55). This is in line with what Erickson (1992) argues in a paper discussing family dinner talk as collective activity. Erickson writes that "given that actual talk must be done in real time, rhythmic organization of speech production appears to be the social integument by which coordinated action among interlocutors is held together in performance" (Erickson 1992:396).

In search of features by which the 'rhythmic organization of speech production' could materialize, I looked at the two encounters to compare instances of overlapping talk. There was much more overlap in the on-site encounter. In the first, telephone-interpreted encounter, only 11 instances of overlap can be found. The overlap was always very short in duration and five of the instances were subject to what conversation analysts have termed 'self-initiated self-repair' (Schegloff *et al.* 1977:364), instances where the speaker provides an alternative word or formulation for something just said. For example, at the beginning of the encounter the client says "I don't know how to start", and the officer replies "Do you want me to ask you. Put questions" (P3:1). The interpreter here starts to translate immediately after the officer's "ask you", thereby overlapping with the last two words in the officer's utterance. In the on-site encounter, there was constant parallel talk. I counted 155 instances of overlap, many of which lasted not just over a word or two, but over longer sequences of talk.

Consider, for instance, the following excerpt, taken from the second half of the on-site encounter. The police officer asks Katya if she recalls any more details about how her husband cut himself.

Excerpt 8 (P4:8)

	377	Katya	я:: ммм пришла,
			I:: mmm came,
	378	Katya	буквально это всё произошёл. ○ ну я не знаю.○
			literally this all happened. well I don't know.
→		Irina	jag kom dit, och så:: hände det.
			I came there and the::n it happened.
	379	Katya	двацать трицать минут . (.) пятьнацать.
			twenty, thirty minutes. (.) fifteen.
→	380	Irina	tjugi, tretti, femton minuter.
			twenty, thirty, fifteen minutes.
		Katya	всё очень быстро.
			all so quickly.
→	381	Irina	det gick allting så fort.
			it went all so quickly.
	382	Peggy	mm. jag vet att tiden är väldigt svår å uppskatta,
			mm. I know that the time is very difficult to estimate,
	383	Peggy	sådär när det händer nåt.
			like that when something happens.
⸴→		Irina	я знаю что тяжело так прикинуть во времени,
			I know that it's hard to estimate like that the time,
	384	Irina	когда произходит что-то такое.
			when something like this is happening.

As can be seen in the above example, the interpreter's translations overlap considerably with the interlocutors' talk. Moreover, the rhythmical organization of her contributions does not seem to have disturbed the speakers in terms of producing new utterances. The interpreter starts to translate when the current speaker is in the process of talking, not just anywhere, but in micro-pauses or shifts in intonation curves, in what Schegloff (1996:97) calls 'transition spaces' (cf. Apfelbaum 1998). In other words, Irina's translations appear in synchrony with the other participants' talk.

Evidently, this would not have been the case had it not been for the interpreter's sense of timing. Overlap is mostly initiated by the interpreter. More-over – and this is of particular interest – the participants' turns at talk (not only the interpreter's turns) generally start in synchrony with the rhythmic organization of the preceding speaker's speech production (see, for example, Katya's utterance (8:380) above). When there is no overlap, speakers' utter-ances often latched onto the following utterance with a minimal space of time in between. In the telephone-interpreted encounter, by contrast, mo-ments of transition occurring between participants' turns at talk are mostly longer in duration.

The significant difference, which explains why the on-site encounter in-volved talking faster, was thus not that the participant had speeded up in talking tempo, but that they spoke faster *together*.

3. Conclusion

In order to explore the nature of telephone-interpreted discourse and the way it differs from on-site interpreter-mediated talk, many studies of a more de-tailed nature than this one are needed. The present comparison between a telephone- and an on-site interpreter-mediated hearing indicates, however, that the three interlocutors' participation in a shared physical environment facilitates a shared rhythmic framework in their conversation. The impact of conversational rhythm on the organization of interpreter-mediated interac-tion is a subject that requires further investigation, but in the case under study it appears to have substantially facilitated the collective speaking activity, including the client's account of the event under investigation.

In the on-site interpreted encounter, the participants' exchange of turns at talk (the management of access and transition) was smoother than in the telephone-interpreted encounter. The pattern of vocal prosodic emphasis be-tween the participants' turns at talk, i.e. how speech production was organized rhythmically, was also more even.

It is evident that the two encounters provided different conditions for the coordination of the exchange and the synchronization of talk, i.e. who speaks when and for how long, and how – in time – participants' turns follow each other. This can be explained, at least partly, by a specific characteristic of interpreter-mediated face-to-face interaction. Since the interpreter's very act of interpreting assures the current speaker that what is said has been under-stood, the interpreter's contributions may partly serve a similar function to that served by feedback in ordinary, non-mediated conversation. As men-tioned above, feedback often occurs in overlap. At times, the speaker – who doesn't understand the content but can register the progression of ongoing (interpreter's) talk – may understand this feedback as a 'you-may-continue' type of confirmation.

Investigating naturally occurring social interaction calls for attention to the uniqueness of a situation. This does not necessarily imply that one looks for 'reasons' that would make two situations non-comparable. I have found it fruitful to compare two encounters that took place at a Swedish police station. On both occasions the same woman provided (at an abstract level) the same story. It was delivered in situations which were similar: in her native language, in a conversation with the same police officer, and with the assistance of the same interpreter. More striking than the differences in content was the difference in fluency of the accounts.

Provided the interpreter's task in face-to-face interaction is seen as involving both translation and the coordination of others' talk (Wadensjö 1998), on-site interpreting, I would argue, offers a clear advantage when it comes to performing the coordinating function. One implication is that in a telephone interpreted encounter interlocutors would be well advised to make a special effort to express themselves clearly and verbalize any non-verbal activities that may have an impact on the ongoing interaction. This would partly make up for the loss of visual impressions, which – under normal circumstances – can help and guide the interpreter, in translating as well as in coordinating the talk exchange. But what cannot be compensated for is the sense of immediacy inherent to face-to-face interaction, which is essential for coordinating talk. With an interpreter on-site then – an interpreter with enough integrity, language and interpreting skills and sense of timing – the participants stand a better chance of synchronizing talk, and thus experiencing a 'normal' (i.e. direct-talk-like) fluency, than with an interpreter working over the phone.

CECILIA WADENSJÖ
Department of Communication Studies, University of Linköping, S-581 83 Linköping, Sweden. cecwa@tema.liu.se

Notes

Work on this paper was supported by a grant from the Swedish Council for Social Research (93-2002:1A). I am indebted to two anonymous reviewers and to Ian Mason for valuable comments on an earlier draft of this article.

1.   Traditional telephone interpreting organized and distributed by local interpreting service bureaux, as in the Scandinavian countries, is not included in their listing.
2.   In Swedish police-talk the word for 'hearing' (*förhör*) sometimes refers to the written record resulting from a hearing, and sometimes to the very activity of hearing someone.
3.   A turn at talk is counted from the moment a person starts talking until someone else (here normally the interpreter) takes over.

References

Apfelbaum, Birgit (1998) 'Instruktionsdiskurse mit Dolmetscher-beteiligung. Aspekte der Turnkonstruktion und Turnzuweisung', in A. Brock and M. Hartung (eds), *Neure Entwicklungen in der Gesprächsforschung. Vorläge der 3 Arbeitstagung des Pragmatischen Kolloquiums, Freiburg,* Tübingen: Gunter Narr, 11-36.

Aronsson, Karin and Ann-Christin Cederborg (1994) 'Co-narration and Voice in Family Therapy: Voicing, Devoicing, and Orchestration', *Text* 14(3): 345-70.

Bakhtin, Michail (1979) *Estetika Slovesnogo Tvorchestva,* Moscow: Isskusstvo.

Drew, Paul and John Heritage (eds) (1992) *Talk at Work: Interaction in Institutional Settings* (Studies in Interactional Sociolinguistics 8), Cambridge: Cambridge University Press.

Duranti, Alessandro and Donald Brenneis (1986) 'The Audience as Co-author', *Text* 6(3):239-347.

------ and Charles Goodwin (eds) (1992). *Rethinking Context - Language as an Interactive Phenomenon* (Studies in Social and Cultural Foundation of Language), Cambridge: Cambridge University Press.

Englund Dimitrova, Birgitta (1997) 'Degree of Interpreter Responsibility in the Interaction Process in Community Interpreting', in Silvana Carr, Roda Roberts, Aideen Dufour and Didi Steyn (eds) *The Critical Link: Interpreters in the Community,* Amsterdam & Philadelphia: John Benjamins, 147-64.

Erikson, Frederick (1992) 'They Know All the Lines: Rhythmic Organization and Contextualization in a Conversational Listing Routine', in Peter Auer and Aldo di Luzio (eds) *The Contextualization of Language,* Amsterdam & Philadelphia: John Benjamins, 365-97.

Goffman, Erving (1981) *Forms of Talk,* Philadelphia: University of Pennsylvania Press.

Goodwin, Charles (1984) 'Notes on Story Structure and the Organization of Participation, in J. Maxwell Atkinson and John Heritage (eds) *Structures of Social Action,* Cambridge: Cambridge University Press.

Gumperz, John J. (1982) *Discourse Strategies,* Cambridge: Cambridge University Press.

Jönsson, Linda (1990) 'Förmedlade samtal: Om återkoppling i tolkade rättegångar', in Ulrika Nettelbladt and Gisela Håkansson (eds) *Samtal och undervisning. Studier till Lennart Gustavssons minne* (Linköping Studies in Arts and Science 60), Linköping: Department of Communication Studies, 71-86.

Linell, Per (1997) 'Interpreting as Communication', in Yves Gambier, Daniel Gile and Christopher Taylor (eds) *Conference Interpreting: Current Trends in Research,* Amsterdam & Philadelphia: John Benjamins.

------ (1998) *Approaching Dialogue - Talk, Interaction and Contexts in Dialogical Perspectives,* Amsterdam & Philadelphia: John Benjamins.

------, Cecilia Wadensjö and Linda Jönsson (1992) 'Establishing Communicative Contact through a Dialogue Interpreter', in Annette Grindsted and Johannes Wagner (eds) *Communication for Specific Purposes - Fachsprachliche Kommunikation.* Tübingen: Gunter Narr, 125-42.

Ochs, Ellinor and Lisa Capps (1996) 'Narrating the Self', *Annual Review of Anthropology* 25: 19-43.

Pointon, Tom, Uldis Ozolins and Chris Doucouliagos (1998) *TIS in Europe 1976-2001*, Victoria, Australia: Deakin University and London, England: The Pointon Partnership.

Polanyi, Livia (1985) 'Conversational Storytelling', in Teun van Dijk (ed) *Handbook of Discourse Analysis*, Vol. 3, London: Academic Press.

Sacks, Harvey, Emanuel A. Schegloff and Gail Jefferson (1974) 'A Simplest Systematics for the Organization of Turn-taking for Conversation', *Language* 50: 696-736.

Schegloff, Emanuel A. (1996) 'Turn Organization: One Intersection of Grammar and Interaction', in Ellinor Ochs, Emanuel A. Schegloff and Sandra Thompson (eds) *Interaction and Grammar*, Cambridge: Cambridge University Press, 52-133.

------, Gail Jefferson and Harvey Sacks (1977) 'The Preference for Self-correction in the Organization of Repair in Conversation', *Language* 53: 361-82.

Tannen, Deborah (1981) 'New York Jewish Conversational Style', *International Journal of the Sociology of Language* 30: 133-49.

Wadensjö, Cecilia (1997) 'Recycled Information as a Questioning Strategy: Pitfalls in Interpreter-Mediated Talk', in Silvana Carr, Roda Roberts, Aideen Dufour and Didi Steyn (eds) *The Critical Link: Interpreters in the Community*, Amsterdam & Philadelphia: John Benjamins, 35-54.

------ (1998) *Interpreting as Interaction*, London & New York: Addison Wesley Longman.

The Translator. Volume 5, Number 2 (1999), 265-283   ISBN 1-900650-21-5

"Nicole Slapped Michelle"
Interpreters and Theories of Interpreting at the O. J. Simpson Trial

ANTHONY PYM
Universitat Rovira i Virgili, Spain

Abstract. *The public perception of court interpreters operates through theories located in discourses both within and around the court. Analysis of interpreting at the 1995 criminal trial of O. J. Simpson shows that such theories are able to explain apparent linguistic shifts in terms of lexical non-correspondence, intralingual discursive coherence, sociocultural bias, variety alignment, a 'user-expectation' principle, the fiction of non-hermeneutic rendition as a mode of professional demarcation, the priority of the cultural component, and various appeals to linguistic and academic expertise. Although all these approaches can provide explanations of apparent shifts, only cost-beneficial theories are found to be successful within the court context. It is concluded that any scholarly intervention in this field should be in terms of theories able to provide explanations adequate to the amount of analytical effort to be invested.*

> *Darden said, and I hope it was in the record, "I object to anybody who starts off saying 'I'm a scholar'".*
> Johnnie Cochran at the sidebar, 3 March 1995

I'm a scholar interested in the public perception of dialogue interpreters, in this case court interpreters. The 1995 criminal trial of O. J. Simpson provides suitable matter for this interest in that it was an international cultural event, indeed an occasion for considerable social debate. It helped air people's ideas about the way courts operate, no matter how unfounded those ideas might be with respect to more run-of-the-mill justice. The trial also used interpreters in the week from 27 February to 3 March 1995, when Rosa López, a housekeeper from El Salvador, chose to testify in Spanish rather than English. The intense public attention on the trial thus fleetingly presented interpreting as a contentious object of knowledge. I am interested merely in how that object was constituted.

ISSN 1355-6509

As such, I remain a relatively external scholar. I claim no special expertise in the practice of court interpreting. And given the fairly atypical nature of my material, I cannot pretend to speak here about what interpreters normally do or should be trained to do. I am merely a scholar trying to grasp the social sense of one particular object, in fact just one fairly brief dialogue from the trial in question. I take the phenomenological position that the object as noumenon (a thing in itself, uninterpreted) is unknown; its sense is to be constructed through a series of epistemological precepts and processes. My tools for recovering and attributing those precepts and processes will partly be the loose metaphors of visibility and concealment – such are the terms currently dominant in interventionist translation studies – but will more seriously be 'theories', broadly in the sense of problem-solving 'passing theories' of the kind used in the dialogic construction of any meaning (cf. Davidson 1984). This means, first, that I personally do not pretend to know what this object is; I can only try to show sets of hypotheses or provisional models by which one might come to some kind of knowledge of the object. It also means that a whole range of social agents, including interpreters, can be seen doing the same thing, and from similar positions of initial ignorance. I will attempt to locate the 'theories' of court interpreting operative in the court itself, in the social debates that surrounded the events, and in the solicited opinions of a linguist and an interpreter-teacher. All those theories are assumed to help constitute the rationalist content of public perceptions. I will close with a suggestion about how to distinguish good from bad theories, leading to a rather cautious plea for scholarly intervention in the general field of dialogue interpreting.

1. The story so far

Just as great dramatic conflicts like Calderón's *La vida es sueño* and Corneille's *Le Cid* begin with a slap, so my account of this, the public drama of our own age, begins with something similar: Nicole slapped Michelle. It may be recalled that Nicole was O. J. Simpson's former wife, whom Simpson was accused of murdering. Michelle was the Simpsons' maid (Am. 'housekeeper'), a friend of Rosa López, who was a maid in the same neighbourhood. These facts are of some importance because, at the stage of the trial that interests me, Rosa López is the only person prepared to provide Simpson with an alibi: she says she saw his car somewhere else at the time of the crime. If she is telling the truth, Simpson is probably innocent. So the prosecution, in the person of counsel Christopher Darden, is intent on showing that she is lying. She might be lying because she likes O. J. Simpson. And she might like him because she disliked Nicole Simpson, O.J.'s murdered wife. And she might have disliked Nicole because, argues the prosecution, Nicole slapped Rosa's friend, the maid Michelle.

Such is the context of the following fragment of the court transcript (taken from Jack Walraven's website). The questions are by prosecuting counsel Darden; the answers are by witness Rosa López; objections are from Johnnie Cochran, one of the defence counsels; 'the Court' is Judge Lance Ito; the terms in italics are the ones that particularly interest me:

1	Mr Darden	Well, you do know that Nicole *slapped* Michelle one day, correct?
2	Rosa López	Because she told me that.
3	Mr Darden	Okay. And Michelle was very upset when she told you that, correct?
4	Rosa López	She was very sad.
5	Mr Darden	Okay. And she told you that she hated Michelle or rather she hated Nicole, correct?
6	Mr Cochran	Objection. Hearsay. Also irrelevant and immaterial, your Honor.
7	The Court	Overruled.
8	Rosa López	She didn't tell me she hated her.
9	Mr Darden	Pardon me? What was the answer?
10	Rosa López	She didn't tell me that she hated her.
11	Mr Darden	Well, she was crying when she told you that she had been *slapped*, correct?
12	Rosa López	Anyone would cry, sir.
13	Mr Darden	Well, was she crying?
14	Rosa López	Yes, sir. A lot.
15	Mr Darden	And were you upset that Nicole had *slapped* Michelle?
16	Rosa López	No. I just try to console her.
17	Mr Darden	Well, isn't it true that you didn't like Nicole?
18	Rosa López	I only saw Nicole once. I can't say that I don't like her.
19	Mr Darden	Well, didn't you tell someone that you did not like her because –
20	Mr Cochran	Objection, your Honor.
21	Mr Darden	– because she *slapped* Michelle?
22	Mr Cochran	Vague, your Honor.
23	The Court	Sustained.
24	Mr Darden	Did you ever tell anyone that you disliked Nicole because Nicole had *slapped* Michelle?
25	Mr Cochran	Objection. Objection.
26	The Court	Overruled.
27	Rosa López	It's true. Nobody likes to get *slapped*, sir.
28	Mr Darden	And so you were angry at Nicole for having *slapped* Michelle, correct?
29	Rosa López	No. She didn't *hit* me. Because if – I would have *hit* her back.

Darden's moderately successful strategy here is to push the witness into a more antagonistic frame, repeating questions so as to encourage her to express a more violent attitude toward Nicole, perhaps emblazoning the act in the mind of the jury. He mentions the verb *slapped* no less than four times, using every available occasion to do so before he finally gets the witness, through the interpreter, to use the same term. No matter how much defence counsel Johnnie Cochran intervenes to slow down the pace of the exchange, to protect his witness, Darden knows that if he can keep Rosa opening her mouth, she will eventually put her foot in it. And she does, in a way. Apart from the increasing rhythm and mounting intonation on both sides (the tension is released in public laughter after line 29), the main shift visible here is the final move from *slap* to *hit* (line 29), with the latter term being used in subsequent exchanges before moving briefly, at Darden's instigation, to *strike*. Tactically significant, this is one of a series of small shifts that raised serious doubts about Rosa's credibility and meant that her evidence, the potential alibi, would not be used later in the trial.

2. Where is the interpreter?

The transcript shows no sign of interpreting occurring in this particular passage. The interpreters (there were at least three involved in the Rosa López week) are nevertheless named elsewhere in the proceedings; they are frequently referred to; they often ask for questions to be repeated; on at least two occasions they interrupt proceedings to consult among themselves; on two further occasions they successfully ask for the speakers to be admonished for interrupting their renditions. In this particular case there can be no immediate decrying of anonymity, passivity or invisibility. Of course, in the television version of the trial the interpreter of this fragment is excluded from view, although one senses she is seated somewhere between the witness and the jury, who are similarly protected by rigorous invisibility. The top of a blonde head does bob over the edge of the screen occasionally, and the interpreter's voice suggests a woman who speaks specifically Central American Spanish and has traces of this in her English (a few instances of inappropriate grammar are in lines 16 and 18 above). But little more identity can be gleaned on the basis of this fragment.

The television version of the above passage gives us two-way consecutive renditions between English and Spanish for all the above interactions between Darden and the witness. It sounds like good professional interpreting; it makes sense; there are no visible deletions; and despite what has been found in other analyses of Spanish-English court interpreting (Berk-Seligson 1990, Hale 1997a, 1997b), there is no particular sign of register being shifted up into English or down into Spanish, no doubt thanks to the rather informal English used by both prosecution and defence. In fact, had I not used the

video in class and seen my students struggle to find certain Spanish replace-
ments, I would not be looking at this fragment at all. One of the best ways to
locate problems is to try to do the interpreter's work over again. So, with
thanks to my students, here is what we found.

3. What the interpreter does

Since my focus is really on just one semantic field, the range of variants used
to describe the slap, I will not transcribe the whole of the interpreting. It
should be enough to reproduce the key renditions and tie them to the numbered English exchanges given above.

The most obvious kind of intervention here involves the creation of equivalents. When Darden repeats the verb *slapped*, the interpreter uses *una bofetada
en la cara* (a relatively non-violent hit on the face) on the first occasion (line
1), switches to the alternative *una cachetada en la cara* (something similar,
also explicitly on the face) on the second mention (line 11), then uses *cachetada* as the working equivalent for subsequent mentions (lines 15, 21, 24).
The shift is perhaps best understood as a move from an international Spanish
term (*bofetada*) to a more locally acceptable variation (*cachetada* has more
to do with American Spanish than with Iberian Spanish). Whatever the reasons, here and elsewhere the interpreter fishes around before proposing the
equivalent and having it situationally accepted. This is not a question of drawing on any dictionary of pre-determined correspondences.

The interpreter then does something rather strange. Having established
an equivalent, and having done so in terms of regional variation, she resists
movement away from that equivalent, as we see here:

27	Rosa López	a nadie le gusta que le pegue
		nobody likes that people pegar *them*
	Interpreter	nobody likes to get slapped

The witness now volunteers the verb *pegar* (generally, to hit), saying in effect 'nobody likes to be hit', whereas the entire previous discussion has
repeatedly used the verb *to slap* and its proposed equivalent. Why does the
interpreter render *pegar* as *slap*? The rendition would appear to involve a
slight toning down of intensity. Something similar happens in the very next
line, when Darden says:

28	Mr Darden	And so you were angry at Nicole for having slapped
		Michelle, correct?
	Interpreter	...porque había pegadole a Michelle, ¿verdad?
		because she had pegar *Michelle, correct?*

Now the English *slap* is rendered as the Spanish *pegar* (hit) rather than the previously accepted equivalent. In effect, the Spanish version of the exchange has shifted to a new equivalent, from *dar una cachetada en la cara* to *pegar*, which is repeated twice, while the English discourse is allowed to remain with the one humdrum verb *slap*. Is this just for the sake of a shorter term? Of course, in the very next line, the Spanish moves again, as the witness may indeed have put her foot in it:

29   Rosa López   No. No me pegó a mí. Porque si... le daría patadas.
                     No. She didn't hit me. Because if... I would kick her
     Interpreter   No. She didn't hit me. Because if... I would have hit her back.[1]

Rosa López appears to have moved to the even more violent register of kicking (*le daría patadas*, I would kick her repeatedly), which the interpreter, after at last allowing *pegar* to mean *hit*, now renders as the more general and distanced *to hit back*, deflecting away not only the kicks but the present-tense conditional as well. Again, why?

To give a more synoptic picture of what is happening here, consider the sequence of terms used in the English dialogue:

   slap, slap, slap, slap, slap, slap, slap, hit, hit

For a hearer following only the Spanish, this sequence would be rather more varied and violent:

   bofetada, cachetada, cachetada, cachetada, cachetada, pegar, pegar, pegar, dar patadas

which roughly means:

   slap, slap, slap, slap, slap, hit, hit, hit, kick

I suggest the interpreter has kept the English discourse at one degree of semantic intensity lower than the Spanish. She has worked to counter precisely the escalation that the prosecuting counsel was trying to impose. This looks like a rather subtle kind of intervention. But why should it have occurred? What theory can account for it?

This is the problem that interests me. We might all agree that interpreters help create equivalents, we might even agree that good interpreters play with variations, but here we find an interpreter using what appear to be outright non-equivalents: *pegar* (hit) as *slap*, and *dar patadas* (kick) as *hit*. What kind of intervention is this? Before considering answers to this question, let me briefly discuss the institutional setting, which might offer a few motivational clues.

4. The interpreter's role

It would be moderately unfair to criticize this interpreter in terms of a model that saw a Sender creating a Meaning that had to be delivered to a Receiver. Such models (they abound in the textbooks) are often embedded in unfortunately common assumptions like the following:

1. Interpreters belong to the target language and culture.
2. Interpreters work into their mother tongue.
3. Interpreters work for people who do not know the source language.
4. The purpose of interpreting is to enable one speech community to communicate with another.

In the case we are considering, none of these assumptions really applies. At best they could be rewritten as follows:

1. The interpreter is between numerous communication participants: a horizontal axis involving counsel and witness (as in the normal models of communication), but also a vertical axis including defence counsel and judge (who may block any question), the accused, the court clerk, the jury, and a television camera taking the interpreter's words to millions around the globe, even to the eyes of prying scholars. If the interpreter belongs anywhere, it is to all that, as an institution which, on this occasion, has placed her in a central overlap, an intercultural space. If we were to discuss her allegiance, it would be difficult to do so in terms of any absolute either/or binarism.
2. The interpreter is working both ways, in and out of two languages. Yet there are contextual reasons to believe she is situated more one side than the other. On 27 February one of the interpreters was named as 'Alicia Luper Gallant' (Hispanic given name and father's family name) and described as "the best Salvadorian-born interpreter we have available"; on 28 February another interpreter is named as 'Cecile Cerda' (Anglicized given name, Hispanic family name). Both, it seems, were brought in specifically to replace the previous interpreter, named as 'Doris Weitz' (nothing blatantly Hispanic there), who worked on 24 February and was much criticized, ostensibly because she did not speak Salvadorian Spanish. If we were to discuss the cultural belonging of our interpreter, this preference for birthright, and the assumptions it apparently conveys about dialect, would seem to have outweighed any strict analysis of two-way linguistic competence. The 'Salvadorian' interpreter is there precisely so that she can be culturally aligned with the witness.
3. The interpreter is not really working because of any primal linguistic

opacity. Rosa López knows English (she has been in California for more than twenty years); at one point in the above exchange (line 14) she actually replies directly in English, and such occasions are common in the extended transcript. The interpreter is there because English is not the witness's *native* tongue (discussed at the sidebar on 27 February 1995) and interpreting should thus, ideally, help to redress a lingual power imbalance. To that extent, the very purpose of having an interpreter is to protect, to some degree, a witness in need of protection. In fact, if we pushed the logic a little further, we might say that the interpreter is paid by an ostensibly monolingual institution (the court, to which she belongs as a paid officer) to be symbolically aligned with a speaker of another language and another culture. Whether or not linguistic justice is done, it must appear to be done.

4.   This relative transparency works both ways. Rosa López knows English, but much of California also knows Spanish (thanks in part to a Spanish presence of some 400 years, the formal lack of an official language, and a bilingual education policy revoked in 1998). Despite apparent invisibility, the interpreters are being checked on all sides. Here, for example, is prosecution counsel Marcia Clark theorizing about translation:

> Ms. Clark: The problem, though, that we were aware of, is the translator was interpreting instead of translating what she [Rosa López] was saying and changing words and cleaning up her language, not even interpreting some of the things she was saying at all. (27 February 1995)

If this kind of awareness is possible (and we will soon see further ways in which courtroom theorists manipulated the verbs *to translate* and *to interpret*), the role of the interpreter would seem to be not to mediate *between* speech communities but to redress symbolic power relationships *within* the one multilingual community. Although this specific parameter certainly does not apply to the whole of dialogue interpreting, its basic features are common enough. Any understanding of what interpreters do should thus at least ask if such relative transparency is operative, if there is indeed an institutionally and symbolically functional visibility of intervention, before we condemn out of hand a few apparent non-equivalents smuggled in unseen.

5. Why did the interpreter do what she did?

My account of the interpreter's situation might have led to the conclusion that she toned down Rosa López's language so as to protect the witness from traps laid by the prosecuting counsel. She might well have done this out of solidarity: a Salvadorian representing the words of a Salvadorian; a woman protecting a woman (all the questioners in this scene are men); an intellectual skilled in communication protecting a worker not so skilled in communication; an institutional polyglot protecting a foreigner, and so on. But also, I suggest, she is paid to express such solidarity. The interpreter is there symbolically to cover over precisely the disadvantages of the foreign woman worker unskilled in communication. She is deploying a certain institutionalized advocacy, as sought in neighbouring fields by theorists such as Barsky (1993, 1996). This is not necessarily unethical behaviour. The interpreter was perhaps only doing what the institution was paying her to do.

That is one kind of explanation. We might call it something like critical sociology, although it would have to be developed further to merit that name. Yet there is more than sociology in this; more than one kind of theorizing. Let me sketch two further explanations that have been offered, the first by a linguist, the second by a researcher who is also a practising court interpreter.

For Juan Sager, who very correctly took linguistic umbrage at my sociology (specifically during a seminar at UMIST, Manchester, on 29 April 1996), the interpreter was quite justified in rendering *pegar* as *slap* and *patada* as *hit*, quite simply because the lexico-semantic fields are different in Spanish and English. This could involve Hjelmslev-like non-correspondences of terms, mainly allowing *pegar* to cover more semantic space than *hit*. But research conducted in polite lunchtime conversations (practical demonstrations are not recommended, particularly with respect to the bodily location of slaps) suggests it could be more a question of superordinates, with *pegar* operating on levels that may indeed cover *cachetadas* and even metaphorical *patadas*. We might then get something like the following schema:

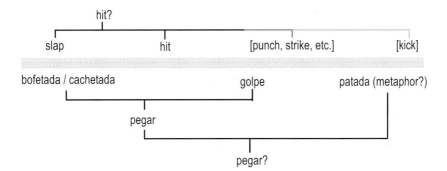

Without trying to defend the schema with heavy artillery from dictionaries and corpora, we might legitimately ask what this kind of linguistics is actually saying about the interpreting. It certainly describes something, but the descriptions are by no means neutral or value-free (for me, no description is value-free). Most obviously, this kind of schema helps to justify this particular interpreter, backing up her spontaneous decisions in terms of some kind of reasoned competence. In fact, it is saying there should be no real argument here, since there are no significant differences to argue about. The interpreter is essentially right.

This is a good kind of theory. It is nevertheless static; it takes no account of the movement of discourse; it has not considered that the stuff to be represented might involve significant discursive shifts on the level of form (*slap* to *hit*, *hit* to *kick*) rather than semantic extensions; and it precariously assumes that the two language systems are entirely separate. Apart from that, the theory might be entirely valid for certain kinds of problems.

A further explanation was offered by Miriam Shlesinger in the same seminar. She pointed out that interpreters often seek to ensure cohesion within each language-discourse, such that what is said in Spanish should make sense in terms of what has previously been said in Spanish, with the same backstitching process occurring for English. This would explain why the interpreter refuses the more obvious equivalents (*hit* for *pegar*, *kick* for *dar patadas*), preferring instead to pick up the terms previously used in English. In that she thus attains greater cohesion for the listeners, the interpreter would once again appear to be quite justified. Indeed, this would be just one of a number of accommodation procedures that Shlesinger has described elsewhere (see Shlesinger 1991).

Once again, this is an appealing theory. It might only fall short if we take seriously the suggestion that there are significant degrees of mutual transparency between these languages, such that it is misleading to pretend there are two parallel discourses at work, one in English and the other in Spanish. In terms of the parameters I have proposed above, there is really only one discourse here, jumping across languages, with many people following many of the shifts, well beyond assumptions of simple monolingual senders and receivers. Nevertheless, Shlesinger's basic point sounds eminently practical; in terms of her theory, too, the interpreter could be quite right.

We thus have at least three theories able to offer some kind of explanation for the interpreter's apparent intervention. One might be described as relatively external with respect to the interpreter's linguistic work (sociological parameters), the second is relatively internal (lexico-semantics), and the third is eminently pragmatic in that it crosses the internal/external divide. Since I have no infallible reasons for excluding any of these levels of theorization, I am more interested in a way of bringing them into the one conceptual package.

Here, then, is a quick suggestion as to how one might get sociologists to look at language, lexico-semanticists to consider situational dynamics, and pragmatists to go beyond the precarious separation of language-discourses. It concerns the concept of discourse best suited to dialogue interpreting of the kind we are looking at. Of all the numerous definitions of *discourse*, the one I prefer was put forward some time ago by Greimas and Courtès (1979: *s.v.* discours): (*dis-currere*): "a constant selection between possible alternatives, opening up a path through networks of constraints" (my translation of "une sélection continue des possibles, se frayant la voie à travers des réseaux de contraintes"). That, I suggest, is a very beautiful idea: *discurrere*, like a river meandering down to the sea, picking its way around rocks and high ground, except that people are not rivers, so the choosing of paths is a subjectively active process, and not all the constraints are stable and passive. If I were to apply that idea to dialogue interpreting, picking its way between constraints in two languages, between questions (Q), answers (A), lexico-semantics, cohesion, coherence, and all the situational participants with all their theories about interpreting, the picture might be something like the following (allowing that the arrows indicate the backward movement of representation, to avoid any suggestion of primal meaning transfer):

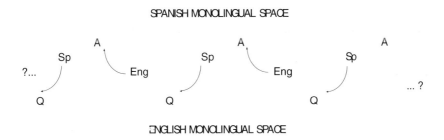

SPANISH MONOLINGUAL SPACE

ENGLISH MONOLINGUAL SPACE

There is enough room in there for all the theories we have discussed so far, plus a few more as well. We can write in the superordinates and the formal shifts; a gradient scale could shade the overlap of languages. However, in refusing any *a priori* separation of language-discourses, this model should also curtail many presumptions of primal meanings, thus blocking the 'conduit' metaphor and potentially meeting up with the critical dialogics broadly espoused by Wadensjö (1992, and especially 1996).[2] It is a model that allows and relativizes many possible descriptions.

What I want to do now involves a slight change of gears. Instead of looking at the actual decisions and their dialogic path, I want to reconsider the 'networks of constraints' that help move this bilingual discourse in some directions rather than others. Further, I want to consider these constraints not immediately in terms of specific people, norms or institutions, but more consistently in terms of 'theories' as sets of passing explanatory hypotheses. Such theories would include both the hypotheses used by interpreters and a range of more public ideas about interpreting, including the ones we have just seen. More important, the theories can be seen as active constraints on discourse, since if they describe, justify or condemn certain behaviour (once again, I believe value-free description is an illusion), they are certainly helping discourse move some ways more easily than others. Minor passing theories help direct the particular discourse of slaps and hits; larger and more lasting theories help orient the general discourses of dialogue interpreting. We too are intervening, along with the interpreters. And perhaps happily, we are not the only people who think we know about interpreting.

6. Who knows about interpreting?

Let me briefly evoke the theories of interpreting that can be found within the scene of the trial. There are many cases of what we might call practical translation criticism, in fact objective manifestations of constraint, from a range of external and internal positions.

First, although defence counsel Johnnie Cochran apparently has no Spanish and is thus relatively external, this does not stop him from questioning the interpreter in some cases. For example, he objects to 'Mr Jones' as a rendition of 'Mr Johnnie', upon which the interpreter duly corrects and apologizes (24 February). Proper names and discourse length being more or less accessible to all, even people in monolingual space can presume to evaluate interpreters. The basic theory in this case is that names and lengths should be about the same in the two languages, although Cochran's assessments are also based on a rule of thumb that we might call users' expectations: "I hadn't noticed [the interpreter's interventions]. But the answers seem to be about what we had expected" (27 February). The underlying theory says that if the interpreter's words are what we expect, they are acceptable.

Second, prosecuting counsel Marcia Clark, whom we have already seen denouncing one interpreter's interventions, feels bilingual enough ("essentially I also speak Spanish") to distribute praise as well: "This [interpreter] is really translating and not interpreting as was occurring yesterday". Note that 'to interpret' here apparently means to intervene in one way or another, so the theory says that good interpreters do not intervene. But this is not just her opinion: "Unlike yesterday, we haven't received any complaints as far as accuracy" (27 February). And where would the complaints come from? Ms Clark continues, "I have someone present in the courtroom fluent in Spanish who has been listening for accuracy..." (27 February). This new theory proposes that what counts when 'really translating' is accuracy, and bilinguals can tell. Of course, the defence also has its experts at work. At one stage Johnnie Cochran reports a fax ("from Skip Taft's office") indicating "that the interpreter was terrible and she was interpreting everything instead of translating". Same terms, same theory. And "some people who speak Spanish on the 12th floor had said we're still having problems with – even though it's a different interpreter.... Apparently it has to do with Salvadorean dialect or something" (27 February). So we have at least three peripheral experts whose theorizing is reported in the trial.

Third, the real expert here is Judge Ito, who apparently knows Spanish and likes to show it. At one point he himself asks Rosa López if she said *hot* or *hard*; she replies, in English, "Hard"; to which he replies, in Spanish, "Duro, ¿sí?" (27 February). So for a brief moment we actually have the Court speaking Spanish and the witness speaking English. This is indeed intercultural space. Judge Ito is also prepared to identify concealed problems and teach about certain arcane arts:

Mr Darden	Was Mr Cochran animated at all during the conversation that you had with him?
The Court	Remember we are using an interpreter.
Rosa López:	No.
The Court	Madam Interpreter, how is *animated* translated in Spanish?
Interpreter	Not very clearly, your honor.
Mr Darden	Since I don't speak Spanish, your honor –
The Court	All right. Using an interpreter with a witness is an art.
Mr Darden	The 'art' word again, hum?
Ms Clark	Oh, no, not that one.
The Court	I'm just familiar, that particular verb in Spanish is very difficult – never mind. Forget I mentioned it. Proceed. (24 February)

Judge Ito apparently knows more about Spanish than he has time to reveal. Yet as far as I know, the English *animated* here is quite efficiently rendered by the Spanish *animado*, be it Salvadorian or otherwise.

More than this, Judge Ito is an expert in how to foresee interpretation problems. Right at the beginning of Rosa López's testimony he invites the non-Salvadorian interpreter to chat with the witness: "As you know, there are sixty major dialects within the Spanish language and I would like her to become acquainted with that" (24 February). But foreseeing the problem does not mean the interpreter can entirely solve it. A Salvadorian-born interpreter was still brought in, since 'dialect' was Ito's main theory for the difficulties observed. The judge then goes to some lengths to protect the Salvadorian-born interpreter from the criticisms of all those who know 'a little' Spanish (including himself?):

The Court	You know, knowing a little Spanish in this situation is dangerous. But as Chair of the Judicial Advisory Council of Court Interpreters, I'm very familiar with the problems. And the problem that we're dealing with, most people don't know there are sixty major dialects of the Spanish language... (27 February).

This could be read as an instance of Judge Ito protecting the interpreter from non-expert theories such as those of Johnnie Cochran and Marcia Clark. Then again, we might also see the judge arguing so as to protect his own theory. Since all problems are supposed to ensue from his 'sixty major dialects', anything else must be a relative non-problem. He can thus explain and rejoice in a certain creation of equivalents (his theory is very good for the move from *bofetada* to *cachetada*), and the rest are red-herrings raised by people with inadequate internal knowledge. Ito's theory not only cannot see things like *hit* as *slap*, but limits the range of people with sufficient authority to see such things. If the one major constraint is in place, if we have the correct equation of birthplace and variety, all else should flow. But the interpreting does not flow; the complaints continue; rival theories abound; and Ito's only real back-up theory is that the speed of the exchanges is too fast. On numerous occasions he asks Rosa López not to listen to the English questions but to wait for the Spanish renditions. As we have noted, the interpreters themselves are quite able to protect themselves in this way.

One final theory erupts right at the end of the Rosa López week:

Mr Cochran	Your Honor, I have received a letter from a Vincent C. Gilliam, a Ph.D. [...] I would like to read a paragraph from that letter and I would ask the Court for permission to get an interpretation from the interpreters.
The Court	You mean a comment?
Mr Cochran	Yes, I'm sorry, a comment. This is from the letter. "First, a point that may easily be lost to Americans is the difference in cultures being manifested by Miss Lopez' responses. Not only does she display a tendency to defer somewhat meekly to people in authority, ([such as] Mr Darden) by saying, quote, 'If you say so, sir', as one might expect from someone from a humble background and from El Salvador at that, but Spanish-speaking cultures are much more subtle than one such as the U.S. Thus, when Miss Lopez says 'No' and then 'No, I don't remember having said that, sir', with further prodding, it is not an equivocal response, nor is it prevaricating that she change her response. It is simply that [she] comes from a more indirect and less confrontational type of culture. And moral [sic.] importantly, quote, 'No, I don't remember having said that,' end quote, does not mean 'Possibly yes' as Mr Darden was attempting to make it mean." (3 March)

The letter is first mentioned on Friday morning, then again late Friday afternoon. It seems the status of theories alters in accordance with how badly people want to go home (Ito: "Come on, guys. It's late. It's been a long week."). This particular theory, insultingly reduced to '*I don't know* means

No', is simply not going to be accepted. Ito doubts its authority ("We don't know what this person's qualifications are"); Darden reportedly mistrusts "anybody who starts off saying 'I'm a scholar'", as Vincent C. Gilliam apparently did; and even Cochran, once he realizes Gilliam's theory will make his witness even less believable, calls it "the rankest kind of irrelevant, immaterial hearsay" (3 March). But even if it had not been read on a Friday, there are two basic problems with Gilliam's theory.

The first is that, if the theory is correct, a whole week of testimony has to be re-read and no one is quite sure to what effect (Darden: "She's only said 'I don't remember' 128 times, and each time she – I don't know if it's good, I don't know if 'no' is bad."). The theory is thus inapplicable in practical terms; it asks for enormous effort in exchange for unpredictable results.

Second, if the theory lacks authority as it stands, it must be corroborated by someone with authority. Judge Ito suggests calling in "an expert witness on linguistics", "somebody from UCLA School of Interpretation", "Dr Rheinhoff from UCLA or somebody from USC". Proper scholarship, from the right academic department, will decide the toss. Yet none is forthcoming, with the end of the week and all. Who should they ask instead? Why, a native speaker, Rosa López, of course! Despite Ito's doubts ("... but to ask this woman who doesn't speak English well, who doesn't read or write Spanish or English, to ask her about, you know, semantics ... of interpreting ..."), that is precisely what they do:

Mr Darden	Is there a phrase in Spanish that means 'I do not remember'?
Rosa López	That 'No'.
Mr Darden	Can you say –
Rosa López	That's the phrase, 'No'.
Mr Cochran	Well, your Honor –
Rosa López	I don't remember in Spanish.
Mr Cochran	That's irrelevant, what dialect –
The Court	Overruled. Overruled.
Rosa López	It is the same in Spanish. I don't remember that, no, sir. No, I don't remember and I don't remember, it's the same thing, sir.
Mr Darden	Thank you. That's all.

And half a minute later Rosa López was out of there and they were all going home. The 'Don't know' theory would of course continue in comedian Jay Leno's nightly jokes about Rosa *no sé* López, doing as much damage as possible to American awareness of cultural alterity. No one would attempt to go back and reinterpret the whole of the Rosa López week.

I mention this farce for the sake of one quite obvious point. At the beginning of that Friday, Cochran asked for the *interpreters* to be consulted on the 'Don't know' issue. In all the discussion that followed, through all the naming of authorities and the debunking of the witness, the transcript shows no sign of the interpreters actually being consulted. It was as if authoritative theories of interpreting were exclusively the stuff of academics and native speakers.

7. Conclusion: good and bad interventions from theories

Why not ask the interpreters? No doubt because, for the hands-on theories of the court, interpreters are not supposed to 'interpret'. What this means, beyond the contradictory semantics and massive simplification of linguistic difficulties, is that interpreters should leave the 'interpreting' to the lawyers, in effect conforming to the fiction that interventionist interpretations are required intralingually but not interlingually (see Morris 1995: 42). As bad as this theory may appear, it does successfully draw a line between two professions: interpreters do one thing ('verbatim translation'), lawyers do another ('interpretation'). When Cochran asks for the interpreters to be consulted (for a 'comment', not an 'interpretation'), he is effectively challenging this basic theory of professionalism; he is stirring up possible antagonism between interpreters and lawyers (see Berk-Seligson 1990:195). That should not be done. If there are to be 'comments' on the problems of cross-lingual rendering, it seems they should ideally come from a further profession, that of experts and scholars, whose theories need not directly challenge those of lawyers, since the latter can then 'interpret' them as well.

There is thus a significant degree of power-play underlying the various levels of theorization, most prominently in the silencing of interpreters' theories. Exclusivist types of interpretation are made to belong to institutionalized professions, which of course have every interest in maintaining that public image (cf. Weber 1987:25). This professional demarcation might be slightly upset by approaches that run roughshod over traditional distinctions, as indeed I have tried to do in describing all opinions and verbalized norms as 'theories'. Even more upsetting, however, is the position of experts and scholars who, although volunteering theories from beyond the court, openly take the side of interpreters, not only in justifying some of their decisions (as we have seen) but more importantly in calling for interpreters to be professionalized in a way that approaches the status of lawyers (cf. Morris 1995, Fenton 1997, Fowler 1997). This is a significant and potentially antagonistic intervention; it is the major input that scholars may yet make to the general field of dialogue interpreting; it no doubt owes its sociological basis to the fact that those experts and scholars are increasingly either practising interpreters or interpreter trainers. Let me now close with a few remarks on why this intervention is positive but should be undertaken with care.

A certain deconstructionist liberalism might suppose that the more theories we have, the better. After all, the more theories, the more can be seen from different perspectives, and the more alternatives and freedom we create. If I can point out or even create things like the shifts from *slap* to *hit*, or if a 'scholar' can claim that 'I don't know' means 'No', whatever theory is used will thus be valid to the extent that it adds to the range of possible interpretations. And yet the various theories we have located remain highly unequal, and not just because of external politics. Some, like Rosa López's final explanation, are ineloquent enough to be totally ineffective. Others, like the interpreter who just explains that *animated* is interpreted 'not very clearly', are merely unhelpful. And still others, like the judge who intervenes to explain *animado*, or the scholar who claims that a whole week of testimony has to be reinterpreted, are outweighed by a situation in which they remain without foreseeable value ("I don't know if it's good, I don't know if 'no' is bad"). There is thus a set of theories that, for various reasons, are defeated because they can only add to a directionless diversity. The constraints are weakened; the discourse has more latitude; the meandering takes much longer to reach any kind of goal. In many situations, theories that blindly require that everything be made visible, or that interpreters be pushed towards other professions, stand to meet much the same fate.

An alternative perspective might look more carefully at the way different theories effectively work together so as to create degrees of consensus. Here I am thinking of things like the 'user-expectation principle' ('the answers seemed to be more or less what we expected', so the interpreting is acceptable), or the critique of non-experts ('knowing a little Spanish in this situation is dangerous'), or again, the various assessments of something as vague as 'accuracy' which then give no accurate details, or even Judge Ito's megatheory of dialect, which does intervene to the extent that a new interpreter is brought in but which then is prepared to lie fairly quiet: Ito actually dismisses debate on this question by saying "If there's any dispute, we can solve it at the appropriate time if necessary" (27 February). In all these cases, what is being accorded to interpreters is a kind of default trust (cf. Chesterman 1997:181), saying in effect that *their* theories, no matter how silent and unseen, are to prevail for as long as they do not run up against any major opposing theory. Let the discourse run free for as long as it does not meet a major constraint.

The problem of the Simpson trial, with its plethora of theories, was that it made far too many constraints visible, pushing issues well beyond any criterion of importance. Oppositional passing theories were allowed to prevail over stronger consensus-building approaches. If scholars are now to intervene in such processes, I suggest it should be within this second kind of frame, investing default trust in the work of interpreters and helping to solve problems only if and when they arise, rather than offering principles and advice that may stand to create antagonism.

Of course, renditions of *slap* in subaltern Spanish are still very difficult – never mind. Forget I mentioned it. Proceed.

ANTHONY PYM
*Departament de Filologia Anglogermànica, Universitat Rovira i Virgili, Plaça
Imperial Tàrraco, 1, E-43005 Tarragona, Spain. ap@fll.urv.es.*

Notes

1. The English rendition here would correspond to the American Spanish '*le
    daría pa' tras*' (lit. 'I'd give her [the same] back'). That this may indeed be
    the phrase misheard by my more Iberian ear should underline the impor-
    tance of variety alignment. My thanks to final-year Spanish students at the
    Forlì translation school for pointing this out.
2. A few implications of the dialogic approach were brought out in the 1997/
    98 cominterp debate (comminterp@web.apc.org) on revising codes of eth-
    ics for community interpreters. As Wadensjö pointed out (11 December
    1997) many of the proposed ethical principles were based on the notions of
    'what is (to be) understood', without locating the people involved in the
    understanding. Here, since I am proposing that all understanding passes
    through theories, the scope of people involved is much larger than a simple
    ethics of direct participants might assume. Does this mean we should give
    up on neat principles altogether? I suspect part of the solution is to be found
    in Andrew Chesterman's negative ethics, drawn from Popper, where the
    translator's task is based not on understanding but on "the minimization of
    misunderstanding" (1997:184). This would seem to comply with the gen-
    eral view that the court interpreter's task is "to remove any barriers which
    prevent understanding or communication" (Judge Samuels, cited in Morris
    1995:41), although in many cases I feel we should also talk about ways of
    skirting around or avoiding barriers. The only further point I would add in
    the present context is that not all 'misunderstanding' really needs elimina-
    tion. If the main aim is cooperation between the communication participants,
    'errors' such as *hit* as *slap* require more effort to be eliminated than would
    be the potential gain from the ensuing cooperation (cf. Pym 1997:123).

References

Barsky, Robert (1993) 'The Interpreter and the Canadian Convention Refugee
    Hearing: Crossing the Potentially Life-threatening Boundaries between
    'coccode-e-eh,' 'cluck-cluck,' and 'cot-cot-cot'' *TTR* 6(2):131-57.
------ (1996) 'The Interpreter as Intercultural Agent in Convention Refugee
    Hearings', *The Translator* 2(1):45-63.
Berk-Seligson, Susan (1990) *The Bilingual Courtroom: Court Interpreters and
    the Judicial Process*, Chicago & London: University of Chicago Press.

Chesterman, Andrew (1997) *Memes of Translation. The Spread of Ideas in Translation Theory*, Amsterdam & Philadelphia: John Benjamins.

Davidson, Donald (1984) *Enquiries into Truth and Interpretation*, Oxford: Clarendon Press.

Fenton, Sabine (1997) 'The Role of the Interpreter in the Adversarial Courtroom', in Silvana E. Carr, Roda Roberts, Aideen Dufour and Dini Steyn (eds) *The Critical Link: Interpreting in the Community*, Amsterdam & Philadelphia: John Benjamins, 29-34.

Fowler, Yvonne (1997) 'The Courtroom Interpreter: Paragon *and* Intruder?', in Silvana E. Carr, Roda Roberts, Aideen Dufour and Dini Steyn (eds) *The Critical Link: Interpreting in the Community*, Amsterdam & Philadelphia: John Benjamins, 191-200.

Greimas, A. J., and J. Courtès (1979) *Sémiotique: dictionnaire raisonné de la théorie du langage*, Paris: Hachette.

Hale, Sandra (1997a) 'The Treatment of Register Variation in Court Interpreting', *The Translator* 3(1): 39-54.

------ (1997b) 'The Interpreter on Trial: Pragmatics in Court Interpreting', in Silvana E. Carr, Roda Roberts, Aideen Dufour and Dini Steyn (eds) *The Critical Link: Interpreting in the Community*, Amsterdam & Philadelphia: John Benjamins, 201-211.

Morris, Ruth (1995) 'The Moral Dilemmas of Court Interpreting', *The Translator* 1(1): 25-46.

Pym, Anthony (1997) *Pour une éthique du traducteur*, Arras: Artois Presses Université / Ottawa: Presses de l'Université d'Ottawa.

Shlesinger, Miriam (1991) 'Interpreter Latitude vs. Due Process. Simultaneous and Consecutive Interpretation in Multilingual Trials', in Sonja Tirkkonen-Condit (ed) *Empirical Research in Translation and Intercultural Studies*, Tübingen: Gunter Narr, 147-55.

Wadensjö, Cecilia (1992) *Interpreting as Interaction. On Dialogue-Interpreting in Immigration Hearings and Medical Encounters*, Linköping: Department of Communication Studies, Linköping University.

------ (1996) Review of Berk-Seligson *The Bilingual Courtroom* and Dueñas Roseann González et al. *Fundamentals of Court Interpretation, The Translator* 2(1):104-109.

Walraven, Jack. n.d. *Simpson Trial Site*. www3.islandnet.com/~walraven/simpson.html.

Weber, Samuel (1987) *Institution and Interpretation*, Minneapolis: University of Minnesota Press.

The Translator. Volume 5, Number 2 (1999), 285-302   ISBN 1-900650-21-5

Police Interpreting
Politeness and Sociocultural Context

ALEXANDER KROUGLOV
Diplomatic Service Language Centre
Foreign & Commonwealth Office, London, UK

Abstract. *Police interpreting is somewhat unjustly neglected by most recent linguistic studies. As an act of necessary and therefore intense interpersonal and intercultural communication, police interpreting provides an excellent example of the way in which an interpreter deals with colloquialisms and hedges, as well as forms of address and other forms of politeness. This paper is based on the analysis of four short extracts from interviews with Russian witnesses conducted at a police station by English speaking detectives and interpreted by four different interpreters. The findings suggest that interpreters often avoid or change colloquialisms and hedges, which could provide evidence of pragmatic intention. The extracts also confirm that interpreters tend to misrepresent the speaker by introducing more polite forms, which in turn can make the testimony of a witness either less certain or more definite. A brief analysis of some in-group terminology in interpreting is also offered.*

Dialogue interpreting involves a significant element of sociocultural analysis, where interpreters mediate "linguistically as well as culturally" between speakers of different languages (Dollerup 1993:139). A number of scholars have examined the ways in which interpreting is performed in various settings, such as legal encounters, immigration and employment interviews, schools, public safety, community agency services and public health.[1] But dialogue interpreting nevertheless remains insufficiently researched in comparison with other types of interpreting.

This article is based on a study of dialogue interpreting as performed in the rather extreme circumstances of a police interview, in which examining detectives and testifying witnesses participate in question-and-answer interaction. The information presented is based on a corpus of data gathered during the police investigation of a murder case in which the witnesses, the suspect and the victim were all Russian sailors. Since the incident took place in the port of an English-speaking country, interpreters were called upon to help with the investigation. The interviews of witnesses and the suspect were conducted at a police station by English-speaking detectives. We shall be looking at some of the key factors which may affect the outcome of the police interview. These are:

- alteration/preservation of speech styles in interpretation;
- deletion, addition or modification of politeness (hedges, address forms, diminutives and other in-group identity markers);
- the availability of a situational context;
- the interpreter's awareness of linguistic and cultural features of both source and target languages.

Interpreters in police investigations are entrusted with enabling meaningful communication to take place between speakers who belong to different cultures. Culture-specific linguistic items such as colloquialisms, forms of politeness (including hedges), and forms of address all play an important role in shaping this type of interaction. The analysis and discussion will be based on four short extracts from the first round of interviews performed by four different interpreters and will focus on the interpreters' use of colloquialisms and their treatment of hedges, forms of address and politeness, as well as their awareness of the socio-cultural context.[2]

1. Colloquialisms

During police interviews interpreters are often faced with having to translate a number of lexical, stylistic and grammatical colloquialisms common to the interviewees' speech. Witnesses try to use their verbal skills in order to appear credible and sincere, while police detectives form their line of questioning in such a way as to induce witnesses to talk. Problems generally arise when witnesses and interpreters diverge in their linguistic and cultural spheres of experience, with a resultant difference in usage and variety of the lexical units they employ.

In the first interview below, the witness uses a number of colloquialisms and hedges, some of which are interpreted into the target language while others are not.

Record of interview: witness 1
(D = Detective; I = Interpreter; W = Witness)

1	D	So what happened when V came on board the ship?
2	I	Itak, chto sluchilos', kogda V prishel na korabl'?
		So, what happened when V came on the ship?
3	W	Sho, kto ego znaet, kogda on prishel. No, kogda ya uslykhal shum,
3a		ya vstal i dver' otkryl.

		What, who knows when he came. But, when I heard the noise, I got up and opened the door.
4	I	I don't know when he came. But, when I heard the noise, I got
4a		up and opened my door.
5	D	Did you see V?
6	I	Vy videli V?
		Did you see V?
7	W	Nu, da. On stoyal u kayuty A.
		Well, yes. He stood near the cabin of A.
8	I	Well, yes. He stood at the door of uhh A's cabin.
9	D	What did he do then?
10	I	Chto on delal potom?
		What did he do then?
11	W	Sho on delal? On skazal A: "Ya tebya uroyu."
		What did he do? He said to A: "I'll dig you".
12	I	He said to A: "I'll kill you."

Witness 1 speaks informal Russian, with some elements of the southern Russian dialect: for example, he uses *sho* instead of the standard Russian *chto* ('what'; lines 3, 11). Another feature which is characteristic of the speech style of this witness is the repetition of the phrase uttered by the previous speaker. For example, when the detective asks him what he did then (line 9), he reiterates by responding *Sho on delal?* (lit.: 'What did he do?'; line 11). This stylistic feature disappears in the interpreted version. The witness repeats the question as a way of confirming that the question has been understood correctly. Sometimes this repetition can be partial, as in line 3, when the witness repeats only the question word *sho* ('what'), which again is omitted in the interpreted version. All of these features of cohesive, naturally-occurring conversation, which are peculiar to the speech of the first witness, are either diminished or disappear in interpretation.

Hatim and Mason (1990:42) argue that interpreters who work in courts with "interlocutors of vastly differing social status (e.g. barrister and accused person), find themselves tempted to neutralize social dialect for the sake of improved mutual comprehension, and to avoid appearing patronising". There is evidence of this tendency in the current data, as more colloquial SL forms such as *uslykhal* ('heard', line 3; instead of *uslyshal*) or unusual word order as in *dver otkryl* (lit.: 'door opened'; line 3a) are not matched by corresponding colloquial equivalents in the interpreted version. Another example of what might be described as 'neutralization' in the TL interpretation can be found in lines 3 and 4, where the colloquial phrase *Kto ego znaet* (lit.: 'who knows it'; line 3) is interpreted by the stylistically neutral 'I don't know' (line 4), rather than 'who knows', a more informal expression which would perhaps reflect the speaker's style more closely. The phrase 'who knows' is less face-threatening in Russian than it is in English, and in Russian the phrase would also be more appropriate in a less formal register. The native Russian interpreter was probably unaware of the pragmatic difference between SL *Kto ego znaet* and TL 'I don't know' (line 4).

The analysis of the data for this study suggests that subconscious omission, inclusion or modification of colloquialisms and particles that are void of lexical meaning is quite a common phenomenon in interpreting.

The second interview provides more examples of the transformation of SL colloquial speech into a more formal register in the TL.

Record of interview: witness 2

1	D	When did you hear the noise?
2	I	Kogda vy uslyshali shum?
		When did you hear the noise?
3	W	Gde-to v chetvert' vtorogo nochi.
		At roundabout quarter past one at night.
4	I	At around quarter past one in the morning.
5	D	What did you actually hear?
6	I	Chto vy uslyshali?
		What did you hear?
7	W	Razreshite ob'yasnit', nachal'nik. Ya ochen' ustal. Moya smena
7a		zakonchilas' pozdno vecherom. Potom my sideli s druz'yami.
7b		Reshili popit' nemnogo vodochki. A tut takaya kuter'ma
7c		nachalas'. Kto-to upal. Slyshu - krichit kto-to.
		Allow to explain, chief. I was very tired. My shift finished late in the evening. Then my friends and I were sitting. Decided to drink a little vodka. And here such rigmarole began. Someone fell. Hear – someone is shouting.
8	I	Sir, will you allow me to explain myself, please. I was tired. My
8a		shift finished late at night. Then I spent some time with my friends.
8b		We had a few drinks. And then such a commotion began. Someone
8c		fell. I heard that someone shouted.
9	D	Do you remember the exact words?
10	I	Zapomnili li vy tochno slova?
		Did you remember the words exactly?
11	W	Chego tam, pomnyu. Govorit: "Uroyu ya tebya".
		Why, remember. He says: "I'll dig you".
12	I	Yes, I do. He said: "I'll get you".

The second interviewee employs even more lexis and syntax of a less formal tenor. The witness in this interview uses a number of colloquialisms at both syntactical and lexical levels, for example, the colloquial Russian lexical unit *kuter'ma* (line 7b; dictionary equivalents are typically 'commotion', 'stir', 'bustle', 'hubbub') and *chego tam* ('why not'; line 11), the latter being substituted by a stylistically neutral 'yes' in the TL. In two cases the Russian witness employs present tense verbs to describe past events, which are transformed into past tense actions in the interpreted version: *slyshu* (line 7c; interpreted as "I heard", line 8c), *govorit* (line 11; interpreted as "he said", line 12). In both cases the witness omits personal pronouns in Russian, but they are implicit in the verb endings and the interpreter includes them in the English version. When past tense forms of the verb are employed, it is sometimes possible to establish the missing pronoun only from the context or previous sentence, as in line 7b, where the verb *reshili* ('decided') is not preceded by a personal pronoun. However, it becomes obvious from the previous utterance that the verb has the same subject pronoun *my* ('we'; line 7a). The use of verbs without independent personal pronouns and the use of the present tense to describe past events is another example of an informal tenor, and again this is not reflected in the English interpretation.

The use of the present tense by the second witness can be interpreted as a positive politeness device aimed at minimizing a potential face threat "by assurance that in general S (speaker) wants at least some of H's (hearer) wants" (Brown and Levinson 1978:70). In other words, the second witness demonstrates his willingness to collaborate and make events in his responses more interesting. The use of the present tense to make past events more interesting to the hearer is also marked for social class in both Russian and English. All three values (i.e. willingness to collaborate, more interesting presentation of events and social class identification) are lost or diminished in the interpreted version.

The second witness also uses inversion in the above extract. For example, lines 7c and 9 contain inverted clauses, with the Russian verbs *krichit* (7c) and *uroyu* (9) preceding the subject. The interpreter does not reproduce the inverted word order because English syntax does not readily lend itself to this type of inversion. However, the simple and rather short sentences of the Russian witness are preserved in the TL interpretation, thus conveying the impression that the witness is speaking in a more colloquial style.

Another example of SL colloquial speech can be found in line 7b in the use of the diminutive noun *vodochka* (derived from *vodka*). Russian diminutive forms not only denote 'smallness' but may also express emotional nuances such as affection, disparagement, irony, etc. Thus, depending on the context in which such a form is used, the same diminutive noun may convey affection or reflect an ironic attitude. In the case of *vodochka* (7b), which is used here in association with *nemnogo* [lit.: 'a little', 'some', 'not much'), this diminutive denotes, first of all, 'a small amount' and, secondly, some sort of affection or endearment in relation to the subject being talked about, here the drink. In translating the SL phrase *Reshili popit' nemnogo vodochki* (lit.: 'Decided to drink a little bit of vodka'; line 7b) the interpreter resorts to generalization and opts for "We had a few drinks" (line 8b). This TL interpretation is wider, less specific than the SL phrase and loses some of the nuances of the original text. By using the diminutive form of *vodka* in line 7b, the second witness wants to imply that he was not drunk by the time he heard the phrase pronounced by the suspect. He wants the detective to believe that his account of events is true. The strategy of generalization or, in Newmark's terms 'undertranslation' (1981, 1988), hardly seems appropriate in the context of a police interview.

2. The treatment of hedges in police interpreting

In their analysis of witness testimony, O'Barr and his associates (O'Barr and Conley 1976; Erickson *et al.* 1978; Conley *et al.* 1978; Lind and O'Barr 1979) established a set of specific traits which constitute witness style. They called this the "powerless" style, because when these traits were present "the witness gave the impression of being less convincing, less truthful, less competent, less intelligent, and less trustworthy than when his speech was lacking in these traits" (Berk Seligson 1990:20). Included among these traits are hedges, non-committal cautions, or ambiguous expressions, such as "well", "it seems to be", "I guess", etc. 'Hedges' have been defined in various ways by linguists. Lakoff (1975:66), who has analysed the use of hedges in women's speech, came to the conclusion that hedges function to create an option for the addressee "of deciding how seriously to take what the speaker is saying. It is for this reason that 'John is sorta short' may be in the right context, a polite way of saying 'John is short', rather than a scaled-down comment on John's actual height". Brown and Levinson (1987:145), as part of their theory of politeness, summarize the literature on hedges and give a definition of a hedge as "a particle, word, or phrase that modifies the degree of membership in a set; it says of that membership that it is partial, or true only in certain respects, or that it is more true or complete than perhaps might be expected".

Hedges encoded in particles are of particular interest to us because both Russian and English have quite a number of commonly used particles which, depending on the context in which they are used, may contain a variety of potential meanings and express a number of intentions. The present study is based on Brown and Levinson's (1987:147) subdivision of all hedges encoded in particles into "strengtheners (those that mainly act as emphatic hedges, 'exactly' or 'precisely' or 'emphatically') and weakeners (those that soften or tentativize what they modify)".

The interpreter in the first interview includes in his interpreting, perhaps subconsciously, an additional element of hesitation or a weakener – *uhh*, which is not present in the SL version (line 8). The hesitation *uhh* is probably a side effect of either mental concentration or strain that the interpreter experiences due to the fact that he has been interpreting for a whole hour by that stage. When this particle is coupled with the hedge *well* (line 8), it leaves open the possibility that the interviewee may appear to the interviewers as less definite and confident about his recollections.

It should be mentioned that the pragmatic value of the particle *nu* (line 7) in the SL is misinterpreted in the TL. Quite often interpreters automatically substitute the English hedge *well* for the Russian particle *nu*, without a proper appreciation of the latter's pragmatic value. The particle *nu* can be either a strengthener or a weakener: its pragmatic potential depends on the immediate linguistic and extra-linguistic environment. *Well*, by contrast, usually signals a dispreferred response or shows surprise, doubt or annoyance. Russian particles, which are a feature of the colloquial language, are used to express a variety of emotions and subjective attitudes and assessments, thereby adding emotive meaning and expressiveness to speech. In line 7 the hedge *nu* is used in the SL as an intensifier, rather than a hesitation particle. What the witness is stressing here is that he did indeed see V, an emphatically expressed assertion of absolute certainty which is not conveyed as such by the interpreter in the TL. Consequently, a lack of interpreter awareness of the pragmatic function of the Russian particle *nu* and the pragmatically inappropriate use of the English *well* change the nature of the speech event.

The use of the particle *zhe* is probably the most complicated case. It may express insistent affirmation, specify precisely a place or time denoted by an adverb or adverbial phrase, impart to a verb a peremptory nuance or one of insistence, implying astonishment, indignation or disapproval when qualifying interrogative words (Wade 1993:519). What is common to all these meanings is the strengthening function. For example, witness four uses *zhe* in sentence 15:

| 15 | W | Ya zhe uzhe skazal, chto ne pomnyu. |
| 16 | I | I 've already told you, that I do not remember. |

Zhe denotes here a categorical affirmation by the witness. In the TL version, however, the idea of insistence disappears and the affirmation becomes less categorical.

Da ('yes') is another commonly used particle which may function as a linguistic hedge. It is used as a strengthener and may, for example, stress negation in combination with *net* ('no') or *ne* ('not'). Let us compare the phrase in line 7 in interview four (cited in full in section 4 below and repeated here for convenience) with its TL interpretation.

5	D	What did you talk about?
6	I	O chem vy govorili?
		What did you talk about?
7	W	Da, ne o chem. A khorosho vypil, da i mne khotelos' spat'.
		Oh, not about anything. A had drunk a lot, and I too wanted to
		sleep.
8	I	Well, about nothing. A was drunk and I felt like going to bed.

Here, when the witness says "da, ne o chem" he is trying to stress that he did not in fact discuss anything. In the English interpreting (line 8), the hedge *well* introduces doubt or uncertainty. The opposite happens in the following example, also from interview 4:

21	D	Did you have an argument with A?
22	I	Vy porugalis' s A?
		Did you have a quarrel with A?
23	W	Da, net. My oba byli piany... V etoj fraze nichego osobennogo
23a		net... Vy ne ponimaete...
		Oh, no. We were both drunk... There is nothing particular in this
		phrase... You don't understand...
24	I	Not at all. We were both drunk... There is nothing particular in
24a		this phrase... You do not understand...

In line 23, *da, net* is interpreted as a categorical negation of the question posed by the detective (21, 22) – "Not at all" (24).

The analysis so far then suggests that hedges encoded in particles present significant difficulty in dialogue interpreting. Misinterpretation, deletion or addition of these particles may lead to an inadequate perception of the interviewee, especially in terms of his or her commitment to what is being said, and may therefore somewhat modify the illocutionary force of an interviewee's utterances.

Examples of tentativisers can be found in both detectives' and witnesses' speech. In example 13 (interview four) the English phrase "you could have said ..." is interpreted as "mozhet byt', vy skazali" ('Maybe you said'; line 14) and vice versa (as in lines 19 and 20).

13	D	You could have said something else ...
14	I	Mozhet byt', vy skazali chto-to drugoe ...
...		
19	W	Ya ne pomnyu. Mozhet byt' i skazal.
20	I	I don't remember. I could have said it.

The modal *could* is a tentativizing hedge which could be used both in questions and statements and "seems often to indicate the presence of an implicature" (Brown and Levinson 1987:153). The Russian indefinite pronoun *chto-to*, when used as a hedge, conveys the meaning 'somewhat' and behaves as an adverb in the sentence. An example of its use is found in the interview with the third witness:

7	W	Spal ya. Chto-to nevazhno mne bylo i ne spalos'. Uzhe vtorye
7a		sutki.
8	I	I slept. I did not feel well and couldn't sleep for the last two days.

In the interpretation, the hedge *chto-to* is deleted and its meaning is lost.

By deleting elements such as these interpreters actually 'dehedge' SL speech, thus transforming, reducing or omitting use and user variables in the speech event. Berk-Seligson, who examined the work of court interpreters in the judicial process, suggests that for some interpreters "these elements seem extraneous to the "meat and potatoes" of the sentence – that is, the subject and predicate – for they do not refer to who did what to whom" (1984:142). Police detectives and other consumers of such interpretation may eventually lose important information, since "both hesitation forms and hedges are part of the constellation of features that constitute powerless testimony style" (ibid:131). As a result, the witness's answers as expressed in the TL interpretation may sound somewhat weaker than they did in the SL. It is possible that the degree of certainty expressed, which may be augmented or reduced in the interpretation, is a highly significant element in terms of what the police rely on in establishing facts related to a crime.

3. Nominal forms of address and forms of politeness

The witness in interview two makes an effort to be conventionally polite by paying attention to the face of the hearer. Consider the following exchange, repeated here for convenience:

7	W	Razreshite ob'yasnit', nachal'nik. Ya ochen' ustal. Moya smena
7a		zakonchilas' pozdno vecherom. Potom my sideli s druz'yami.
7b		Reshili popit' nemnogo vodochki. A tut takaya kuter'ma
7c		nachalas'. Kto-to upal. Slyshu - krichit kto-to.

Allow to explain, chief. I was very tired. My shift finished late in the evening. Then my friends and I were sitting. Decided to drink a little vodka. And here such rigmarole began. Someone fell. Hear – someone is shouting.

8	I	Sir, will you allow me to explain myself, please. I was tired. My
8a		shift finished late at night. Then I spent some time with my friends.
8b		We had a few drinks. And then such a commotion began. Someone
8c		fell. I heard that someone shouted.

In line 7, in order to establish a better rapport with the detective, the interviewee uses the address form *nachal'nik* [lit.: 'chief'], which, though belonging to the colloquial register, is both deferential and friendly at the same time. Address forms always contain some type of social marker, where "the social component consists of the speaker-addressee relationship, the speaker's evaluation of the addressee (and situation), and of the speaker's social background, as expressed in the use of a given form of address" (Broun 1988:258). A closer look at this form of address suggests that in using it the interviewee underscores the asymmetrical power relations of the co-locutors.

Yet, at the same time this address form indicates a friendly or polite attitude of the speaker towards the police detective. This is not a violation of address norms, since "informal forms are used in Russian in asymmetrical relations even referring to strangers. It sometimes creates a friendlier atmosphere, by introducing less asymmetry in the relations of the collocutors" (Krouglov 1996:93). In the TL interpretation, *nachal'nik* is substituted by *Sir* (line 8), which is quite formal and distant. By adding the conventional politeness tag *please* (line 8), which does not appear in the source utterance, the interpreter tries to achieve a degree of mitigation. However, a native speaker of English would have probably said something like "allow me to explain" – not *"will* you allow me to explain *myself"* (my emphasis). The witness is not under suspicion, so there is no need for him to "explain himself". It is not his actions that are in question. In fact, the interpreter's formulation may ultimately have reflected negatively on this witness's account.

It is worth noting that in the case of the SL stretch in line 7 above, the introduction of markers of distance and formality in the TL interpretation (line 8) could be explained by the fact that Russian distinguishes between what are known as 'polite' and 'familiar' forms of address, as manifested in the pronoun system (Russian "vy/ty" is similar to French "vous/tu") and personal verb endings. Prior to using the address form *nachal'nik* the interviewee had used the imperative form of the verb *razreshite* [lit.: 'allow'] in the second person plural, which renders the Russian phrase more distant.

In some contexts, when interpreters are short of time or wish to keep the TL text concise for any reason, they will often omit politeness forms, on the assumption that these forms are irrelevant and do not change the meaning of the original utterance. In other situations, interpreters tend to insert politeness forms, especially when they interpret from Russian into English; they assume English speakers to be generally 'more polite' based on sets of rules of conduct elaborated by English society. It is possible that interpreters who introduce additional politeness forms or omit them in their interpretation misrepresent the illocutionary force of the client's utterances, a particularly important issue in the context of a police investigation. Berk-Seligson (1990:137) considers politeness "one of the features characteristic of powerless testimony style, and persons who use powerless speech on the witness stand tend to be evaluated more negatively than do persons who use the powerful style". During police investigation it is important for interpreters to provide a true representation of the interviewee's speech and communicative intent. Misrepresentation may lead to pragmatic inappropriateness, complications in police investigation and loss of time.

Record of interview: witness 3

1   D   So, how long have you been on this boat?
2   I   Itak, kak dolgo vy rabotaete na etom sudne?
         So, how long have you been working on this boat?

3	W	Polgoda.
		Half a year.
4	I	Six months.
5	D	What did you do yesterday after midnight?
6	I	Chto vy delali vchera posle polunochi?
		What did you do yesterday after midnight?
7	W	Spal ya. Chto-to nevazhno mne bylo i ne spalos'. Uzhe vtorye
7a		sutki.
		I slept. Somehow I did not feel well and I could not sleep. Already for the second 24 hour period.
8	I	I slept. I did not feel well and couldn't sleep for the last two days.
9	D	Could you hear what happened in A's cabin?
10	I	Vy slyshali, chto sluchilos' v kayute A?
		Did you hear what happened in the cabin of A?
11	W	Slyshal. V zakrichal: "Ya tebya uroyu". Nu i nomer on vykinul.
		Heard. V shouted: "I'll dig you." Quite a stunt he pulled.
12	I	I heard, V said "I will stitch you up." He pulled a stunt.

The witness in the third interview uses colloquial language, for example the inversion in line 7: *spal ya* (lit.: 'slept I') which is interpreted into the TL as "I slept" (line 8). Generally speaking, the interpreter preserves the stylistic characteristics of the witness. Colloquial phrases find their equivalents in the interpretation, for example "Nu i nomer on vykinul" (line 11) becomes "He pulled a stunt" (line 12), though in this case the particle *nu*, which is used in the source utterance for emphasis, is lost in the interpreted version.

Although the interpreter in this interview manages to find the colloquial equivalents of some lexical units and tries to preserve the style of the source utterances, the use of full forms of English auxiliary verbs, such as *will* (line 12) and *did not* (line 8), results in a more formal style. Such stylistic shifts may lead to inaccurate social or psychological evaluations of witnesses (O'Barr 1982).

4. Sociocultural context in interpreting

The absence of a context can result in misinterpretation or several readings of the same stretch of text. Three interviews with the witnesses, held simultaneously at the police station, produced three different interpretations of the SL phrase "Ya tebya uroyu", heard at the crime scene on the night of the murder:

> Interpreter 1: I'll kill you
> Interpreter 2: I'll get you
> Interpreter 3: I will stitch you up

All three interpreters indicated that this phrase presented certain difficulties because (a) the witnesses were not completely aware of the full context in which it was used, and (b) this phrase is not a standard lexical unit; it belongs to sailors' jargon, probably having its roots in criminal argot. But it is the absence of the context in which witnesses heard the phrase uttered that most probably accounts for the three different interpretations.

The chief detective received the scripts of the three interviews in question just before the interview with witness 4 was due to resume. The interpreter of the interview knew nothing about the phrase when the interview started.

Record of interview: witness 4

1	D	What did you do, when you saw A?
2	I	Chto vy sdelali, kogda vy uvideli A?
		What did you do when you saw A?
3	W	Nichego. Ya poprosil u nego sigaretu, i my pokurili vmeste.
		Nothing. I asked him for a cigarette, and we smoked together.
4	I	Nothing. I asked for a cigarette, and we smoked together.
5	D	What did you talk about?
6	I	O chem vy govorili?
		What did you talk about?
7	W	Da, ne o chem. A khorosho vypil, da i mne khotelos' spat'.
		Oh, not about anything. A had drunk a lot, and I too wanted to sleep.
8	I	Well, about nothing. A was drunk and I felt like going to bed.
9	D	And did you say: "I will kill you"?
10	I	A vy skazali: "Ya tebya ub'yu"?
		And did you say: "I'll kill you"?
11	W	Net, ya etogo ne govoril.
		No, I didn't say that.
12	I	No, I didn't say that.
13	D	You could have said something else …
14	I	Mozhet byt', vy skazali chto-to drugoe …
		Maybe you said something else …
15	W	Ya zhe uzhe skazal, chto ne pomnyu. Ya govoril, chto do etogo
15a		ya vypil s druz'yami v parke.
		I've already said that I don't remember. I've said that before that I had drunk with friends in the park.
16	I	I 've already told you, that I do not remember. I told you, that I
16a		had a few drinks with my friends in the park.

At this stage the chief detective points to the SL phrase from the transcript of one of the three interviews and asks the interpreter to read the phrase in Russian to the witness.

17	D	Did you say it to A?
18	I	Vy skazali eto A?
		Did you say it to A?

19	W	Ya ne pomnyu. Mozhet byt' i skazal. Ne znayu. A chto tut
19a		takogo? U nas u moryakov eto obychnaya fraza.
		I don't remember. Maybe I said. Don't know. And so what? With
		us, sailors, it is a usual phrase.
20	I	I don't remember. I could have said it. I don't know. So, what?
20a		This is a usual phrase with us, sailors.
21	D	Did you have an argument with A?
22	I	Vy porugalis' s A?
		Did you have a quarrel with A?
23	W	Da, net. My oba byli piany... V etoj fraze nichego osobennogo
23a		net... Vy ne ponimaete...
		Oh, no. We were both drunk... There is nothing particular in this
		phrase... You don't understand...
24	I	Not at all. We were both drunk ... There is nothing particular in
24a		this phrase ... You do not understand ...

At this point the chief detective provided a verbal 'caution' informing the interviewee of his right to remain silent and that anything said may be taken as evidence in a court of law. Afterwards, what started out as a friendly police interview turned into a more formal one, since from that point on the interviewee was treated as a suspect.

This extract from the police record of the interview can be divided into two parts:

- Part 1 (lines 1-16a) – the witness seems to be more relaxed; he uses complex sentences in his speech; his answers are clear and he seems pretty sure of his position.

- Part 2 (lines 17-24a) – the witness becomes nervous; he uses only simple sentences and some sentences are unfinished; his main goal is to explain that the phrase "ya tebya uroyu" does not carry any threat.

Since the Russian phrase "Ya tebya uroyu" was crucial to this investigation, both police and interpreters made significant efforts to establish its illocutionary meaning, trying to recover what it really 'meant' in the SL text from the entire range of possible meanings (or meaning potential, which Halliday (1978:109) defines as "the paradigmatic range of semantic choice that is present in the system, and to which the members of a culture have access in their language"). The phrase originated in criminal jargon and later came into use among some sailors and members of certain other occupations and groups.

When interpreting the phrase "I will kill you" (line 9) from English into Russian, the interpreter in interview four used the common verb *ubit'* ('to kill'; line 10). This substitution of a key verb in the phrase may be the reason the fourth witness denied uttering the phrase (lines 11, 12). The chief detective had to produce the original phrase "Ya tebya uroyu", quoted by other witnesses, for the interpreter and ask him to read the phrase to the interviewee. Only then did the interviewee admit to having uttered the phrase (lines 19, 19a). In the answers which followed he tried to explain that in his view the phrase did not carry any threat to the victim, that it was not his intention to kill him. By using a slang term, the witness probably wanted to "evoke all the shared associations and attitudes that" he and the victim had towards the event; "this may be used as FTA redress" (Brown and Levinson 1987:111).

The main problem was that, in order to establish the meaning potential of the phrase, interpreters had to identify and analyse the wider linguistic and extra-linguistic context in which it was used. Unfortunately, neither the detectives nor the interpreters were able to do this because this information was not available, the intentions of the speaker being inaccessible. This is as much a problem for the linguist as for the law. At the debriefing after the first round of interviews, this fact was acknowledged by both detectives and interpreters. Since the phrase was critically important for the investigation, the police asked the interpreter, who worked with the suspect, to provide a sociocultural analysis of the interview, in order to investigate further the use and pragmatic value of the phrase and to disambiguate it. The analysis performed by the interpreter included the following factors: physical state of the suspect at the time the phrase was uttered; relative social status/characteristics of both interlocutors; tenor of discourse; cultural factors, including (a) cultural inheritance, and (b) life experience.

As a result of this analysis two groups of contradictory factors were identified: on the one hand, the suspect exhibited the speech patterns of a well-educated individual. The fact that he generally avoided jargon and colloquialisms attested to his appreciation of the tenor of the interview. His speech patterns also demonstrated that he had experience of interacting with a wide range of speakers belonging to different layers of society. On the other hand, it is possible that his social status at the time, i.e. a sailor on a Russian fishing trawler, as well as the circumstances in which he found himself, encouraged the suspect to express a greater degree of threat than might otherwise have been the case. The physical state of the suspect, who was drunk at the time, might also have had a significant impact on the meaning potential of the phrase and the level of threat it carried.

The final debriefing which took place in the presence of all detectives and interpreters helped to identify and resolve residual issues and enabled the police to decide on what further steps were necessary in the investigation. The interpreter's conclusion in relation to the meaning potential of the Russian phrase "ya tebya uroyu" was taken into account and was eventually presented in court.[3] It revealed two conflicting positions: on the one hand, it suggested that the phrase in question did not carry a significant threat to the victim, because the use of in-group terminology may indicate that no threat to face is intended. On the other hand, it pointed to the fact that the suspect had a higher educational level than his fellow sailors, minimal experience as a sailor and fewer shared in-group associations, all of which could pose some threat to the victim.

Languages do not function outside cultural and situational contexts (Halliday 1981:48), so an interpreter can only perform adequately when a variety of factors ranging from the ritualistic (which assumes great importance in traditional societies) to the most practical aspects of day-to-day existence are taken into account (Malinovski 1923, 1935). Interpreters constantly have to consider the social and cultural implications of their work. It is therefore vital for police interpreters to predict and explain to the parties involved certain cultural aspects which may arise during the interview. The opportunity of a briefing before the interview enables an interpreter to avoid certain problems of this type.

5. Concluding remarks

The preceding analysis of the speech of Russian witnesses and its English interpretation during police interviews shows that interpreters often alter the meaning potential of the utterances they are required to interpret. Interpreters tend to delete or sometimes change, in their interpretation, certain colloquialisms and hedges which provide evidence of pragmatic intention, thus transforming the source text into a series of neutral utterances. In other instances interpreters introduce additional particles or polite forms, which may misrepresent the speaker or make a witness's testimony seem less certain or more definite, a situation which can ultimately lead to an inaccurate perception and possibly even to the loss of important information in police investigations. It is therefore important to preserve, as much as possible, the stylistic markers of the SL text. In police interpreting, accuracy is of extreme importance and generalizations are often not helpful. Berk-Seligson (1990) and Gentile (1991) suggest that the omission of elements, whether of a linguistic or cultural nature, should be avoided in interpreting.

A second finding of this study is that the absence of a situational context may result in several different readings of the same phrase, especially when dealing with specific in-group terminology. Textual as well as sociocultural and situational analyses play an important role in establishing the meaning potential of a phrase or stretch of text. Such analyses should make use of sociolinguistic factors which are relevant to the situation. These may include the relative social status of both interlocutors, the tenor of the discourse, as well as cultural factors such as cultural inheritance and life experience. It is important to distinguish the propositional and pragmatic meanings of any stretch of language in order to understand the potential intentions of a speaker. The use of in-group terminology, for example, could significantly mitigate threat to face.

Interpreters involved in police investigations should attempt as best they can to produce a TL interpretation which preserves the linguistic and cultural characteristics and nuances of the source utterances. If a Russian speaker sounds certain or hesitant, for example, the interpreter should attempt to convey this in his or her interpretation. The results of this research demonstrate that, in the case of police interpreting, Hatim and Mason's conclusion (1990:190) with reference to the translation of legally binding texts is also true, namely, that only minimal changes can be allowed: "The whole matter of structural modifications and the degree to which they are permitted needs to be considered with the text producer's purpose in mind. In particular, degrees of evaluativeness in the source text are of overriding importance when it comes to deciding what structure to preserve and how".

ALEXANDER KROUGLOV
Diplomatic Service Language Centre, Foreign and Commonwealth Office, Cromwell House, Dean Staley Street, London SW1P 3JH, UK

Notes

1. See Berk Seligson 1990, D'Argaville 1991, Downing and Helms Tillery 1992, Laster and Taylor 1994, Shackman 1984, Wadensjö 1992, 1995, and Zimman 1994.
2. The names of all participants in the police interviews quoted here are omitted in order to protect the privacy of witnesses, police interpreters and detectives.
3. Since neither the phrase nor the verb itself are registered in dictionaries, the report also discussed the derivational morphology of the verb. *Uryt'* is derived from the imperfective verb *ryt'* ('dig'). The addition of prefixes most often results in perfectivization as well as additional meaning being imparted to the verb. When prefixed the imperfective verb *ryt'* changes both its aspect and meaning. The general meaning of the prefix *u-* can be either 'leaving' or 'removing', as in *brat'* ('take'), *ubrat'* ('remove', 'take away'; coll. 'kill'); *idti* ('go'), *ujti* ('leave', 'go away'). Special attention was paid to the analogy between the verb *ryt'* and the verb *bit'* ('beat', 'strike', 'hit'), which when coupled with the prefix *u-* transforms into the verb *ubit'* ('kill'). This analogy between *ubit'* and *ubrat'* demonstrated that the verb *uryt'* had been formed in accordance with the rules of word formation in Russian and the prefix *u-* with the verb *ryt'* produces another verb, which expresses similar semantic characteristics with both *ubrat'* and *ubit'*, i.e. both with the meaning 'to kill'.

   Suspect V was eventually acquitted by the court due to lack of evidence. The prosecution had no witnesses at the trial: the Russian sailors had gone back home and failed to appear in court.

References

Berk Seligson, Susan (1984) 'Subjective Reactions to Phonological Variations in Costa Rican Spanish', *The Journal of Psycholinguistic Research* 13: 415-42.

------ (1990) *The Bilingual Courtroom. Court Interpreters in the Judicial Process*, Chicago: The University of Chicago Press.

Conley, J. M., W. M. O'Barr and E. A. Lind (1978) 'The Power of Language: Presentation Style in the Courtroom', *Duke Law Journal* 78: 1375-99.

D'Argaville, M. (1991) *Cross-cultural Communication Issues and Solutions in the Delivery of Legal Services*, Melbourne: Centre for Community Languages in the Professions, Monash University.

Broun, Frederike (1988) *Terms of Address*, Berlin: Mouton de Gruyter.

Brown, P. and S. L. Levinson (1987) *Politeness: Some Universals in Language Usage*, Cambridge: Cambridge University Press.

Dollerup, Cay (1993) 'Interlingual Translators and Issues in Translatology', *Perspectives: Studies in Translatology* 2: 137-154.

Downing, Bruce T. and Kate Helms Tillery (1992) *Professional Training for Community Interpreters: A Report on Models of Interpreter Training and the Value of Training*, Minneapolis: Center for Urban and Regional Affairs.

Erickson, B., E. A. Lind, B. C. Johnson and W. M. O'Barr (1978) 'Speech Style and Impression Formation in a Court Setting: The Effects of "Powerful" and "Powerless" Speech', *Journal of Experimental Social Psychology* 14: 266-79.

Gentile, A. (1991) 'Working with Professional Interpreters', in A. Pouwels (ed) *Cross-Cultural Communication in Medical Encounters*, Melbourne: Centre for Community Languages in the Professions, Monash University.

Halliday, M. A. K. (1978) *Language as Social Semiotic: The Social Interpretation of Language and Meaning*, London: Edward Arnold.

------ (1981) *Explorations in the Functions of Language*, London: Edward Arnold.

Hatim, Basil and Ian Mason (1990) *Discourse and the Translator*, London & New York: Longman.

Krouglov, Alexandr (1996) 'Transformation of Nominal Address Form Systems in Russian and Ukrainian', *International Journal of the Sociology of Languages* 122: 89-106.

Labov, W. (1969) 'Contraction, Deletion and Inherent Variability of the English Copula', *Language* 45: 715-62.

Lakoff, R. (1975) *Language and Woman's Place*, New York: Harper & Row.

Laster, Kathy and Veronica Taylor (1994) *Interpreters and the Legal System*, Sydney: Federation Press.

Lind, E. A. and W. M. O'Barr (1979) 'The Social Significance of Speech in the Courtroom', in H. Giles and R. St. Clair (eds) *Language and Social Psychology*, College Park, Md.: University Press.

Malinovski, Bronislaw (1923) 'The Problem of Meaning in Primitive Languages', in C. K. Ogden and I. A. Richards (eds) *The Meaning of Meaning*, London: Routledge.

------ (1935) *Coral Gardens and Their Magic, Vol.2, The Language of Magic and Gardening*, London: Allen & Unwin. Reprinted, Bloomington: Indiana University Press, 1965.

O'Barr, William M. (1982) *Lingustic Evidence: Language, Power and Strategy in the Courtroom*, New York: Academic Press.

O'Barr, W. M. and J. M. Conley (1976) 'When a Juror Watches a Lawyer', *Barrister* 3: 8-11, 33.

Shackman, Jane (1984) *The Right to be Understood*, Cambridge Mass.: National Extension College.

Wade, T. (1997) *A Comprehensive Russian Grammar*, Oxford: Blackwell.

Wadensjö, C. (1992) *Interpreting as Interaction – On Dialogue Interpreting in Immigration Hearings and Medical Encounters*, Linköping University: Department of Communication Studies.

Wadensjö, C. (1995) 'Dialogue Interpreting and the Distribution of Responsibility', *Journal of Linguistics* 14: 111-29.

Zimman, Leonor (1994) 'Intervention as a Pedagogical Problem in Community Interpreting', in Cay Dollerup and Annette Lindegaard (eds) *Teaching Translation and Interpreting 2: Insights, Aims and Visions*, Amsterdam & Philadelphia: John Benjamins.

The Translator. Volume 5, Number 2 (1999), 303-326   ISBN 1-900650-21-5

The Interpreter on the (Talk) Show
Interaction and Participation Frameworks

FRANCESCO STRANIERO SERGIO
University of Trieste, Italy

Abstract. *This paper analyses dialogue interpreting in the context of the televised talk show. In the first part I examine some basic issues related to broadcast talk. Among these are the television speech context, the distinction between on-screen and off-screen participants, the function of the presenter, the use of language and the goal of communication. In the second part of the article – using a framework which draws on conversational analysis, and taking data from a large corpus of Italian talk shows – I explore how the interpreter's role and identity are interactionally constructed by participants. I argue that the talk show features a greater visibility and involvement of the interpreter in terms of meaning negotiation, topic management and turn-taking behaviour, all of which calls for extra competence as compared to other institutional settings. Finally, I point to the need for research to adopt a sociolinguistic approach in order to gear training to the realities of the interpreting profession.*

This article, part of a much larger research project, examines the interactional aspects of TV interpreting, and more specifically the talk show. The data for the larger project is partly drawn from the archives of RAI (Italian Broadcasting Corporation) and partly provided by professional interpreters in the form of private video recordings of their past assignments for state and commercial networks. The project is designed to trace back the history of the interpreter on Italian television from the early days up to the present, including such momentous events as the first landing on the moon (1969), Kennedy's assasination (1973), Lady Diana's and Mother Teresa's funerals (1997), and the Anglo-American attack on Iraq (1999). This history will be examined in relation to interpreting modalities, television genres and media events, programme times, and various other parameters.

In the study reported here, I will be using methods and concepts developed by disciplines such as discourse analysis, conversational analysis and ethnomethodology, which view language as action and as an instrument of social interaction. Context in this framework is seen not only as a constraint on the production of talk but also as itself a product of the use of language.

ISSN 1355-6509

The dynamic character of context means that participants are able to evoke alternative contextual frames during interaction, and the analyst must therefore recognize the mutual role played by language, context and participant cooperation in shaping speech events.

The data analysed in this study consists of a transcript of a talk show where I myself acted as interpreter in 1986. This particular case study is part of a corpus of more than 200 episodes, from more than 40 different Italian talk shows, involving 6 languages and 30 interpreters (working both in simultaneous and consecutive modes). The episode has been selected because it illustrates a number of issues related to the conceptual and methodological approach I intend to adopt for analysing the corpus as a whole. The issues I will be focusing on in the present study are: (a) how the interpreter and the talk show host change their footings (Goffman 1981) in framing their speech activities; (b) how the interpreter manages his face wants (Brown & Levinson 1987); and (c) how the interpreter contributes to the successful outcome of the interaction in terms of topic introduction and management, meaning negotiation and turn-taking behaviour.

1. Talk show interpreting

Media discourse has been described as "techno-communication" (Berger 1992: 8) because it is not based on physical or personal experience and involves no direct face-to-face interaction; instead, "[t]he impression of presence is created through the construction of a shared space [and] of a shared time" (Morse 1986:62). The sender has no direct access to the receiver and the receiver can never directly respond to the sender. Both, however, project their own self images and that of the interactional exchange *into* the text. Communication takes place *through* the text, and speakers' roles are constantly (re)defined through the relationships established between the text and the audience. Broadcast talk has also been defined as talk for (absent) overhearers (Hutchby 1995) and as more specifically "designed to display the orientations of speakers to the 'presence' of a distributed set of recipients" (Hutchby 1997:177).

The talk show is an electronic space which simulates the physical environment and constructs relations of intimacy and confidentiality with viewers via the presentation of an individual's private life. This may be achieved through camerawork, body language, and/or the decor (which duplicates either the typical home or the town square). The audience may variously be referred to as 'the people', 'the consumer', 'electors', 'women', and so on, hence the continuous need to define the participation framework and goals of communication. The fact that there is a tele-viewing audience may be indicated implicitly by audiovisual language (shots and camerawork, decor, posture, voice) that assigns the audience a certain place or positioning in the text; it may also be indicated explicitly, as in the following extract (*Tappeto*

Volante, Telemontecarlo, 7.5.1996), where the presenter (C) is interviewing
a French director (O), with the help of an interpreter (I):

C chiediamo alla cortesia di Josiane di raccontarci per quanto possibile il
   contenuto di questo film che fa riferimento a un trian/

O   c'est tout public?

C eh?

O c'est tout public?

C sì

O (*turning towards I*) j'ai demandé si c'est des questions pour tout public je fais
   des réponses pour tout le public ou je fais des réponses ehm [normales]

I   [ah (.) dice] le le risposte
   che deve dare devono essere rivolte ad ogni tipo di pubblico oppure ehm a un
   pubblico partico [lare?]

C →   [sì] dunque noi in questo momento siamo stiamo trasme- se
   vuole tradurre ehm Rosanna così la mentre io parlo così guadagnamo qualche
   secondo di tempo dunque noi stiamo trasmettendo evidentemente a quest'ora
   del pomeriggio abbiamo un pubblico familiare ehm (*titters*) [ora]

O   [je vais faire une
   réponse [public familial]

C   [ecco per]
   il [pubblico familiare perchè i contenuti sono come dire un po'] arditi per la
   verità

I   [quindi darò una risposta destinata a un pubblico familiare]

English Gloss

C we would like to ask Josiane to tell us as far as possible about the content of this
   film which is based on a trian/

O   is it for any audience?

C eh?

O is it for any audience?

C yes

O (*turning towards I*) I'm asking if these questions are for any audience I'll make
   answers for any audience or I'll make my answers ehm [normal]

I   [ah (.) she] says that (.)
   the answers she is to give (.) are they to be addressed to every type of audience
   or ehm to a special audi [ence?]

C→   [yes] well right now we are broadca- (*addressing I*)
   Rosanna (.) would you please translate so that while I'm talking we can save a
   few seconds (.) so (*looking at O*) (.) well clearly we're on the air at this time in
   the afternoon (.) we have an audience made up of families (*titters*) [so]

O   [I'll give you
   a family] [public] answ[er]

C   [here we are] [for] fa [milies since the content of this film is you
   know] a bit racy I'd say

I   [so I'll give you an answer for family viewers]

  The audience of a talk show, moreover, are frequently consulted and questioned by presenters who may even answer the questions themselves, speak

as their interlocutor, act as their spokesman or pretend they are themselves the audience. Viewers participate in an act of communication which is secondary with respect to the primary act, that between the on-screen participants. Theirs is more a matter of spectatorship than of participation. More often than not, presenters have already heard the guest talk, as is evident in references such as "before the beginning of the show you told me ...". The construction of the televisual space then is made up of two discourse levels: "the plan of reporting interaction", which is the relationship between the speakers and the overhearing audience,[1] and "the plan of reported interaction", or the relationship between the speakers themselves (Bondi Paganelli 1990:45-55). This pragmatic feature, peculiar to audiovisual communication, is crucially important for understanding the speech context it creates, since what is being discussed, narrated, (re)presented (the **plan of reported interaction**) is constrained by the frame within which discussing, narrating, (re)presenting takes place (the **plan of reporting interaction**). The televised text is at the same time the object to be communicated and the electronic place of communication which constrains and orients the object to be communicated. This means that in the televised text the narration of an event often turns out to be more important than the event itself.

The talk show, like other TV programmes, is thus a narrating event. The participants talk among themselves and at the same time talk to the audience: what they talk about are narrated events. In this speech context, the interpreter is not the only person to speak through the words of others. At the interface between on-screen and off-screen participants is the presenter who has a dual identity, speaking as an institutional voice and with the voice of the man or woman on the street. The presenter mediates events and people in terms of popular speech, providing his or her "own version of the language of the public to whom talk is mainly addressed" (Hall *et al* 1978:61). This is particularly evident, for example, when the presenter, pretending to be someone from the audience, 'acts out' ignorance, naivety, astonishment, curiosity, etc. It is the presenter who, with his or her discourse register, personality and conversational style, ultimately determines the participation format, the identity and success of this specialized form of talk.

Talk show interpreting requires a specific job profile and special skills compared not only to conference interpreting but also to other forms of dialogue interpreting. Interpreters are increasingly required to translate the discourse of ordinary people rather than experts, people who are invited to share their personal experiences and emotions with a large audience. Moreover, talk shows take on a variety of forms. Some authors make a distinction between "monothematic" and "polythematic" talk shows (Charaudeau and Ghiglione 1997:135), while others, like Dahlgren (1995:62), distinguish between "élite talk shows" and "vox pop talk shows". However, an important characteristic of contemporary television is the hybridization of genres, so that information, entertainment and opinion are all mixed together. Discourse strategies employed in genres such as the interview, the debate, the testimony, the stories about victims, the reportage, the story-telling or the game all have in common a conversational format. As the study described here will demonstrate, advertising and promotional discourses are also part and parcel of the televised text.

A distinctive feature of the talk show, particularly in multiparty settings, is that there is not necessarily a logical or consequential development of the *content*. Topics continuously shift, and what counts is the development of the *situation*. It is the latter which gives rhythm to the show and keeps viewers glued to the TV screen. Local attention is focused not so much on propositional as on relational aspects: to cause a reaction, to embarrass someone, etc. The same is true for unexpected events: the more unexpected the occurrences (whether technical or human), the better the show. The presenter announces, recalls, describes and comments in a dynamic context of 'things that happen'. This means that disproportionate emphasis is placed on the relational level and phatic communication to the detriment of the referential level. In fact, contemporary television is increasingly turning into meta-television, which is more interested in speaking about the relationship it is establishing with its audience than in speaking about the outside world.

The phatic exchanges between the presenter and the interpreter may go beyond the usual microphone check and become an ad-libbed sketch, as in the following example in which the presenter is about to interview an American pop music band, assisted by the simultaneous interpreter (*Domenica in, Rai 1,* 17.11.1996):

C   Io leggo qui addirittura otto milioni di dischi d'oro venduti nel mondo più (*the compere's assistant approaches C*) ah sì grazie ma tanto ci capiamo lo stesso sapete che io parlo tutte le lingue (*touching her earphone*) non sento il traduttore

I   eccomi Mara

C   eccoti qua (.) come stai?

I   bene grazie e tu?

C   è un piacere sentirti ogni volta

I   il piacere è mio

C   ma figurati non c'è di che vogliamo (*laughs*) parlare con loro?

I   pronti

C   disco d'oro disco d'oro negli Stati Uniti (.) otto milioni di dischi venduti nel mondo

English Gloss

C   I'm reading here eight million gold records sold throughout the world and also (*the compere's assistant approaches C and fits her out with the earphone for the translation*) ah yes thank you but anyway we understand each other you

	know I can speak any language (*touching her earphone*) I can't hear the translator
I	here I am Mara
C	oh there you are (.) how are you?
I	fine thanks and you?
C	it's always a pleasure to hear you
I	the pleasure is mine
C	oh come on don't mention it (.) shall we (*laughs*) talk to them?
I	I'm ready
C	gold record gold record in the Unites States (.) eight million records sold throughout the world

Small talk sequences of this type are consistent with the playful macro-function performed by television. The rules of this form of interaction (including current affairs or journalism talk shows involving politicians and experts) seem to require "serious political talk not to be sustained for more than a few seconds without being 'lightened' by humour" (Fairclough 1995: 172). Moreover, given that entertaining can be seen as "the supraideology of all discourse on television" (Postman 1985:8), the talk show may be said to share many of the features of "talk-as-play", where "the main goal ... is the construction and maintenance of good social relations, not the exchange of information" and "[t]he second goal ... is that participants should enjoy themselves. The fun of talk arises as much from *how* things are said as from *what* is said" (Coates 1995:85).

No wonder then that broadcasting organizations expect interpreters not just to have the relevant linguistic skills but also to be good 'performers'. The presence of the interpreter is a contextual resource utilized for introducing new topics and providing vignettes, with ad-libbed sketches often playing on elements of farce, all of which exploits the fact that the event is 'live'. This means that the interpreter must be aware that the 'text' he or she delivers can become a form of pre-text for the presenter (and other participants) to develop and manipulate – in short, 'mediatize'. Even such a private form of interpreting as chuchotage can be transformed into a public visual event. Close camera shots of the interpreter in chuchotage mode are sometimes used to stage a sort of 'chuchotage show'. At the level of register, an interpreter who expresses something in an unmarked language may find it being reformulated by the presenter in a more colloquial and television-friendly way. The interpreter's text may also go beyond the limits of the event itself and become part of the media discourse in general. Not only are interpreters' performances commented on, (mis)quoted, praised and criticized in the press, but their blunders, facial expressions or gestures, individual utterances, un-witting comic or bizarre situations in which they may find themselves, are also re-contextualized into comic TV collages through skilful editing. There are even now comedians who mimic interpreters in satirical programmes. More recently, these events have become more personal, with one comedian in Italy impersonating a popular TV interpreter.

2. The case study

In 1986, when the Berlin wall had not yet collapsed, a Bulgarian family sought political asylum in Italy. Thanks to the Italian Radical Party and the Italian Embassy in Sofia, the refugees were allowed to come to Italy. The woman, with her two small daughters, were invited to participate in *Buona Domenica* ('Have a Good Sunday'), a typical afternoon infotainment programme broadcasted by Mediaset, the largest Italian private television company. In order to help the refugees settle down in Italy, a fund-raising campaign was mounted and some corporations were asked to contribute and participate in the show with the Bulgarian woman, ostensibly to publicize her predicament but in reality, as we shall see, this was a mediatized performance, a platform to publicize the companies' products.

Five fragments of this episode will be examined, where Maurizio Costanzo (MC), the most popular of Italian TV-show presenters, meets three commercial representatives. The setting in this programme is such that there are always two parallel speech activities, which are also spatially marked: the main action takes place at the centre of the studio (stage), where the presenter welcomes the commercial representatives; the other, on which the camera occasionally focuses, takes place at the sofa (backstage), where the interpreter and the Bulgarian woman are seated.

2.1 Footing and interactional identity

The term **footing** refers to "the alignments that people take up to each other in face-to-face interaction" (Goffman 1981:67), "the alignment we take up to ourselves and others present as expressed in the way we manage the production and reception of an utterance" (ibid:128); different footings "provide contrast to what the text itself might otherwise generate" (ibid:174). As noted above, the presenter acts as a narrator and as the person responsible for the narrative construction of the interactional identity of those who appear on the screen, including the interpreter. This task may be accomplished in a variety of ways. For example, through identification and (self)-presentation rituals, as well as modes of address and the use of pronouns, which have important interactional values in terms of footing. Let us start with the first extract in which the host is talking to the sales manager of Cirio, a famous Italian food company. *MC* stands for Maurizio Costanzo (the host), *I* for the interpreter and *FR* for the food company representative.

Extract 1

13	MC	E quale è stato il prodotto leader in questi mesi in questo anno?
14	FR	Beh diciamo che il nostro prodotto di punta al di là dei pelati che sono
15		un prodotto tradizionale senz'altro la passata verace Cirio che è il

16		nostro cavallo di battaglia grazie anche alla fiducia di tanti consumatori
17		[in Italia]
18 →	MC	[Aspetti] che mi voglio divertire (.) senta Straniero scusi traduca in russo
19		perchè lei sta parlando in rus [so con la signora]
20	I	[sì in russo perchè lo parla benissimo]
21	MC	ecco passata verace (.) verace voglio vedere in russo come glielo dice
		verace no
22		per curiosità
23	I	(*whispering in Russian*) special'nost [ ] etoj firmy [ ] ehm eto nastojasee
24	MC	[eh] [sì] sì non mi
25		prenda in giro come glielo dice verace no [perchè eh
26	I	(*glances towards MC*) [non mi dà il tempo di tradurlo
27		(*continues in Russian*) eto nastojasee smesivanie [ ] pomidorov
28	MC	[sì]
29		Però è bravo eh?

English Gloss

13	MC	So what's been your top-selling product these last months this year?
14	FR	Well I suppose that our best-seller apart from peeled tomatoes which are
15		a traditional product by now is no doubt the Cirio "verace" tomato purée
16		which is our core product thanks to the loyalty of our many consumers
17		[in Italy]
18 →	MC	[Hang on a moment] I'd like to have a bit of fun here (.) Francesco[2]
		translate
19		this into Russian as you are speaking in Rus [sian with the lady]
20	I	[yes in Russian as she speaks it
		perfectly]
21	MC	ok then "verace" purée (.) I'd like see how you say "verace" in Russian
		(.) no I mean
22		sheer curiosity
23	I	(*whispering in Russian*) the speciality [ ] of this company [ ] ehm is a
		true
24	MC	[huh] [ok] ok but
		don't
25		mess about how you say "verace" in Russian no because you know
26	I	[*glances towards MC*] you're not giving me the
		time to translate
27		[*continues in Russian*] it is a true [ ] tomato sauce
28	MC	[yes]
29		Not bad though eh?

In line 18, MC signals that he is 'interrupting' and indirectly apologizes for the interruption. The act of interrupting is prefaced by "Hang on a moment". The utterance "I'd like to have a bit of fun here" creates the frame for the request "translate"; as a pre-formulating segment, it is a comment on the host's face-threatening act of making a request and signals both for the audience and the interpreter the recognition of the possibility of a negative evaluation of this interactional move and that, in this case, no hostility is intended. Moreover, by drawing the audience's attention to the presence of the interpreter, MC ratifies his participation. The effect is that instead of being carried out unnoticed (and in parallel with the main action), the interpreter's work is highlighted. The prompt to translate in 18 can only be understood in terms of the sequencing of speech activities, because the interpreter is already translating (in chouchotage). So MC is simply creating a new frame, and the injunction to translate is not to be taken literally. The imperative mode could be interpreted as an overt expression of authority, but the accompanying metamessage signals that the utterance is to be interpreted in a "play frame" (Bateson 1972, Goffman 1974), where the move "I'd like to have a bit of fun here" actually means "I want the audience to have a bit of fun". MC temporarily discontinues the exchange with the food company representative (lines 13-17) to directly address the interpreter. In uttering "Hang on a moment" (line 18), he turns his body and gaze towards the sofa, where the interpreter is seated. This action is also captured by the movement of the camera. Line 18 then represents a boundary of an interactional unit (Philips 1986) or a discourse juncture (Goffman 1974).

The distinctive participation mode (or talk format) created by line 18 is also conveyed by prosodic traits. The utterances from line 18 to line 25 are pronounced with a mischievous, ironical, Roman dialect. The structure of role relationships is embedded not only in the language but also in the spatial organization of interaction. Spatial positioning and alignments are influenced by and reflect communicative roles enacted in public institutional scenes. The person controlling and regulating the activity faces those whose participation is being regulated (Philips 1986:229). Coded spatial arrangement, together with the personality and status of the presenter, are important pragmatic elements in the televised text.

So, when MC talks to the interpreter he initiates an exchange, and this is marked by a shift in his position. When the interpreter assumes the speaker's role, he turns towards the centre of the studio. Positional changes are used as "framing devices" (Goffman 1974) to convey to participants that a juncture is occurring in the ongoing interaction. They are "motivated by changes in the role relationship among those present in the same speech situation" (Philips 1986:232). At 18 MC inserts himself in the exchange between the interpreter and the Bulgarian woman, who are having a sort of parallel and private conversation. MC, whose role is to regulate the communication flow and monitor the interaction, asks the interpreter to "stage" his translation for the benefit of the overhearing audience.

Once again, the utterance "as you are speaking in Russian" (line 19) is a metamessage which means something like "you are participating in the show, aren't you?"; it is a remark that conveys "in-frame activity" (Schiffrin 1993:250) or rather the plan of reporting interaction. The information it conveys is already known to the interlocutors, its inclusion can only be understood as audience-directed. The whole sequence "as you are speaking in Russian with the lady/yes, in Russian as she speaks it perfectly" (lines 19-20) is more phatic than topical, in the sense that the exchange is not focused on discussing a particular topic but serves to maintain the footing both among participants and, above all, with the overhearing audience. Through continuous prompting and challenging activities MC projects his role as a bystander who watches the scene with the audience. On the other hand, these conversational moves, including backchannelling moves of the type in line 24, are also aimed at preventing extended silences (dead air); even the normal few seconds of silence that occur in ordinary conversation are intolerable on TV.

MC grants and at the same time denies the interpreter the authority to translate: "translate ... I'd like to see how you say ... don't mess about ... how you say in Russian?". The interpreter responds by appealing to the extralinguistic context: "you are not giving me the time to translate" (line 26). He refers to the rules of the game, to the procedures regulating interpretation, focusing attention on an expectation which his interlocutor has failed to comply with, i.e. he should be given the time to satisfy MC's request, which he seems to perceive as a face-threatening act. The notion of **face** has to do with our sense of identity, the image of our self we wish to project during interaction. According to Goffman's definition (1963:5), face is "the positive social value a person effectively claims for himself by the line others assume he has taken during a particular contact". Brown and Levinson (1987) distinguish between a **positive face** (in Goffman's sense) and a **negative face**, which has to do with our need to be independent, to have freedom of action, and not to be imposed upon by others. The interpreter's negative face is therefore threatened when he is challenged in his work. MC does draw the interpreter into the interaction, but he does so by encroaching upon his territory and forcing him to defend himself. Indeed, the interpreter's "you're not giving me the time to translate" (line 26) is accompanied by a strained smile, suggesting unease and nervousness, and may be seen as a 'counter-face-threatening act'.

The 'teasing framework' described above could also be seen as a means by which MC intends to build a complicity alignment with the interpreter (and the audience). The face-saving act accomplished in line 29 ("not bad though, eh?") serves this purpose. By praising the interpreter's work in his presence and addressing his comments to the audience, MC is apparently excluding the interpreter from the conversation (the interpreter is treated as an unaddressed recipient). In fact, third-person reference is used by the speaker to sustain the footing with the audience. On the other hand, through the presenter's affiliative assessment, the interpreter becomes the object of discourse and thus even more involved in the ongoing interaction.

Provoking and teasing are part of the narrative structure of the talk show, with the interpreter being both the subject and the object of narration. In this sense, we can apply Propp's narrative theory (1975) and Greimas's narrative semiotics (1985) and look upon the interpreter as playing the narrative role of the hero, who is requested to accomplish an action the outcome of which is approved or disapproved by an acknowledged authority (the presenter). Thus the process may be described according to the three phases which characterize narration: reference is made to the subject's Competence (Manipulation), and that Competence is acted out, put to the test (Performance) before being accepted (Sanction). All three phases are reflected in the position attributed to the viewers, whose participation format in the interaction consists of enjoying the interpreter's performance.

At another point in the show, soon after the manager of a bottled mineral water company has offered the Bulgarian family a free crash course in Italian, MC adopts the same teasing practice, again using the third person with reference to the interpreter, who responds non-verbally this time. In the following two extracts, *B* stands for the Bulgarian woman and *MW* for the managing director of the mineral water company.

Extract 2

1	MC	Aspetti un attimo (*turning to the sofa*) ecco Straniero gli ...
2	I	(*is already translating into Russian*)
3	MC	loro s'impegneranno a frequentare la scuola seriamente?
4	I	(*whispers in Russian*)
5	MC	eh?
6	B	oh
7	MC	sì eh?
8	B	sì (*in Italian*)
9	MC	perchè poi fra tre mesi dovete venire a parlare italiano qui
10	I	(*translates into Russian*)
11	B	(*laughs*)
12 →	MC	contento l'interprete ma insomma eh
13	I	(*shrugs*)
14	MC	no no no ma per dire non si preoccupi

English Gloss

1	MC	Hang on a moment (*turning to the sofa*) ah Francesco transla ...
2	I	(*is already whispering his translation in inaudible Russian*)
3	MC	they will make sure that they'll really attend the school won't they?
4	I	(*whispers his translation in inaudible Russian*)
5	MC	eh?
6	B	oh
7	MC	will they?
8	B	Yes (*in Italian*)
9	MC	because in three months you'll have to come back here and speak Italian
10	I	(*whispers his translation in inaudible Russian*)
11	B	(*laughs*)
12 →	MC	the interpreter won't be so happy but anyway
13	I	(*shrugs*)
14	MC	no no no don't worry just joking

Both the compliment in line 29 in extract 1 ("Not bad though eh?") and the joke in line 12 above ("the interpreter won't be so happy but anyway") are part of a positive politeness strategy, the aim of which is "to soothe the other party's needs for association [...] to minimize social distance, as the speaker wants to come closer to the listener by showing solidarity and in-group relationship" (Villemoes 1995:302). The "no no no don't worry just joking" in line 14 responds to MC's own provocative remark in line 12 ("the interpreter won't be so happy but anyway") and testifies to the strength of the emerging relationship between the two interlocutors.

Third-person reference, together with the teasing activity in line 14 ratify the interpreter's interactional identity. These conversational moves signal involvement, familiarity and complicity. Furthermore, considering the asymmetrical relationship between the two speakers (MC besides being the host is the interpreter's employer), in uttering "don't worry" (line 14), the presenter is actually projecting his institutional identity to reassure the interpreter about future assignments. Like "I'd like to have a bit of fun" (line 18 in extract 1), "just joking" (line 14 above) frames the intent to provide the public with an opportunity to enjoy themselves. Lines 12-14 above highlight the intersubjective nature of interaction and how the construction of a single turn is the product of cooperation among participants. The current interactional identity of participants is being signalled not only through language but often through gaze, gesture and posture. Linguistic behaviour is not the only way to accomplish an interactional move; as Goffman (1971:151) explains, "it is not communication in the narrow sense of the term that is at the heart of what is occurring. *Stands* are being taken, *moves* are being made, *displays* are being provided, *alignments* are being established".

Frequent metadiscursive references to the interpreting setting are typical of this type of interaction. In this episode, MC always keeps the two discourse levels separate, marking the shift from stage to backstage both with prosody and body movements and with paralinguistic means, as in lines 11-12 of extract 3 below.

Extract 3

1	MC	Il centro studi Sangemini offre 10 milioni e un soggiorno da stabilire la durata del
2		medesimo in un albergo di (*looks questioningly at MW*) Sangemini
3	MW	Sangemini alle terme di Sangemini
4	MC	ecco alle terme di Sangemini quindi possono fare anche un periodo di riposo la
5		famiglia Filipov dopo ehm gli stress di questa attesa gli stress [di della]
6	MW	[gli suggerisco in modo=]
7	MC	[prego]
8	MW	=particolare verso l'autunno verso settembre
9	MC	ecco verso sett [embre]
10	MW	[che è] il periodo più bello in quella zona

11 →	MC	Va bene (*turning towards the sofa and lowering the tone of his voice*) verso settembre
12		Straniero dice che è meglio stare là (*turning again to MW*) ehm parliamo di
13		questo centro studi della Sangemini di cosa di occupa?

English Gloss

1	MC	The Sangemini centre is offering 10 million lire and holiday dates to be finalized
2		at a Sangemini hotel (*questiongly looking at MW*) Sangemini
3	MW	Sangemini at the Sangemini health resort
4	MC	Ok at the Sangemini health resort so the Filipov family can also have some time to
5		relax after ehm the stress of waiting the stress [of of the]
6	MW	[I'd strongly recommend=]
7	MC	[yes?]
8	MW	=around autumn around September
9	MC	there we are around Sep [tember]
10	MW	[which] is the best period in that area
11 →	MC	Ok (*turning towards the sofa and lowering the tone of his voice*) around September
12		Francesco (.) he says it's the best to stay there (*turning again to MW*) so ehm let's
13		talk about this Sangemini centre (.) what's it all about?

As in line 18 in extract 1 ("Francesco, translate this into Russian ..."), lines 11-12 above are semantically redundant but interactionally important. They are whispered in a confidential manner, as if the speaker were saying "we will have to remember this". The relation in which the interpreter is cast by this mode of address is not that of the man in the middle, the neutral link, who doesn't side with either party, but that of an assistant, someone who collaborates with the presenter. In fact, when introducing the guests at the beginning of the show MC referred to the interpreter as "our interpreter", followed by first name and surname. In this case the interpreter apparently belongs to the talk show cast.

2.2 Repair and story-telling

Repair and meta-discourse are important interactional resources for maintaining, restoring and monitoring mutual understanding among participants. Unlike "substantive acts [which] provide the substance or essence of conversation" (Hellspong 1988:47), they are "regulatory acts" (ibid) which perform a coordinating function in dialogue (see also Wadensjö 1993).

It is important to note that unlike the conference hall, the courtroom or the police station, the talk show is basically a showplace which features a very special form of monitoring. Translation is not the exclusive right of the interpreter, but is a (meta)discoursal activity, an interactional space open to all participants, who can at any time shift roles and temporarily act as competing mediators; they may bypass, question or even ridicule the interpreter in order to entertain the audience or themselves. Moreover, translational strategies such as omissions, additions, semantic and communicative equivalence, etc. are not pre-established categories but are locally and interactionally managed moment-by-moment during the exchange. Before the beginning of the show, the interpreter may be instructed to make the guest's words 'more interesting'. Guests are often nervous on television and it is up to the interpreter (besides providing psychological support) to 'clean up' or 'polish' their utterances by leaving out hedges, self-corrections, hesitations and false starts, or to 'embellish' or complete what the guest cannot say or articulate. As our corpus appears to indicate, interpreters tend to add textual material and, at times, even improve upon the original style in terms of lexical choices and register. This is clearly different from interpreting in other settings, such as the police station or the courtroom, where the interpreter is expected to translate verbatim.

A further point concerns the interpreter's choice to retain or explain an ambiguity in the source utterance. It would be very difficult, if not impossible, for talk show interpreters to follow the recommended protocol for court interpreters, namely that in the case of ambiguity "the interpreter should state "Your Honor, the question/answer is ambiguous and the interpreter cannot proceed without clarification" (Gonzáles *et al.* 1991:485), "ask the court permission to inquire with the witness", or "call the matter to the court's attention by requesting a side-bar conference" (ibid:487). For, as already noted, metalinguistic activity means first and foremost phatic communion and sociability. In a talk show setting, where there is no "side-bar conference" to retreat to, the 'right' interpretation of an ambiguous term would be negotiated by participants themselves, who may even play with the very ambiguity of the word. We must also remember that controversy and disagreement are often fictionalized on television, and participants argue for the sake of arguing, being well aware that they are actors playing 'on the stage'.

Here is an example from extract 3 (which starts with line 29 at the bottom of extract 1), where the presenter and the interpreter engage in a defining activity.

Extract 3

29	MC	Però è bravo eh?
30	I	*(turning towards MC and speaking aloud)* [ha capito benissimo]
31	MC	[che le ha detto scusi?]
32 →	I	Le ho detto che è una vera autentica perchè verace vuol dire poi vera
33		autentica [ ] passata di pomodori che è quello che poi [è il suo]
34	MC	[eh] [ecco]
35	I	non era poi tant [o]

36	MC		[sì] è che a Napoli insomma verace vuol dire [proprio=]
37	I		[verace vero]
38	MC	=sincero	
39	I	sincero	
40	MC	ecco since:ro	

English Gloss

29	MC	Not bad though eh?
30	I	(*turning to MC and speaking aloud*) [indeed she understood perfectly]
31	MC	[Sorry what did you tell her?]
32 →I		I told her that it is ehm real authentic because verace actually means really
33		authentic [ ] tomato purée which is actually [it's]
34	MC	[huh] [there we are]
35	I	=actually it wasn't [so]
36	M	[yes] but in Naples "verace" means [exactly=]
37	I	["verace" true]
38	MC	=sincere
39	I	sincere
40	MC	there we are since:re

The meaning of *passata verace* becomes the topic of the exchange and the object of negotiation. Because of its strong connotations, 'the taste and feel of 100% genuine Neapolitan tomato pureé', *passata verace* may be considered a culture-bound term. The expression conjures up the image of Mediterranean sunshine and typical (Southern) Italian cuisine. After a first explanation given by the interpreter, aimed at responding to the request made by MC and managing his face wants, the host insists on the difficulty of translating *verace* by locating a problem in the interpreter's previous talk. Put in conversationalist terms, the hearer redefines something the speaker has already said as 'incomplete', i.e. he treats his action as 'repairable'; a request for clarification of meaning is always a bid for repair (White 1997).

MC attempts to 'other-initiate' a repair ("yes but in Naples ...") but then, since he cannot find the right word to define *verace*, he '**self-initiates**' a repair which is '**other-completed**' by the interpreter ("verace, true"), with overlap between the two (lines 35-39).[3] The two speakers compete for the right definition, but they both accept each other's suggestions. Interruptions are supportive, being perceived as reinforcing communication. The fragment under analysis is characterized by a double **repair format** (Schiffrin 1987) which shows a division of responsibility for the information management task.[4]

In line 40, MC and the interpreter apparently reach an agreement on the meaning of *verace* as synonymous with *sincere* on the basis of their shared knowledge and as a result of a joint negotiation process. However, the interpreter subsequently self-selects for the next turn (line 41 in extract 4 below) with a marker ('but') which prefaces a new interactional move.

Extract 4

40	MC	ecco sinc [ero]
41 →	I	[bè] ma in russo c'è un aggettivo stupendo perchè il russo è una lingua ricchis
42		[ ] sima e quindi c'è un aggettivo che esattamente indica autentico vero reale=
43	MC	[sì]
44	I	=anche di qualità per cui proprio:
45	MC	in russo?
46	I	verace
47	MC	[questo aggettivo?]
48	I	[nastojasij] [nastojasij]
49	MC	[com'è?]
50	I	NASTOJASIJ
51	MC	nastojasij (*everyone laughs*) vabé quando volete aprire il il mercato (*laughs*)
52	FR	(xxx)
53	MC	ecco il mercato in Russia allora dice:
54	FR	nastojasij
55	MC	nastojasij poi Gorbaciov mi sembra ha dato un nuovo corso [quindi al contrario]
56	FR	[appunto quindi]
57	MC	[questa=]
58	FR	[non è detto che] si possa sfruttare
59	MC	=passata nastojasij servire calda (*everyone laughs*)

English Gloss

40	MC	there we are sinc [ere]
41 →	I	[but] in Russian there's a really great adjective because Russian is a
42		language really rich [ ] and so there's an adjective which exactly means authentic=
43	MC	[yes]
44	I	=also quality so it fits exactly:
45	MC	in Russian?
46	I	"verace"
47	MC	[this adjective?]
48	I	[nastojasij] [nastojasij]
49	MC	[sorry?]
50	I	NASTOJASIJ
51	MC	nastojasij (*everybody laughs*) Ok whenever you want to open the market (*laughs*)
52	FR	(xxx)
53	M	I mean the market in Russia you say:
54	FR	nastojasij
55	MC	nastojasij also I believe that Gorbachev has opened up a new direction [so I guess]
56	FR	[exactly so=]
57	MC	[this=]
58	FR	[=we may] take advantage of it
59	MC	=nastojasij purée serve hot (*everyone laughs*)

The interpreter initiates an action of controlling the topic of discourse with a metalinguistic explanation which means 'I am the linguistic expert'. He thus foregrounds his 'interlinguistic' authority with respect to the host's institutional authority. The move can be understood as a form of "authority display" (Schiffrin 1987). By choosing a favourable topic, the interpreter secures the possibility of presenting his arguments, placing MC in the position of assuming that the interpreter is speaking knowledgeably, and that MC does not have the competence to challenge what is said.

The word *nastojasij* ('authentic') uttered by the interpreter twice in line 48 above and repeated in line 50 is repeated in the successive moves both by MC (51, 55, 59) and by the food company representative (54). Unlike other settings, where repetition may be aimed at preventing potential or actual misunderstandings, repetition here serves to ratify the interpreter's contribution, i.e. his participation (Tannen 1989:59-74). Besides performing a topic-setting function at the beginning of each speaker's turn, the repetition of the Russian adjective also establishes a sense of affiliation between the three speakers by their echoing of each other's use of the word. This type of alignment work between speaker and hearer is a form of "cooperative topic building" (Schriffrin 1987:240). Moreover, code-switching here is a conversational strategy. The word *nastojasij* takes on an exotic meaning, in tune with the entertainment goal of the ongoing interaction. In line 51, MC incorporates the foreign word into his own discourse "in order to savour it" (Tannen 1989:64); in line 55, he goes back to the firm representative and shifts the topic to Gorbachev and marketing strategies. Finally, in 59, he appropriates the word to crack a joke, make the audience laugh and close the exchange in order to call the next guest.

The sequence in lines 41-50 is structured as typical storytelling. The story is preceded by specific moves by both the teller (the interpreter) and the recipient (the presenter). The interpreter provides a preface, offering to tell the story, while the presenter makes a request to hear the offered story. The utterance in line 41 anticipates a new developing content. Like all pre-formulations, it has a topic-fixing property (Heritage and Watson 1980:255). Once again, the collaborative nature of the interaction emerges, where conversational tasks are managed through a process of hearer participation, expressed not only through body-stance, head-nodding or eye-contact but also through backchannelling signals such as 'huh', 'yes' and 'that's ok'.

2.3 Turn-taking and agenda policing

Unlike other institutional settings characterized by a rigid question/answer format, the talk show has a relatively more flexible structure in terms of topic and turn-taking organization. It is similar in some respects to natural, spontaneous conversation, even though, being a form of institutionalized chat, speaking turns must be adjusted to the specific requirements of television. Depending on the presenter, and the type and rhythm of the programme, the interpreter may be requested to translate utterance by utterance or perform a form of simultaneous translation without headphones. In some cases, if the interpreter delays the delivery to listen to longer portions of the source utterance the presenter may explicitly ask him or her to start translating. In other cases the interpreter may be asked to postpone, speed up or summarize because of commercial breaks and other time restraints.

Roy (1996) analysed the different strategies adopted by the interpreter in deciding who should have priority in case of overlapping and showed that this turn-mediation function is a result of sociolinguistic choices made by the interpreter on the basis of his or her understanding of the ongoing social situation. She explains that "both speakers and the interpreter create unique kinds of pauses, lags, overlaps and turns. Turns taken by the interpreter [are] shown to be a mixture of the interpreter's decisions as well as the primary speakers' tacit agreement to accept those decisions" (ibid:63). The last fragment (extract 5) will illustrate further aspects of turn-taking and topic management.

Extract 5

1	MC	dottor Vivaldi noi ci rivediamo a fine trasmissione ancora per un saluto
2		però la settimana prossima [ancora]
3	MW	[va bene] spero di essere presente io stesso grazie
4	MC	ma faccia il possibile
5	MW	[senz'altro]
6	MC	[faccia il possibile] per esserci ricordo che (*turns to the sofa*)
7 →	I	voleva dire una cosa sull'acqua minerale
8	MC	che ci ha qualcosa da ridire?
9	I	anzi voleva dire [ ] mi stava raccontando una cosa
10	MC	[no ecco]
11	B	kogda my delali pervuju zabastovku my posovetovalis' c doktorom kakuju
12		vo [du nado pit' on skazal Sandzemini]
13	I	[allora quando hanno fatto lo sciopero della fame] il dottore gli ha consigliato
14		di bere l'acqua Sangemini l'acqua Sangemini
15	MC	ecco io mi augur [o]
16	MW	[diciamo] che quella è una cura dimagrante un po' drastica
17		però anche per le cure dimagranti va bene
18	MC	io voglio sperare che nessun nostro simile (*turning towards sofa*)
19	B	(xxx)
20	I	(*translating*) perchè le qualità dell'acqua sono buone per questo allora
21	B	[dlija detej]
22	I	[per i bambini va benissimo]
23	MC	[ecco io voglio dire] apprezzando la Sangemini e la Ferrarelle voglio
24		veramente che nessun nostro simile debba bere Sangemini o Ferrarelle

		perchè sta
25		facend [o lo sciopero della] fame
26	MW	[apposta apposta]
27	MC	questo lo dico proprio (*turning towards sofa*)
28	I	l'ha conosciuta in quell'occasione
29	MC	l'ha conosciuta in quell'occasione adesso invece la conosce in un'occasione
30		assolutamente lieta
31	MW	un tantino più lieta
32	MC	eh ah ma molto più lieta

English Gloss

1	MC	Mr. Vivaldi we'll meet again at the end of the programme to say goodbye
2		but next week [again]
3	MW	[fine] I hope to be here myself
4	MC	do your level best
5	MW	[no doubt about it]
6	MC	[you'll do your level best] to be here I just want to remind you that (*turns to the sofa*)
7 →	I	she wanted to say something about mineral water
8	MC	she's got something to complain about?
9	I	no on the contrary she wanted to say [ ] she was telling me something
10	MC	[that's ok]
11	B	when we started our first hunger strike we asked the doctor which
12		water [to drink and he said Sangemini]
13	I	[well when they were on hunger strike] the doctor advised them
14		to drink Sangemini mineral water Sangemini mineral water
15	MC	well I sincerly ho [pe]
16	MW	[let's] say that that's a slightly drastic diet
17		but it's also good for diets
18	MC	I don't want any of us (*turning towards the sofa*)
19	B	(xxx)
20	I	(*translating*) because the properties of the water are good for this so
21	B	[for children]
22	I	[for children it's perfect]
23	MC	[now let me make it clear that] I know we like Sangemini and Ferrarelle but I don't
24		want anybody to drink Sangemini or Ferrarelle just because
25		they're on [hunger strike]
26	MW	[absolutely] just what I said (xxx)
27	MC	Actually I say this because (*turning towards the sofa*)
28	I	she tried it at that particular time
29	MC	she tried it at that particular time but now she can drink it at really
30		happy moment in time
31	MW	just a teeny bit happier I'd say
32	MC	come on now much happier by far

In line 7 the interpreter considerably expands his turn-allocating role, going as far as interrupting the presenter at a crucial discourse juncture. MC is taking his leave of the mineral water representative. By interjecting, the interpreter challenges two important institutional prerogatives of the presenter: the power to sanction the closing of the exchange and to allocate turns. The act of interrupting is set within spatial factors peculiar to this type of video communication. MC has indeed no direct visual access to the interpreter and the Bulgarian woman, seated on the sofa. Thus the interpreter decides to draw the host's attention by aurally signalling that the guest wishes to intervene ("she wanted to say something about mineral water").

Line 8 contains two moves: the first is a response to the interpreter's summons, the second formulates a request aimed at eliciting a justification for the interruption. Lines 21, 22 and 23 are characterized by overlapping talk: the woman speaks in Russian, the interpreter begins to translate and MC interjects with 'now', signalling his intention to claim the turn. Although the interpreter's and MC's interruptions are both competitive in nature, the aim of the first is to let the woman speak, turn opportunities for the woman being very limited. Thus the interpreter takes a turn to allocate a turn, but MC steps in to re-assert his role as the controller of verbal initiatives, all of which suggests that interruption is indeed "a construct, a category which participants can make use of to deal with currently prevailing rights and obligations in actual situations" (Bennett 1981:176).

The Bulgarian woman's story about her drinking 'Sangemini' water during her hunger strike is perhaps not the best advertisement for the company. It is clued by MC as a threat to the positive face of the company and, more generally to the frame in which the show is embedded. The act through which the host expresses his authority is marked by explicit performatives ("I don't want", "I do hope", "I know", "let me make it clear"), that allow him to regain control of the exchange and decide what topics are appropriate to the agenda.

Note how in lines 16-17 ("let's say that that's a slightly drastic diet but it's also good for diets") the mineral water representative topicalizes the hunger strike in terms of slimming diet, thereby accomplishing a face-saving act, aimed at toning down the conflictual import of the woman's utterance. Thus the episode is emptied of all political meaning. Ironically, it was the hunger strike which brought the Bulgarian family to television, making it a human rights issue. The confrontational nature of the exchange is further evidenced in lines 28-29 above, where the interpreter sides with the woman, attesting the truthfulness of her story (and his translation). MC, on the other hand, echoed by the commercial representative (line 31), foregrounds the new 'happier' television experience the woman is having at *that* moment. In particular, the repetition in line 29 takes on a special interactional meaning; as Orletti (1994:177) explains, repetition followed by negation tends to signal conflict or disagreement.

3. Conclusion

Activities such as facework, topic management, repairing, interrupting, disagreeing, glossing and backchannelling reflect the jointly negotiated identities of interlocutors and play a crucial role in shaping the emerging talk-show. As the interaction unfolds, the host and the interpreter work out their social relationships in relation to the audience and to their conversational goals.

The interpreter's role is dependent on that of the presenter. His conversational behaviour throughout the interaction is determined by the alignment work accomplished by the host. As a speaker, the interpreter alternates between the role of animator (speaking for the Bulgarian woman) and that of author, shifting between self and other. The act of speaking for himself takes on different interactional meanings, as a result of the participation framework created by the presenter, who makes speaking power available to guests. In regulating (and policing) access to speaking time (and speaking modes), the presenter too is an animator who constructs participants' identities, thereby contributing to shaping a positive or negative image of a participant in the minds of viewers. In animating his guests' words, MC performs his interactional task (and institutionalized footing).

As the present study has demonstrated, the presenter of a talk show is actively involved in interaction, playing, to use Heritage's terminology (1985), not only the role of 'report elicitor' but also that of 'report recipient', as indicated by his backchannel behaviour. The interpreter, on the other hand, is not simply the animator of the spoken-for person and, contrary to widely held assumptions about 'neutrality' and 'invisibility', does not refrain from making unsolicited comments. The context of the talk show requires the interpreter to abandon any attempts at maintaining a low-profile, behind-the-scene footing and assume a different participation status in the management of the interaction.

The 'being-ignored-can-be-bliss' principle (apparently the title of a book by Fink, reported in Frishberg 1986) no longer works, if it ever did. What is needed is a new awareness of the interpreter's social competence, i.e. how his or her communicative competence is enacted in the form of appropriate conversational behaviour. For this to happen, a shift from cognitive to sociolinguistic research is necessary. It is only through the empirical observation of regularities of situations and behaviour that it is possible to create corpora which, in turn, enable the determination of norms (in Gideon Toury's sense), a major lacuna in the field of interpreting. The study of authentic interpreted discourse helps lay bare not only some of the normative taken-for-granted principles of interpreters' behaviour but also the 'hidden' assumptions about the nature of the interaction in which interpreters are involved. To this end, ethnographic vs. experimentally produced data have the advantage of avoiding the inevitably controlled laboratory conditions in which research is limited to those variables preselected by the researcher.

One of the objectives of this research project is to elaborate, on the basis of description rather than prescription, 'interpreter profiles' in terms of such parameters as communicative style, interactional capacities, teamwork organization, translation strategies, reaction time, turn-taking, meaning negotiation and cooperation, conflict management, use of register and vocabulary, and so on. In the case of television interpreting, recording interpreters' performances does not influence their behaviour, since recording is an instrinsic feature of this electronic and public means of communication. The findings of the research project should therefore prove useful and reliable in terms of designing teaching modules and materials, allowing students and their teachers to analyse and evaluate authentic texts produced in authentic contexts and demonstrating genuine interpreter performance in action.

FRANCESCO STRANIERO SERGIO
Scuola Superiore di Lingue Moderne per Interpreti e Traduttori, Università degli Studi di Trieste, via Filzi, 14, 34132 Trieste, Italy. stranier@sslmit. univ.trieste.it

Notes

1. The definition of 'overhearing audience' applies both to viewers and to the studio audience who, like the jurors in a trial, are physically but not interactionally present. In most talk shows, the audience is made up of walk-ons. Interactivity is often a form of disguised manipulation. An extreme example of how television organizes the participation of viewers is pre-recorded laughter in sit-coms or cartoons.
2. In Italian, the use of a surname ('Straniero' in line 18 of the original) can be informal and friendly, as in this case, whereas the effect in English would be quite different. I have therefore opted to replace it with the first name 'Francesco' in the English gloss.
3. On the structural organization of repair techniques see Jefferson (1974), Schegloff *et al.* (1977), Goffman (1981), Schegloff (1981) and White (1997).
4. Self-repair is a very common practice in interpreting *tout court*. In our corpus, numerous cases have been found in which the repair is initiated by the presenter, a participant, or even the foreign guest when the latter knows some Italian and realizes that the interpreter has omitted or mistranslated something. The repair is always self-completed by the interpreter in his or her next turn.

References

Bateson, G. (1972) *Steps to an Ecology of Mind*, New York: Ballantine.

Bennett, A. (1981) 'Interruptions and the Interpretation of Conversation', *Discourse Processes* 4: 171-88.

Berger, R. (1992) *Il Nuovo Golem*, Milano: Raffaello Cortina Editore.

Bondi Paganelli, M. (1990) 'Off-Air Recordings: What Interaction? The Case of News and Current Affairs', in R. Rossini Favretti (ed) *The Televised Text*, Bologna, 37-68.

Brown, G. and S. Levinson (1987) *Politeness. Some Universals in Language Use*, Cambridge: Cambridge University Press.

Charaudeau, P. and R. Ghiglione (1997) *La Parole Confisquée*, Paris: Dunod.

Coates, J. (1995) 'The Construction of Collaborative Floor in Women's Friendly Talk', in T. Givon (ed) *Conversation: Cognitive, Communicative and Social Perspectives*, Amsterdam & Philadelphia: John Benjamins, 55-89.

Dahlgren, P. (1995) *Television and the Public Sphere: Citizenship, Democracy and the Media*, London: Sage.

Fairclough, Norman (1995) *Critical Discourse Analysis,* London: Longman.

Frishberg, N. (1986) *Interpreting: An Introduction*, Rockville (Maryland): RID Publications.

Goffman, E. (1963) *Behavior in Public Places*, New York: Harper & Row.

------ (1971) *Relations in Public*, Harmondsworth: Penguin.

------ (1974) *Frame Analysis*, New York: Harper & Row.

------ (1981) *Forms of Talk*, Philadelphia: University of Pennsylvania Press.

Gonzáles, R. D., V. F. Vasquez and H. Mikkelson (1991) *Fundamentals of Court Interpreting. Theory, Policy and Practice*, Durham, NC: Carolina Academic Press:

Greimas, A. (1985) *Del Senso II. Narrativa, Modalità, Passioni*, Milano: Bompiani.

Hall, S., C. Critcher, T. Jefferson, J. Clarke and B. Roberts (1978) *Policing the Crisis*, London, Macmillian.

Hellspong, L. (1988) *Regulation of Dialogue. A Theoretical Model of Conversation with an Empirical Application,* Stockholm: Meddelandedn fran Institutionen for nordiska sprak vid Stockholms universitet, MINS 30.

Heritage, J. (1985) 'Analyzing News Interviews: Aspects of the Production of Talk for an Overhearing Audience', in T.A. Van Dijk (ed) *Handbook of Discourse Analysis* 3, London: Academic Press, 95-117.

------ and D. R. Watson (1980) 'Aspects of the Properties of Formulations in Natural Conversations: Some Instances Analyzed', *Semiotica* 30: 245-62.

Hutchby, I. (1995) 'Aspects of Recipient Design in Expert Advice-Giving on Call-in Radio', *Discourse Processes* 19: 219-38.

------ (1997) 'Building Alignments in Public Debate: A Case Study from British TV', *Text* 17(2): 162-79.

Jefferson, G. (1974) 'Error Correction as an Interactional Resource', *Language in Society* 3(2): 181-200.

Morse, M. (1986) 'The Television News Personality and Credibility: Reflections on the News in Transition', in T. Modleski (ed) *Studies in Entertainment: Critical Approach to Mass Culture*, Bloomington & Indianapolis: Indiana University Press: 55-79.

Orletti, F. (ed) (1994) *Fra conversazione e discorso*, Roma: La Nuova Italia Scientifica.

Philips, S. (1986) 'Some Functions of Spatial Positioning and Alignment in the Organization of Courtroom Discourse', in S. Fischer and A. Dundas Todd (eds) *Discourse and Institutional Authority: Medicine, Education and Law – Advances in Discourse Processes*, Norwood: Ablex, 223-33.

Postman, N. (1985) *Amusing Ourselves to Death*, New York: Penguin Books.

Propp, V. Ja (1975) *Morfologia della fiaba*, Torino: Einaudi.

Roy, Cynthia (1996) 'An Interactional Sociolinguistic Analysis of Turn-Taking in an Interpreted Event', *Interpreting* 1: 39-67.

Sacks, H., E. A. Schegloff and G. Jefferson (1974) 'A Simplest Systematics for the Organization of Turn-taking for Conversation', *Language* 50: 696-735.

Schegloff, E. A. (1980) 'Preliminaries to Preliminaries: 'Can I ask you a question?'', *Sociological Inquiry* 50: 104-152.

------ (1981) 'Discourse as an Interactional Achievement: Some Uses of 'Uh huh' and Other Things that Come between Sentences', in Deborah Tannen (ed) *Analyzing Discourse: Text and Talk*, Washington, D.C: Georgetown University Press, 71-93.

------, G. Jefferson and H. Sacks (1977) 'The Preference for Self-Correction in the Organization of Repair in Conversation', *Language* 53: 361-82.

Schiffrin, D. (1987) *Discourse Markers*, Cambridge, Cambridge University Press.

------ (1993) ''Speaking for Another' in Sociolinguistic Interviews', in D. Tannen (ed) *Framing in Discourse*, Oxford: Oxford University Press, 231- 63.

Tannen, Deborah (1989) *Talking Voices: Repetitions, Dialogue and Imagery in Conversational Discourse*, Cambridge: Cambridge University Press.

Villemoes, A. (1995) 'Culturally Determined Facework Priorities in Danish and Spanish Business Negotiation', in K. Ehlich and J. Wagear (eds) *The Discourse of Business Negotiation*, New York: Mouton de Guyter, 291-312.

Wadensjö, Cecilia (1993) 'The Double Role of a Dialogue Interpreter', *Perspectives: Studies in Translatology* 1: 105-121.

White, R. (1997) 'Back Channelling, Repair, Pausing and Private Speech', *Applied Linguistics* 18(3): 314-43.

The Translator. Volume 5, Number 2 (1999), 327-332   ISBN 1-900650-21-5

Revisiting the Classics

Replies and Response Cries
Interaction and Dialogue Interpreting

MELANIE METZGER
Department of ASL, Linguistics and Interpretation
Gallaudet University, USA

Forms of Talk. Erving Goffman. Oxford: Basil Blackwell and Philadelphia: University of Pennsylvania Press, 1981. 335pp. ISBN 0-631-12788-7 (Blackwell) / ISBN 0-812-21112-X (Pennsylvania).

Erving Goffman has made many classic contributions to our understanding of human interaction. *Forms of Talk* (1981) is, in fact, itself a collection of classics, since it includes the re-printing of three previously published journal articles, followed by two original papers that apply the theories regarding behaviour and communication that were developed in the previous three. By focusing on the study of human behaviour as it pertains to language, Goffman's *Forms of Talk* provides useful information that makes clear a distinction between dialogue interpreting and conference interpreting, and that has provided the basis for a new approach to the study of interpreting in general.

In *Forms of Talk,* Goffman focuses on three themes: ritualization, participation status, and embedding. By ritualization, he refers to the learned and rule-governed but unconscious behaviours discussed by those who study conversational interaction. These can include gestural information, such as glances and postural shifts, as well as oral information such as the intonation, pausing, and restarting of utterances by a single speaker. Goffman proposes that these features of interactive discourse are important to both speaker and addressees, and are frequently used, for example, during retellings of prior events and experiences, to create what Tannen (1989) refers to as involvement strategies, using the language in a theatrical manner to involve the addressees and assist them in inferring those things left inexplicit.

Goffman's first theme, ritualization, while discussed as part of non-interpreted interactive discourse, clearly has implications for dialogue interpreters. If a speaker, in one language, uses gestural and prosodic strategies to involve addressees and hint at implicit meanings in their own discourse, then clearly the dialogue interpreter must have a means to similarly convey the imagery of a retelling and the hinted-at allusions within a rendered interpretation. Whether or not, or how, a dialogue interpreter might do this is beyond the scope of Goffman's work here. But as those in the field of translation and interpreting began to turn their attention to what sociology and sociolinguistics has to offer the field (see Hatim and Mason 1990), Goffman has provided a foundation for researchers to begin to examine the ritualized interactive features of interpreted encounters (cf. Roy 1989, Wadensjö 1992, Metzger 1995, forthcoming).

Participation framework is Goffman's second theme. By this he refers to the fact that all individuals, regardless of their status within an event, have a status with regard to the discourse. That is, one person might be designated as a speaker, another might be designated as a primary addressee, as when a speaker calls someone by name: "Dawson, what do you think of that?". Even those individuals who are not in the room have a designated status. For example, if they are within earshot of a spoken conversation they might be considered overhearers, and as such, have an avenue for taking a turn within the conversation, perhaps answering the question despite being 'unratified' and maybe receiving a reply such as "Are you Dawson?".

Like the ritualization theme, this notion of participation framework also has important implications for dialogue interpreters. Interpreters are often expected to be neutral with regard to the people and discourse that they interpret. However, as individuals present during the interaction, Goffman's notion implies that interpreters do have a participation status within the communicative event. Some theorists have speculated on the interpreter's role within this participation framework, often presuming the interpreter's status to be neutral. For example, Edmondson (1986) proposes that, while interpreters do have some participant responsibilities, such as formulating and producing utterances, they are not responsible for the content of the utterances, and therefore, interpreters have a unique status as neither hearers nor speakers within the participation framework. However, more recently, research based on Goffman's work (e.g. Wadensjö 1992) has begun to demonstrate that the interpreter's status is not nearly so neutral and uninvolved as was once thought to be the case.

The third theme, embedding, refers to the fact that speakers can produce utterances that reflect the words of other people, as well as their own. For example, speakers can construct the dialogue of other people from other times and places (see Tannen 1989). This raises an interesting issue for dialogue interpreters, who relay the dialogue of others at the same time and in the same place (see Metzger forthcoming).

Goffman weaves these three themes throughout the five chapters of *Forms of Talk*. Each chapter contains a wealth of information about the nuances of interactive discourse in dyadic or multiparty encounters. Goffman's insights, and his application of previous findings regarding the structure of interactive discourse, provide a foundation on which interpreted interaction can be discussed in a new light. After years, even centuries, of discussion regarding the nature of translation and interpreting, Goffman's attention to the details and ritual constraints underlying interactive discourse has already sparked innovative approaches to theories of and research in dialogue interpreting.

The implications of Goffman's work can be seen merely by examining one chapter of *Forms of Talk*. In the very first chapter, 'Replies and Responses', Goffman builds a case that both supports and extends the basic units of interaction, namely adjacency pairs. Adjacency pairs are those two-part units of discourse that provide evidence of the sequential nature of interactive discourse. That is, dyadic interaction is not simply two people engaging in monologues while taking turns at talk (though possibly some interactions feel like this!). Turns at talk are related to one another, each turn providing the opportunity for interlocutors to respond to what has previously been said as well as to make a connection to which the addressee can respond in subsequent turns. Greetings provide evidence of these adjacency pairs and the sequential structure they imply, as they generally include a first-part (in English perhaps a "Hello, how are you?") and a second-part response (such as "Fine"). Closings, question-answer pairs and so forth all represent examples of adjacency pairs.

In keeping with prior research, Goffman points out that adjacency pairs provide further evidence of the sequential nature of interaction by 'chaining'. He cites Merritt's (1976) findings regarding the chains in service encounters:

> A: "Have you got coffee to go?"
> B: "Milk and sugar?"
> A: "Just milk."   (quoted in Goffman 1981:8)

In this example, Goffman points out that two two-part adjacency pairs have been condensed into three turns at talk, because one part of the first pair (the answer to the first question, "Yes") can be understood without actually being uttered.

While all of this is not new to discourse analysts, Goffman's contribution is to suggest that the units of interaction are not nearly as precise and identifiable as once thought. In interaction, people do not speak in sentences when, pragmatically speaking, partial utterances are sufficient for mutual understanding. Conversational discourse analysts have tried various ways of approaching the study of interaction, to identify the basic unit of talk in interactive discourse. Goffman suggests that the *sentence*, the *utterance*, and the *turn* are all insufficient measurements. He suggests, instead, that the basic unit of interactive discourse is the *move*. A *move* can be a sentence, utterance, or turn, but need not be. A move can even be accomplished by silence, since pauses are as capable of conveying meaning as is discourse (cf. Tannen 1986, 1989).

The notion of moves as a basic unit of interaction can be very useful to the dialogue interpreter (as well as to the interpreter educator and researcher). This notion clarifies an issue that has plagued the field for some time, namely equivalence. It is sometimes assumed that the only true measure of an interpreter's success at their work is to know that they have conveyed an equivalent message in their rendition of the source into the target language. However, it has long been clear that the notion of equivalence is not straightforward. Moreover, where a translator of written discourse deals with the lexical, syntactic, pragmatic and discourse levels of text, the dialogue interpreter must cope with the additional dimensions that live, real-time participants offer in particular contexts (see Hatim and Mason 1990).

In the case of Goffman's description of interactional moves, a question for the dialogue interpreter might be this: has the move that was intended by the originator of an utterance been conveyed appropriately? And if so, what has this done to the various levels of linguistic equivalence? Or if not, how can the interaction continue, when interactive discourse, as Goffman points out in this classic, is built by participants move by move? While it might be argued that moves can also occur in written discourse, the dialogue interpreter does not have the luxury of a text that has been completed from beginning to end. Interactive discourse is a jointly negotiated process that participants engage in, and though many professional codes of ethics for dialogue interpreters suggest otherwise, dialogue interpreters are, as Wadensjö (1992) points out, centrally involved in this negotiation process (see, for example, Roy (1989) for a study of an interpreter's role in turn exchange).

The fact that dialogue interpreters have a unique participant status is also indirectly addressed in Goffman's chapter entitled 'Footing'. In this chapter (chapter 3), he describes the relationship between participants in interaction. By examining the role of all individuals present in interactions, he makes it clear that even unaddressed bystanders can have an impact on the unfolding of interactive discourse.

In his discussion of participant roles in interactive discourse, Goffman extends the notion of 'speaker-hearer', once presumed to represent the status of interlocutors in interaction. And although it would be easiest to develop a relatively simple structure (such as speaker-hearer) to describe interaction, he attempts, instead, to characterize the dynamic and ever-changing relationships between interactants and the discourse itself. He does this by focusing on the production and reception of utterances. With regard to production, he proposes that the term 'speaker' implies that an individual is animating their own words, ideas, and positions, whereas this might not be the case. For example, when an individual reads a paper at a conference presentation for a colleague who is unable to attend, the reader is animating words but the ideas and positions are not their own. Goffman provides numerous examples of the ways in which a 'speaker' can fulfill one or another, rather than each, of these roles.

This clearly has relevance for interpreters, whose professional responsibility it is to animate in a second language the ideas and positions of others. Hence, a dialogue interpreter is constantly shifting back and forth between these three aspects of being a 'speaker', sometimes animating the words of one participant, sometimes those of another, and still at other times giving voice to ideas and positions of their own (for example when explaining something about the interpreting process to other participants).

This is the basis for Goffman's production format, in which he divides the notion of speaker into three roles, based on distinguishable characteristics. An *animator* is a speaker who functions essentially as a "talking machine" (p. 144). An *author* is responsible for originating the content as well as the form of an utterance. The individual who is responsible for or committed to what is being said is the *principal*. It is clearly possible for a dialogue interpreter to animate the words of another. Nevertheless, when an interpreter is not the originator of the content of an utterance (a rendition), they are still responsible for the form of the utterance, since they render it into a different language. Moreover, it is also possible for them to behave as *principal*, uttering words of their own. The implication for research into dialogue interpreting is that we can use Goffman's taxonomy of speaker roles to examine in greater detail how interpreters function in various types of interactive settings (see Wadensjö 1992, Metzger 1995, forthcoming).

Erving Goffman's *Forms of Talk* provides important insights regarding the structure of interactional discourse. In addition, by adopting a sociological point of view, it deepens our understanding of the nature of such encounters. Ultimately, these are the reasons why Goffman's work is still considered to be a classic today. And perhaps even more importantly for the purposes of this volume, these are the reasons that Goffman's work is so critical to both the theoretical and the empirical foundation of dialogue interpreting.

MELANIE METZGER
Department of ASL, Linguistics, and Interpretation, Gallaudet University, 800 Florida Avenue, N.E., Washington, D.C. 20002-3695, USA. melanie.metzger@gallaudet.edu

References

Edmondson, W. (1986) 'Cognition, Conversing, and Interpreting', in Juliane House. and Shoshana Blum-Kulka (eds) *Interlingual and Intercultural Communication*, Tübingen: Gunter Narr, 129-38.

Hatim, Basil and Ian Mason (1990) *Discourse and the Translator*, London: Longman.

Merritt, M. (1976) 'On Questions Following Questions (in Service Encounters)', *Language in Society* 5(3): 315-57.

Metzger, Melanie (1995) *The Paradox of Neutrality: A Comparison of Inter-preters' Goals with the Realities of Interactive Discourse.* Unpublished Ph.D. thesis, Washington, D.C.: Georgetown University.

------ (forthcoming) *Simultaneous Interpretation: Deconstructing the Myth of Neutrality*, Washington, D.C.: Gallaudet University Press.

Roy, Cynthia (1989) *A Sociolinguistic Analysis of the Interpreter's Role in the Turn Exchanges of an Interpreted Event.* Unpublished Ph.D. thesis, Washington, D.C.: Georgetown University.

Tannen, Deborah (1986) *That's Not What I Meant*, New York: Ballantine Books.

------ (1989) *Talking Voices: Repetition, Dialogue, and Imagery in Conversational Discourse*, Cambridge: Cambridge University Press.

Wadensjö, Cecilia (1992) *Interpreting as Interaction: On Dialogue Interpreting in Immigration Hearings and Medical Encounters*, Linköping University: Linköping Studies in Art and Science.

Publishers of Books Reviewed in this Issue

Addison Wesley Longman, Edinburgh Gate, Harlow, Essex CM20 2JE, UK

Basil Blackwell, 108 Cowley Road, Oxford OX4 1JF, UK

Deaf Studies Research Unit, University of Durham, Elvet Riverside 2, New Elvet, Durham DH1 3JT, UK

John Benjamins, P O Box 75577, 1070 Amsterdam, The Netherlands

University of Ottawa Press, 542 King Edward, Ottawa, K1N 6N5, Canada

University of Pennsylvania Press, 820 North University Drive, University Park, PA 16802-1003, USA

Waterside Press, Domum Road, Winchester, SO23 9NN, UK

The Translator. Volume 5, Number 2 (1999), 333-355   ISBN 1-900650-21-5

Book Reviews

Equality before the Law: Deaf People's Access to Justice. Mary Brennan and Richard Brown. Durham: Deaf Studies Research Unit, University of Durham 1997. 189 pp. Pb. ISBN 0-9531779-0-4. Out of print.

The legal system is society's instrument for solving conflicts of interest between its members and disputes over violations of norms. At least theoretically, in a democratic community governed by law everybody is supposed to be treated equally in court proceedings.

The European Convention for the Protection of Human Rights and Fundamental Freedoms, signed on November 4, 1950, states (article 6.3) that "Everyone charged with a criminal offence has the following minimal rights: (a) to be informed promptly, in a language which he understands and in detail, of the nature and cause of the accusation against him; ... (e) to have the free assistance of an interpreter if he cannot understand or speak the language used in court". This right is acknowledged in the British Police and Criminal Evidence Act 1984, which states that the custody officer must "as soon as practicable call an interpreter if a detained person appears to be deaf or there is doubt about his hearing or speaking ability or ability to understand English, *and the custody officer cannot establish effective communication*" (my emphasis).

The right to an interpreter is obviously not unqualified. Code C, paragraph 13 in the same Act gives another opening to the discretion of the authority: "If a person appears to be deaf or there is doubt about his hearing or speaking ability, he must not be interviewed in the absence of an interpreter *unless he agrees in writing to be interviewed without one ... or Annex C applies*". Annex C states that under certain defined conditions, in exceptional cases urgent interviews at police stations may be conducted in the absence of an interpreter.

The above quotations from British law are taken from Brennan's and Brown's *Equality before the Law: Deaf People's Access to Justice*. The book reports on a research project aimed at exploring the extent to which Deaf people have equal access to justice in today's Britain. Although the studies reported were undertaken in the United Kingdom, the results are no doubt generalizable to other countries as well.

The research project consisted of several studies. One important part was the observation of authentic BSL (British Sign Language)/English interpreting in a great number of court cases, including two major murder cases, and the video-taping of a two-day trial in Scotland. An examination of documentary material related to court proceedings where Deaf people had been involved

ISSN 1355-6509   © *St Jerome Publishing, Manchester*

was conducted, as well as interviews with Deaf people about their experience with courts and the interpreting service provided. Interpreters' experiences of court interpreting and issues of training and qualifications were documented on the basis of a survey and a number of in-depth interviews.

In parallel with the growing recognition of BSL, sign language interpreting has developed into an occupation; professional organizations have evolved and developed rules of professional conduct, and society has set up examining bodies and official registers of interpreters. A central aim of the project was to investigate the current situation regarding availability and qualifications of BSL/English interpreters, and to gain a better understanding of the problems they face when interpreting in court and other stages in the legal process. Surveys were conducted in England and Wales, but not in Scotland.

The emerging picture is not a very bright one. While court interpreting is mostly conducted by qualified, registered interpreters, the survey shows that all too often sign interpreting is undertaken by registered trainee interpreters or unregistered interpreters. In police stations non-registered interpreters are even more frequently employed. Levels of training in sign language interpreting seem to be very low. Hardly any of those undertaking legal interpreting have taken more than very short training courses of one day or a weekend.

One of the recurring questions in court and community interpreting (oral as well as signed) is whether the interpreter should be a 'translation machine' or an 'advocate' (or some other kind of 'intermediary'). Among other related issues which have been discussed in the literature on court interpreting are the conflicting demands made on the interpreter by legal professionals and immigrant clients. The present book gives ample evidence of these and other pertinent problems facing interpreters in the context of sign language court interpreting.

Despite the importance of their role, many interpreters are not given the professional status they deserve, are not given adequate support to carry out their work, are often not adequately trained and are subject to conflicting demands by Deaf people, legal personnel, police and their own professional colleagues (p. 46). Surprisingly, social workers often take on interpreting roles, particularly in police stations, but also in courts. This used to be the norm between the 1950s and the 1980s and, despite the growing professionalization of interpreting, has not ceased: "Social workers still interpret in court. Full stop" (p. 52).

There is an obvious conflict between the role of the interpreter as someone who 'transfers messages', not necessarily ensuring that they are understood, and the social worker who wants to make sure that the messages are fully understood so that appropriate measures can be taken. The conclusion of the authors on the basis of their own research as well as studies in other countries of both oral and signed interpreting is that "we need to rethink the interpreter's role and function generally, but particularly within legal contexts" (p. 52).

It seems rather typical that interpreters take on duties that the courts do not specifically require them to do and possibly would even disapprove of had they known about it. In some cases the researchers found that the interpreters not only provided lawyers with spoken comment but also additional written material to help 'educate' the lawyers, i.e. the interpreter was used as a language and community expert. The authors point out that the Deaf people involved in these cases would not necessarily even know that such advice was being sought or proffered, or what precisely the nature of the advice was (p.70). The authors suggest that Deaf people themselves should be encouraged to give this kind of linguistic and cultural information about the Deaf community. It is unfortunate that Deaf people and their organizations play such a limited role within the legal system (p. 71).

Other issues taken up in the interviews and discussed by the authors include working conditions and the working environment, working alone or working in a team, acoustics, choice of interpreters (if, how many, who?), interpreters as witnesses, and interpreters interpreting for both witnesses and defendants.

From the account in this report, it is striking how ignorant legal professionals are of Deaf people and their language and culture. Deaf defendants or accused often feel that they are not only physically handicapped but also discriminated against. The collocation 'deaf and dumb' is still used, involving the second meaning of the word dumb as stupid or slow-witted. Chapter four in the book draws mainly on unique material consisting of in-depth interviews with Deaf people who have had direct experience of the criminal justice system in the form of police questioning, court appearances and custodial sentences.

The chapter abounds with examples of difficulties which Deaf people have experienced in communicating with the authorities, with or without an interpreter. There is shocking evidence of ignorant lawyers, bad interpreters, or lack of interpreters altogether. Deaf prisoners bear witness to serious issues of inequality of treatment between Deaf and hearing prisoners. There are also examples of practical difficulties, like the fact that it is physically tiring to watch interpreting for long periods, especially if the visual background is poor, and that long stretches of interpreting can be mentally demanding for the Deaf person:

> It was like something out of a book, but with a book you can control it, close the book, if you've had enough, but this just went on and on, ... I can't take everything in that quickly, I need time to think and to translate it for myself. (p. 104)

Several Deaf interviewees indicated that they had difficulty with English and with the extensive use of fingerspelling by some interpreters. Especially in those cases where interpreters used fingerspelling for legal terms, the Deaf client did not have real access to the meaning. For many Deaf people, English is not only a second language, but also a language that they have never heard. It is a silent language, which many Deaf people cannot read or write well. It is sad that the authors have to point out that this does not mean that Deaf people have low linguistic competence in BSL or that they have low intelligence!

Chapter 5 gives a very interesting theoretical and practical account of the linguistic factors at play in BSL/English court interpreting. This is especially valuable for a person who does not know sign language, as the chapter aims at describing some of the peculiarities of sign language compared to oral languages like English, and the implications of these differences for court interpreting.

BSL/English interpreters work not simply between two languages, but between two languages expressed in different modalities.Written statements based on 'verbatim' records of spoken utterances play an important part in court proceedings. Throughout court cases, reference is made to written documentation. This means that the courts are not comfortable with languages without a written form, for example BSL. Courts require sign language to be 'pinned down' in written form, i.e. written English, in a form "which is at least twice removed from the original, i.e. it involves translation into another language, in a different modality, and then a further modality change from spoken to written. Problems can and regularly do occur in each part of this process, yet little account seems to have been taken of this within the courtroom" (p. 120).[1]

As a visual-spatial gestural language, BSL is organized in a very different way from English. A very illustrative example is given: person X recounts how he goes to a pub, buys a pint of beer and is short-changed by the bartender. In English this story can be told and embellished in many ways, but if the story is told in sign language, it would automatically include a great deal of visual information. Much of this visual information is normally excluded in English, but it would be unusual to exclude it in a BSL version. This of course has enormous implications for court interpreting. Court proceedings usually involve reconstructing past events, and minute details are very important. The signer always conjures up a particular visual image of the events being recounted. The BSL interpreter also has to create visual scenarios: "I arrived at his door at half-past seven" may include in BSL that there was a gate which was opened and steps which were climbed. If the interpreter decides to be more 'neutral' and exclude such information, then the Deaf person may assume that a different door is being referred to (p. 122).

Is there a BSL formal register that interpreters try to exploit in court? According to the authors, there is, but the situation is made complex by the interpreters' and other people's uncertainty about the relationship between BSL and English and the fact that they are often being forced to use an informal style because of the Deaf person's linguistic choices.

The picture given here of equality before the law for Deaf people is rather dark. One positive aspect of the research, according to the authors, has been that it has allowed researchers to see the types of successful strategies that interpreters use in court. Successful interpreters take into court and use the rich linguistic and cultural resources of BSL. These interpreters ignore the pressures for 'literal interpretation', giving themselves the time and visual space to exploit the language to the full. They have the confidence to recognize that their interpreting may indeed interfere with the usual dynamics of the court, but they are not afraid to change those dynamics. The book ends with detailed recommendations for improving the practice of BSL/English court interpreting.

Overall, the book offers a thought-provoking, partly shocking and throughout very illuminating account of the harsh reality behind the official expressions of equality before the law, as formulated in laws and political documents. This review has taken up only a few of the interesting questions discussed. Some of the findings have already been used in interpreter training. Hopefully the book will be read by both providers and users of interpreting services, as well as interpreters themselves. Indeed, this should be mandatory reading for several groups, especially those in charge of employing interpreters for courts and other legal settings.

HELGE NISKA
Institute for Interpretation and Translation Studies, Stockholm University, S-106 91 Stockholm, Sweden. Helge.Niska@tolk.su.se

Notes

1. A further complication which the authors do not touch upon concerns the impact of the institutional setting itself. Jönsson (1988) points out in her study of interaction in police hearings that what a dominant party (e.g. the police) does in a reformulation is to summarize aspects of what the interlocutor has just said, reformulate it in other words, draw conclusions from it and very often assign an interpretation that has not been expressed by the interlocutor him/herself.

References

Jönsson, Linda (1988) *On Being Heard in Court Trials and Police Interrogations. A Study of Discourse in Two Institutional Contexts*, PhD thesis, Linköping: University of Linköping.

Interpreting as Interaction (Language in Social Life). Cecilia Wadensjö. London & New York: Addison Wesley Longman, 1998. 312pp. Hb. ISBN 0-582-28911-4, Pb. 0-582-28910-6.

Interpreting as Interaction is a far-reaching, new approach to interpreter-mediated conversations in face-to-face, institutional encounters. Cecilia

Wadensjö presents actual interpreted encounters and asks radically different questions about interpreted conversations, such as: What is going on from the perspective of all the participants? What are their expectations and assumptions about the interaction? In what ways are the participants making sense of the event as it happens? To what degree are interpreters and other interlocutors responsible for the substance and progression of talk?

The heart of the book examines empirical data – audio-recorded, interpreter-mediated encounters within medical, legal, and social services settings – to illustrate and to examine how interpreters and primary parties collude in their conversational activity, creating and responding to the utterances and actions of each other. As the most recent contribution to the *Language in Social Life Series* edited by Christopher N. Candlin, this book furthers thoughts and perspectives first presented in Wadensjö's (1992) Ph.D. thesis, published by the University of Linköping, Sweden. In this revised and crisply written version, Dr. Wadensjö has composed an absorbing account that invites a wide audience to see how ethnographic descriptions and analysis lead to interpretations of discourse processes, demonstrating that talk is a social, reciprocal activity in which the interpreter inhabits a role that requires more than to "just translate". Narrative accounts from her own professional experience intertwined with data and accounts of the data make for an absorbing read.

Wadensjö's work is theoretically grounded in the analytic frameworks of Goffman's work on the nature of social organization and of Bakhtin's work on the dialogic theory of language and interaction. Her perspective of the interpreter as an engaged actor solving not only problems of translation but also problems of mutual understanding in situated interaction is groundbreaking in its approach and superior in its scholarship. Her analysis demonstrates that interpreting consists of two interdependent activities – translation and coordination – established by the fact that interpreters create two kinds of talk: talk that is generated in relaying a message, and talk that is generated by the interpreter to assist (or mediate) the flow of talk. She provides examples of utterances directed *at* the interpreter and *from* the interpreter that are not about the content of the relayed message. Thus, the progression of talk is both a coordinated activity among the participants, and a responsibility of the interpreter: "In an interpreter-mediated conversation, the progression and substance of talk, the distribution of responsibility for this among co-interlocutors, and what, as a result of interaction, becomes mutual and shared understanding – all will to some extent depend on the interpreter's words and deeds" (p. 195).

Elaborating further on interpreter rights and responsibilities, Wadensjö problematizes 'understanding' in conversation and its opposite 'miscommunication' by showing three different ways in which interpreters handle miscommunication events. These reveal their perspective on what constitutes sufficient understanding among the participants. In her discussion of "relaying by displaying" and "relaying as re-playing (or re-presenting)", Wadensjö explores how interpreters behave as narrators of others' speech, either to convey impressions of self as a person using others' words or to "*re*-present the expressiveness of preceding talk" (p. 247).

In Chapter 1, Wadensjö introduces the main themes and organization of the book. First among her themes is the goal of description rather than prescription, to describe how all the participants are making sense of the interaction and thus how interpreting is an activity intertwined with coordinating (her term). Dominant throughout the book is the perspective of dialogism versus monologism, how interpreting is a pervasive and normal activity in modern society, and how interpreted conversations are a give-and-take interactivity: "This book promotes face-to-face interpreting as a field of research in its own right, and suggests directing investigations within this field on *the dynamics of interpreter-mediated encounters*" (p. 15, emphasis in original).

Chapter 2 introduces the ongoing perspective of 'talk as text' and 'talk as activity'. It looks at the nature of talk from various theoretical and analytical perspectives, including translation (both independently and as part of interpretation), and argues for differences between monologism and dialogism, Bakhtin's claim about the nature of discourse and the mind. The relevance of a dialogic perspective to investigations of interpreter-mediated conversations becomes clear.

Chapter 3 provides a background discussion on community interpreting, its professional status, and its emergence as a phenomenon in modern society, including codes of conduct and guides for officials working with interpreters.

Chapter 4 explores the literature of sociology and social anthropology and its concepts of *intermediary, gatekeeper,* and *non-person* as potential roles/ explanations for performing the role of interpreter. It also reviews recent empirical studies of interpreting in face-to-face situations, mostly from legal settings.

Chapter 5 explores the work of Erving Goffman, a sociologist who wrote extensively on the nature of social organization. Goffman argued that groups of people were the appropriate unit of analysis, not the individual. People act in concert with each other and thus everything that is said and done is revealed through the description and analysis of the interaction. Interpreters and those who teach interpreting will be most interested in the analytic and theoretical discussions of 'role'. Wadensjö leads readers into an intense investigation of role concepts, something heretofore lacking in professional discussions, contrasting *normative roles*, roles expressed in official codes, rules and ideas of conduct, with *typical roles*, how people actually perform while in a specific role.

This chapter also explains Goffman's concept of participation *frameworks*, that is, how participants align to self and others while engaged in talk. In his essays, Goffman has painstakingly sorted out the various aspects of speaking, or the role of speaker. Here Wadensjö makes an original contribution to the field of social interaction and linguistics by explicating the aspects of the role of listener, the ways in which interpreters listen in order to repeat, or listen in order to respond, and so on. Lastly the chapter discusses methods for data collection and outlines the analytical method applied to the data gathered.

In Chapter 6 Wadensjö examines the utterances of interpreters and primary interlocutors within actual speech events. Interpreter utterances can be distinguished on the basis of two typologies; firstly, as 'close' or 'divergent' renditions of the primary participants' talk, or secondly, as utterances which function to "mediate" or *coordinate* the ongoing talk. Thus interpreter utterances correspond to the "two intertwined functions interpreters typically carry in interaction, that of *translating* and that of *coordinating* others' talk" (p. 18).

Chapter 7 explores interpreter-mediated conversation as instances of particular kinds of three-party interaction. Considering talk as an activity in which understandings, expectations, and perspectives are part and parcel of how actors make sense of ongoing talk, this chapter enquires about the way in which all the participants jointly organize conversational activity. The analysis demonstrates how the primary participants and the interpreters display various modes of speaking and listening such that their "words and deeds condition one another" (p. 18). In this chapter Wadensjö presents four interpreter-mediated encounters as *"situated systems of activity"*, describing in great detail the coordinating function of the interpreter as it occurs in combination with verbal and other activities of the primary parties and demonstrating that different circumstances change the responsibility or organization of talk either in general or within a turn-by-turn level.

Chapter 8 focuses on *mis-communication* events (Linell 1995), instances where one or more of the primary parties appear to have sensed a misunderstanding: how do interpreters either choose to become responsible for the primary parties' achieving mutual understanding or choose not to?

In Chapter 9 Wadensjö continues to explore the theme of interpreter responsibility by framing the interpreter's performance as an art of reporting others' words. Experienced community interpreters will most likely remember an encounter in which, by verbal means or otherwise, they distinguished between their own and others' responsibility for the utterances they spoke or signed. It is in this chapter that Wadensjö problematizes the notion of neutrality and discusses the twin concepts of *relaying by displaying* and *relaying as re-playing*. She shows how interpreters present others' words and simultaneously either emphasize their personal non-involvement or work to re-present another's utterance with all its attendant emotion, manner and feeling.

Chapter 10 is a summary chapter revisiting the main theoretical and practical implications of dialogism in the study of face-to-face interpreting. Faced with descriptions and analytical insights into how interpreters actually perform necessarily opens discussions about teaching and training as well as certifying and licensing. Wadensjö also makes suggestions for future research.

While the old adage to "just translate and translate everything" is a useful shorthand for explaining interpreting to lay persons and newcomers, it is not useful for explanations needed to define interpreting as a profession and to define the actual rights and responsibilities that characterize the everyday experience of interpreting work. Wadensjö has pioneered a vast new perspective for understanding, researching and teaching the work of interpreters. She offers, in a seminal way, the perspective of the interpreter as an engaged actor solving not only problems of translation but also problems of mutual understanding. Hers is the first full-length work to suggest that we can understand the task of interpreting much better if we look to a perspective that accounts for the *interactivity* of the primary participants, rather than looking only at the interpreter and the interpreted message. The frameworks of social interaction and dialogic linguistics provide, again for the first time, a deeply theoretical understanding of the complex nature of participating in an interpreter-mediated encounter. Wadensjö's detailed, meticulous analysis has thrown open avenues of research that will be explored for years to come.

When Goffman (1981) introduced his notions of participation framework, the complex ways in which speakers participate in a conversation, he did not explore the complexities that exist within the role of listener. Wadensjö does this. She develops the notion of *reception formats*, corresponding to that of 'production formats'. Distinguishing between production roles is a way of making explicit in what sense speakers display their own or others' opinions or attitudes; the gain in distinguishing different modes of listening is to elucidate more thoroughly how individuals demonstrate "their own opinions and attitudes concerning rights and responsibilities in interaction" (p. 92).

An interpreter's role, as both a social role and a role that performs an activity, is realized through interaction with others. With analytical precision and detail, Wadensjö explains how interpreters both listen and speak within shifting stances of their own participation, shifting from relaying to coordinating the interaction. Thus, they change the level and degree of their participation. This is significant because it profoundly changes the current vision of what interpreters are doing. In fact, the *pas de trois* (Wadensjö's term) is the basic, fundamental event of interpreting and other models should be seen as deriving from it. It changes teaching the process of interpreting and certification practices for interpreters.

Wadensjö has written a fascinating book, explaining difficult concepts lucidly. Readers will enjoy the author's telling examples from her own experience, interspersed in ways that make complex theories come to light. This book is a must read for interpreters everywhere, including sign language interpreters. Scholars, researchers, students, and educators in interpreting, translation, linguistics, anthropology, sociology, and other disciplines interested in the interaction of institutional and social life and language will find that *Interpreting as Interaction* throws a new light on all discourse processes.

CYNTHIA B. ROY

ASL/English Interpreting Program, English Department, Indiana University Purdue University Indianapolis, Indianapolis, IN 46202, USA. *croy@iupui.edu*

References

Goffman, Erving (1981) *Forms of Talk*, Philadelphia: University of Pennsylvania Press.
Linell, P. (1995) 'Troubles with Mutualities: Towards a Dialogical Theory of Misunderstanding and Miscommunication', in I. Marková, C. F. Graumann and F. Koppa (eds) *Mutualities in Dialogue*, Cambridge: Cambridge University Press, 176-213.
Wadensjö, Cecilia (1992) *Interpreting as Interaction: On Dialogue Interpreting in Immigration Hearings and Medical Encounters*, Linköping University: Linköping Studies in Art and Science.

The Critical Link: Interpreters in the Community. Silvana E. Carr, Roda P. Roberts, Aideen Dufour and Dini Steyn (eds). Amsterdam & Philadelphia: John Benjamins, 1997. viii, 322 pp. ISBN 90-272-1620-7 (Hb), NLG 158.

An old Chinese proverb has it that it is both a blessing and a curse to live in interesting times. This book presents a snapshot of an interesting time in the development of community interpreting. It consists of a selection of papers from the First International Conference on Interpreting in Legal, Health, and Social Service settings, held in Geneva Park, Canada in 1995. In the Foreword, Brian Harris explains that the conference sought "to bring workers from scattered areas together for the first time in a live international exchange of information and prospects" (p. 2). Aware of the current interest in the professionalization of this field, I prepared for a provocative and stimulating read.

Roda Robert's 'Overview' whets the appetite by posing such questions as "What exactly does community interpreting cover?", " Where is the profession heading?", and "What are the different philosophical approaches to community interpreting and how do they influence the task of the community interpreter?" (pp. 7-8). She then attempts the rather dangerous feat of offering a working definition of community interpreting. In taking as her premise, however, the Collard-Abbas (1989) definition ("the type of interpreting done to assist those immigrants who are not native speakers of the language to gain full and equal access to statutory services"), she takes rather an unfortunate backward step. Some of the papers collected in this book reflect work with indigenous, rather than immigrant, users of marginalized languages. Whilst Roberts does concede that the Collard-Abbas definition "is still a matter of debate" (p. 9), one senses a missed opportunity here. The paper goes on to suggest that "community/cultural/ dialogue interpreting" be seen as a generic term "with at least three specific forms specified by setting" (p. 9). I found this emphasis on the setting in which interpreting takes place tangential to the main argument, though perhaps others would view it as inclusive. The following pages (pp. 10-25) give a remarkably concise, yet reasonably comprehensive account of the state of the art. Here the "machine/advocate/ally" (Baker-Schenk 1986) argument is rehearsed and updated, and issues of recruitment, training and working conditions are outlined. Teachers, trainers, and those new to the field will find this a remarkably accessible introduction.

Whilst it is not clear that all the following papers are working to the same (Collard-Abbas/ Roberts) definition of community interpreting, it is clear that the philosophical underpinnings of the practices and training courses outlined differ considerably. As with all branches of interpreting, philosophy and theory inform our understanding of the interpreter's role and thus, ultimately, our practices. The disparate and isolated nature of community interpreting has meant that there has been, hitherto, little focus on how an understanding of this field might redefine some of the rhetoric of the wider discipline. It is disappointing, then, that only two of the papers in this volume are devoted to role: those by Sabine Fenton and Cecilia Wadensjö.

Sabine Fenton urges that we should "put the person back into the interpreter" (p. 33) and end what Morris (1993) has called the "legal fiction" of interpreters being language conduits in the courtroom. She suggests that one way to achieve this might be to regard the interpreter as an expert witness. Cecilia Wadensjö's paper takes as its premise the interpreter as participant in the activity of the interpreted interaction (Wadensjö 1992). Such a theoretical approach is akin to the work of post-modern critical linguists such as Hodge and Kress (1979), Fairclough (1992), Wodak,(1996) and Lee (1992) in concentrating on discourse as action. Moreover, rather than attempting to describe the activity of community interpreting in ways that concord neatly with existing frameworks, this data-driven paper looks at reality and develops a framework that reflects it. Here one senses a breakthrough which should shape the development of the community interpreting debate, and which could help to take the wider discipline of interpreting into the 21st century. Birgitta Englund Dimitrova's further application of Wadensjö's premise, in her paper on interpreter responsibility (pp. 147-65), suggests the emergence of a Swedish school.

Adolfo Gentile's is another of the rare voices in this volume that question the rubric. Taking issue with the term community interpreting, this paper unashamedly raises more questions than it seeks to answer. This is the kind of stimulation one feels is required since, as Gentile points out, "the degree of cross-fertilization world-wide on this issue is minimal" (p. 118). It could be viewed as disappointing, then, that the rest of this volume contains surprisingly little philosophical or theoretical debate.

In seeking to find commonalities of theory, approach and practice, it seems odd to focus on the minutiae of difference. There is an argument, though, articulated neatly by Gentile, that " [w]ithout examining the different possibilities and versions of this area as they have developed around the world it would be foolhardy and premature to come up with solutions [to the problems of defining community interpreting]" (p. 118). The rest of the papers collected in this volume afford the reader an opportunity to examine this issue.

Most of the papers are straightforwardly informative. Mikkelson and Mintz's (USA) paper is an outline of a training initiative and its attendant programmes, Terry Chesher's a reflection on two decades of community interpreting in Australia, and Penney and Sammons' a fascinating account of the training of interpreters working with a marginalized language (in this case Inuktitut). Whilst the authors offer little comment on their work, there is much worth in its content. Virginia Benmaman (USA), Yvonne Fowler (UK), and Sandra Hale (Australia) all contribute papers that serve to illustrate the complexity of the task faced by community interpreters in legal settings. Hale's paper presents " a sample of the results of a major data based study" looking into "the accuracy of ... interpretation in terms of pragmatic equivalence" (p. 205). This is an interesting paper, though it is marred by the lack of a coherent philosophical framework. Hale talks in punitive terms of the interpreter's 'guilt' and 'failure', yet claims that "at times, the interpreter cannot be held accountable for intrinsic problems of the interpreting process which hinder accuracy" (p. 205). One feels that Benmaman's sound suggestions (pp. 187-188) and Fowler's calls (pp. 198-200) for the improved training of legal interpreters will founder without an appropriate and coherent wider vision which might unite the international field.

Puebla Fortier (USA) and Silvana Carr (Canada) draw attention to the attitudinal, financial and legislative barriers to effective service provision and the difficulties of attempting to regulate an adequate supply of personnel to meet demand. Franz Pöchhacker (Austria) also bemoans the inadequate supply of interpreters in his paper, aptly entitled 'Is There Anybody Out There?'. Ann Corsellis' paper (pp. 77-89) addresses the responsibilities of the public services personnel who work with interpreters.

For those involved in community interpreting, concerns about the complexity and scope of the task, supply and demand, funding, adequate training, recognition, social attitudes, accreditation, and the vagaries of politics are commonplace. The papers collected here are honest and open accounts. As such they are at once therapeutic in a cathartic sense, and also a little disheartening. One imagines that those interested and bold enough to attend the conference in the first instance might represent the cutting edge. Thus it is disappointing to see an old rubric reiterated here. It is popular to cast community interpreting as the Cinderella of the broader discipline. Here, though, the role is that of the Ugly Sister, desperate to force her broad, strong feet into impossibly constricting stilettos. One hopes that community interpreting will soon have the confidence to re-examine good, solid data (such as that presented by Hale) through sensible frameworks (such as that used by Wadensjö).

Sherrill J. Bell's paper on the NAATI system of accreditation in Australia, with its concentration on the 'functional' interpretation of a given number of words (p. 96), would certainly be analogous to the stiletto. Boasting of "standards, which have undergone very few changes between 1977 and 1993", when one suspects this paper was written, Bell applauds the "stability within the system" (p. 96). After working through the painstaking detail of this paper, one is left wondering at what point stability becomes sterility. It is a stroke of neat editing to follow this paper with two more from Australia; those by Elisabeth Lascar and Adolfo Gentile. Lascar's alternative version cites research that questions the scope and depth of the NAATI system (pp. 119-123).

Throughout this book, the reader is challenged to identify common roots. Though these are not too far below the surface as to have become buried in the detail, I was left with a desire for further exploration. Nicholson and Martinsen's paper (pp. 259-271) is a case in point. Whilst ostensibly a description of the state of court interpreting in Denmark, the authors conclude with a fleeting discussion of Danish attitudes towards the current influx of non-Scandinavian immigrants. Issues of power in discourse, emotional neutrality, responsibility and role were writ large in Major Roy Thomas's paper (pp. 249-259) on the stresses and horrors faced by UNMO interpreters working in war-torn Sarajevo. My thoughts go out to colleagues working in the current crisis in the Balkans.

For me, at least two other papers echoed Thomas' issues. Carolyn Bullock and Brian Harris write cheerfully of empowering children by encouraging them to become "Ambassadors" (p. 232) to other minority language children in their school. Their endeavours are rewarded by certification. There is no recognition here that such plaudits might consolidate parents' views that it is both convenient and acceptable to use their children as interpreters in other, less suitable, settings. Similarly, Suzanne Michael and Marianne Cocchini, who regard college students as appropriate interpreters in medical settings (pp. 237-249), seem intent on ignoring the obvious dangers to all concerned. The emotional immaturity of minors and the unpredictable and demanding nature of any form of community interpreting makes for a potentially lethal cocktail. I would encourage these authors to look at any of the material available from CODAs (Children of Deaf Adults) should they need convincing of the long-term damage that can be wrought by such practices.

There is no easy way to organize such a volume. The contents are ostensibly divided into sections on role, training, standards, evaluation and accreditation, issues and practice. These are not, and cannot be, discrete categories. This, together with the variety of voices and the inclusion of tables, questionnaires, transcriptions and diagrams, does not make for an easy, cover-to-cover read. Rather, the reader should approach this volume as the diner might approach the smorgasbord, returning to the table again and again to sample the range and variety.

Despite the preponderance of contributions from Australia and North America, this book succeeds in affording us "an unprecedented panorama and cross-section of what is going on at this time in an ebullient field" (Harris, p. 2). One senses that community interpreting is at a critical point in its development. This volume is an opportunity to take an honest look at what is happening. Beyond the worth of documentation and exchange, though, this is not a book that seeks to develop theoretical frameworks, refine training practices or improve administrative techniques. That said, I guarantee that whether you are a practitioner, a consumer, an employer, an administrator, or a trainer you will find something of interest here.

KYRA POLLITT
Sign Languages International, Huddlestone's Wharf, Newark, England, NG24 4UL, UK. kyra.waving@passersby.freeserve.co.uk

References

Baker-Schenk, Charlotte (1986) *The Interpreter: Machine, Advocate, or Ally?*, Proceedings of the 1991 RID Convention, Expanding Horizons, USA.

Collard-Abbas, Lucy (1989) 'Training the Trainers of Community Interpreters', in Catriona Picken (ed) *ITICO Conference Proceedings*, London: ASLIB, 81-85.

Fairclough, Norman (1992) *Discourse and Social Change*, Cambridge: Polity Press.

Hodge, Robert and Gunther Kress (1979) *Language as Ideology*, London & New York: Routledge, (2nd Edition 1993).

Lee, David (1992) *Competing Discourses. Perspective and Ideology in Language*, London & New York: Longman.

Morris, Ruth (1993) *Images of the Interpreter: A Study of Language Switching in the Legal Process*, Ph.D. Thesis, Department of Law, Lancaster University.

Wadensjö, Cecilia (1992) *Interpreting as Interaction. On Dialogue-Interpreting in Immigration Hearings and Medical Encounters*, Linköping: Linköping University.

Wodak, Ruth (1996) *Disorders of Discourse*, London & New York: Longman.

Interpreters and the Legal Process. Joan Colin and Ruth Morris. Winchester: Waterside Press, 1996. 191 pp. Pb. ISBN 1-872-870-28-7.

Most public service interpreters (PSIs) are employed on a sessional basis, across the whole range of public services. Few, if any, of them restrict their activities to only one area. Indeed, individual assignments may involve dealing with more than one service. An Italian interpreter was once called out in the early hours of the morning, to assist the police in dealing with a hotel guest who was causing a breach of the peace; it quickly became evident that the person concerned was mentally disturbed, at which point it became necessary to hospitalize him. The interpreter needed, therefore, to be able to deal with legal and medical situations in rapid succession.

Many, although not all, PSIs began their careers as 'informal' interpreters, helping friends, family and neighbours with less English deal with the day-to-day requirements of life in Britain. As such, they would have had the average layperson's knowledge of the practice and procedures of the public services, which would have been gradually extended and developed through experience. Few would have had any formal training in the complexities of interpreting and translating.

In the last twenty or thirty years, interpreters and public service providers alike have come to recognize the inherent dangers in making use of untrained interpreters – the horror stories from both viewpoints are legion and range from police requiring an interpreter to act as minder to an accused person to an interpreter advising an appellant how to respond in an immigration interview.

Public services and interpreters both recognized the pressing need to formalize and evaluate the interpreting process as it applied to their particular situation and requirements, and from this was developed the Diploma in Public Service Interpreting.This examination, administered by the Institute of Linguists, assesses the performance of candidates in both interpreting and translating in the context of one aspect of the public services – law, local government or health. Candidates are required to demonstrate their proficiency in both consecutive and simultaneous interpreting, oral translation of written texts and written translation, tasks which reflect the range of activities that a PSI may be asked to undertake. The content of each task is carefully designed to evaluate not only the candidate's linguistic ability but also their knowledge of the terminology and procedures in use in the option they have chosen, in addition to good practice. Successful candidates have their skills evaluated and validated and public service providers have the reassurance of knowing that they are working with trained personnel.

Most Diploma candidates will undertake a course of study before sitting the examination, and it is at this point that many realize for the first time how limited their knowledge of the public services really is. Many words and expressions are familiar from newspapers and television but students have no real understanding of the procedures or personnel involved.

Good reference materials for the 'agency knowledge' aspect of a course are difficult to come by. Information leaflets readily available are, more often than not, too superficial to provide the depth and range of knowledge that PSIs require in order to function efficiently, and specialist training materials are at the other end of the scale, being too complex. Trainers must always bear in mind that they are training interpreters, not lawyers or local government officers – the aim is to make the interpreter as competent a means of communication as possible, not to replace the service provider entirely.

Between them, Joan Colin and Ruth Morris have a wealth of experience in training both interpreters and service providers, and *Interpreters and the Legal Process* is a useful addition to materials already available. It is aimed at "people interested in language, communication, interpreting and translation as they affect legal matters – including interpreters and legal personnel". The contents cover all the areas in England and Wales in which interpreters are employed within the legal system: the police, immigration and asylum hearings and appeals, the courts, the probation service and prisons. In addition, consideration is given to general principles of language, as well as professional standards, and legal interpreting arrangements in parts of Australia, Canada, Sweden and the USA are described.

The text is divided into nine main sections covering the areas within the justice system in which interpreters are used. Some of these main sections are subdivided into Parts I, II and III which are themselves further subdivided into smaller sections to allow the authors to deal with specific points of detail concerning practice and procedures within the wider context of the main section. For example, Section 3, Entry to the United Kingdom, contains, in Part I, subsections on entry procedures, entry and asylum, engaging an interpreter, asylum, dealing with harrowing information, pre-interview briefing, record of interview, immigration appeals, Stage I: Adjudications, engaging interpreters for immigration appeals and Stage II: The Immigration Appeals Tribunal. The other main sections organized in this way are: Interpreters and the Police (Section 2), Interpreters and the Courts (Section 4), Working with the Probation Service (Section 5) and Prisons (Section 6), although this last section is not divided into Parts I, II and III. Section 1 (Language, Communication, Interpreting and the Law) and Section 7 (Professional Standards) deal with more general issues and, again, are not divided into Parts but only smaller sections.

Section 8 describes examples of good practice in other parts of the world (Australia, USA, Sweden and Canada) as concerns the provision of legal interpreting services, training and training materials. Section 9 summarizes some of the issues raised in the book which have yet to be satisfactorily resolved in practice, such as the interpreter's place on the 'court team'.

In addition, there is a short glossary of interpreting terms at the beginning of the book and, at the end, a curious chapter entitled 'Epilogue: a Backwards Look Forwards', which gives some historical examples of interpreting.

Practising and trainee interpreters will find here the clear, concise and comprehensive description of practice and procedures which is of most use to them, while public service providers are given much excellent advice on good practice when working through an interpreter. It is encouraging to see the two sides of the process considered together, rather than in isolation as is frequently the case. As the authors state in their description of guidance notes for interpreters issued by one of the public services, these notes convey "the unfortunate impression that the authorities are having difficulties with their interpreters, who seem to make a habit of arriving late or failing to turn up for engagements, and whose professionalism is in doubt" (p. 66). Experience suggests that, all too often, guidance notes for interpreters and translators (where they exist and are, in fact, passed on) are couched in the same vein, absolving service providers of all and any responsibility in the interpreting process. Trainers of PSIs are also often involved in training service providers; they will wholeheartedly endorse all the points made by the authors in relation to this aspect of provision. Recommendations concerning the choice of interpreter, the necessity of pre-assignment briefing and the emphasis on the importance of providing on-going training apply to all public service providers, without exception, but are infrequently followed.

I cannot help but feel, however, that, desirable though it might be, interpreters and service providers are unlikely to wish to read through the entire volume, but would prefer to be able to select what applies directly to their own situation. The structure of the book does not lend itself easily to such an approach; the focus of the writing tends to switch between the target readerships rather rapidly at certain points and, while this does emphasize their interdependence in the process of interpreting, I suspect that potential readers might simply abandon the effort. The choice of an expanded list of contents over an alphabetical index does nothing to make the task easier.

Nevertheless, I was impressed by the scope of the volume and the user-friendly language used. The authors consider, in some depth, every aspect of the interpreting and translating process in the context of their chosen topic in a way which admirably fills the gap between public information leaflets and specialist publications. Materials of this kind are much to be recommended for PSIs.

ALISON FERRANDO
Community-based ESL, Stevenson College, 4 Duncan Place, Edinburgh EH6 8HW, Scotland, UK

The Origins Of Simultaneous Interpretation: The Nuremberg Trial. Francesca Gaiba. Ottawa: University of Ottawa Press, 1998. 186 pp. ISBN: 0-7766-0457-0, $26 Cdn.

It is no exaggeration to say that without simultaneous interpretation, the 1945-1946 multilingual Nuremberg trial of major figures of the Nazi regime could not have taken place. A form of communication that has become a daily occurrence throughout the world was applied for the first time to a world event. As a legal event, Nuremberg has been criticized as "victors' justice". For the interpreting profession, it was an exemplary – and almost unparalleled – instance of human and technical triumph over the linguistic obstacles that can otherwise impede the implementation of the loftiest sentiments of fairness. As described by the system's manufacturer, IBM, the goal was "that all men may understand" (p. 53, note 15). "All men" included those involved in the trial – defendants, judges, counsel for the prosecution and defence, witnesses, guards and representatives of the media – as well as the world which had just emerged from a lengthy and bloody conflict characterized by great suffering on the part of all sectors of the population of many countries.

Before the trial, both prosecutors and judges reacted with a mixture of concern and scepticism to the proposed use of simultaneous interpreting. The idea was opposed by some of the world's few professional interpreters – the small band of skilled consecutive interpreters. Even those who believed that simultaneous interpreting was feasible wondered if the electrical system would be able to survive the rigours of the trial. Not infrequently the trailing wires on the courtroom floor were tripped over and disconnected. Sometimes languages would become mixed in the interpretation because of technical problems. Eventually the cables would be covered by planks of wood to minimize the need for repairs.

A few statistics will make the enormity of the interpreting task at Nuremberg clear. It has been estimated that some six million original-language words were spoken at the main 1945-1946 trial, which lasted a year. At one point, nearly 300 translators and interpreters were employed in the proceedings – not including the Russian team. The interpreter turnover in the first year at Nuremberg was 104%. Four tons of various electrical 'gadgets' were required for the sound system that enabled the interpreting to be provided. Listeners used the 600 or so headsets with selector switches with which the courtroom was fitted.

The 'aquarium' – the four desks, separated by low glass panels, at which at any one time there sat a total of 12 interpreters – made the interpreting arrangements a highly visible element in the courtroom. This conspicuousness was heightened by the fact that practically everyone at Nuremberg wore headphones in order to follow the proceedings. Interpretation was even needed to allow the judges to communicate with each other. At times many of the defendants conspicuously removed their headphones, such as when evidence was given about conditions in the concentration camps, perhaps because "they could not bear or care to hear about the atrocities" (p. 111). At one point, Göring, in a rage at the way the cross-examination of a German witness was going, pulled at the cord of his headphones so violently that a guard had to remove it from his hands before he ripped it off.

Major efforts were made to recruit the best possible people to interpret at Nuremberg. Some of those engaged were unable to stand the strain of the proceedings; others who showed great talent in the new profession were recruited by the fledgling United Nations in the summer of 1946, before the end of the main trial. Some stayed on for the subsequent bilingual (German-English) trials. Those who interpreted at Nuremberg came from a variety of national, linguistic and professional backgrounds. Some were very young, including an 18-year-old recent high-school graduate, and a fair number were still in their early twenties. Among other things, the Nuremberg interpreting ranks comprised teachers, academics, lawyers, army personnel, professional conference interpreters, including graduates of the School of Interpreters in Geneva, and a future Soviet Ambassador to the United Nations (Oleg A. Troyanovsky, son of the first Soviet Ambassador to the United States). One of the longest-serving interpreters at the Nuremberg Trials, Austrian-born Peter Uiberall, had worked as a stock clerk and farm labourer in the United States after leaving Austria as a refugee in 1938. This experience provided him with a highly valuable work background for an interpreter.

Some of the book's thumbnail sketches of Nuremberg interpreters contain fascinating insights into the foibles and experiences of those 'strange creatures' who performed this seemingly 'impossible' feat, such as George Vassiltchikoff, who was "famous for the fact that he stuttered in normal conversation but not when interpreting" (p. 151). Elisabeth Heyward was literally thrown in the deep end. The day she arrived in Nuremberg she went into the visitors' gallery, where she was astonished to see and hear simultaneous interpreting. The next day in the courtroom she had to launch into simultaneous interpreting herself. She survived this 'baptism by fire' most successfully, eventually being recruited by the United Nations headquarters, where she worked until her retirement in December 1981, and then continuing on and off to work as a freelance interpreter. A fair number of those who worked as interpreters in Nuremberg similarly became and remained professional interpreters.

Certain of the participants made highly critical comments on the interpreters and their performance. The observations by Göring and Norman Birkett, the British Alternate member of the Bench, are the most notorious. Some of Birkett's verge on the unbalanced, but he deserves to be quoted in this review so that modern-day readers can smile in wry amusement. The most infamous citation is his evaluation of what he called "translators" as "a race apart – touchy, vain, unaccountable, full of vagaries, puffed up with self-importance of the most explosive kind, inexpressibly egotistical, and, as a rule, violent opponents of soap and sunlight ..." (p. 114). Gaiba comments that, "ironically", the soundest remarks about the interpreting weaknesses turned out to be those made by Göring, who was more interested in exploiting than correcting them.

While attitudes such as Birkett's have, fortunately, disappeared among the 'consumers' of conference interpretation, some representatives of the judicial professions, at least in Birkett's own country, still harbour similar sentiments towards these undesirable intruders, whom they view as, at best, a "necessary evil" (Herbert 1952:4) in the legal system. One of the Nuremberg defendants, a keen observer of the interpreters' performance and analyst of his co-defendants' linguistic behaviour, even went so far as to write a set of guidelines for speakers, in an admirable effort to facilitate interpreters' work and improve accuracy. In the ultimate accolade, one of the defendants condemned to death in the subsequent proceedings which followed the main trials wrote a letter of appreciation to the interpreters who, he felt, "had given him the chance to understand and be understood in court. He thought he had thus been given a fair trial" (p. 112).

As the main Nuremberg trial proceeded, related administrative procedures and arrangements were honed and refined. At the outset, the translation department – especially in those distant pre-word processing days – was unable to cope with the vast amount of German-language documentation which needed to be translated into the three other languages. In order to overcome this difficulty, an arrangement was worked out under which interpreters would produce instant 'sight translations' of specific passages in documents. This oral technique enabled the material in question to be submitted to the Court even though no written version of the document was available other than in the original language. Later, when the defence was presenting its case, the backlog had been eliminated and it was possible to submit translated documents in writing, without reading selected passages into the record. The defence complained that they were put at a disadvantage by this differential treatment of submitting documentary testimony. The difference in procedure was not, however, a matter of deliberate policy or discrimination, simply the result of changes in a practical situation.

Those responsible for the arrangements as they affected the interpreters tried to ensure that the latter had the best possible conditions for their work, subject to time and space constraints. Having dared take the risk of applying an untried approach – the 'simultaneous' technique had been used in the pre-war period only for the reading out of pre-translated versions of speeches or simultaneously provided multiple-language versions of consecutive interpretation – they tried to build in as many measures as possible to enable the interpreters to do the best job possible. They also recognized the human element. Arrangements were made to provide discreet signals when a speaker needed to slow down, or if it became necessary to interrupt the proceedings for reasons related to interpretation. A monitor in the courtroom constantly kept an ear on all working interpreters, and was prepared to replace anyone who showed signs of fatigue, if necessary interrupting the proceedings to do so.

Acknowledgement of the likelihood of errors led to a system of subsequent quality control in the form of a comparison between the various language transcripts (based on shorthand reporters' notes) and the original spoken material. This checking work was one of the duties of the 'third' team of interpreters. On any one day, two full teams (three interpreters per language 'desk') would work in court, each team working either the first and fourth 85-minute sections, or alternatively the second and third stretches. When not actually interpreting, the other team listened to the proceedings in a separate room. This arrangement was introduced after the trial had begun in order to ensure continuity in terminology and familiarity with the material.

The idea of using simultaneous interpretation – hitherto unheard of in this completely live, unrehearsed form – at the trial came from Léon Dostert, the first Chief Interpreter at Nuremberg. Born in France in 1904, Dostert had served as interpreter for both the German army occupying his town during the First World War and the American Army which liberated it. This 'middleman' situation of the interpreter similarly became clear at Nuremberg, where the interpreters developed a form of rapport (sometimes linguistic, sometimes human) with some of the defendants. A number of the defendants actively cooperated in trying to assist the interpreters' endeavours, for example by passing along notes with the English or German equivalent of a word with which an interpreter was having a problem. After listening for just a few minutes, defendant Albert Speer would give a highly relevant opinion on the potential of a new recruit being tried out as an interpreter. Another example involved Jodl, who had noticed that interpreters' performance was improved if they were provided in advance with a document being read out. He therefore obtained permission to supply the text of his plea in advance and have it pretranslated. Referring to this linguistic 'complicity' between interpreters and a number of the defendants, Gaiba writes that interpreters "were probably the only people in the courtroom who treated the defendants like human beings and accepted their help and suggestions" (p. 129). She points out that the interpreters were providing a specific service: to ensure communication between groups speaking different languages, and "that required cooperation ... with the speakers, including the defendants" (p. 129).

The author, who trained as a conference interpreter at the University of Bologna, has drawn extensively on previously unpublished sources and oral testimony, much of it obtained by considerable perseverance. Over fifty years later, she has succeeded in giving a voice to some of those who worked at Nuremberg and helped give today's modern interpreting profession a flying start. She comments that, "astonishingly", historians have paid no attention to the "miracle of simultaneous interpretation" at the trial (p. 20). A number of papers about the origins of simultaneous interpretation have referred to Nuremberg as a seminal event in the history of the profession, but this is the first book to focus specifically on the interpretation at the War Crimes Trial and those who provided it.

Francesca Gaiba's book touches on many questions which are vital to the running and legal status of contemporary legal proceedings involving the use of interpretation, including transcripts, record of proceedings, electronic recordings, quality control, collegiality, speed of delivery, errors, documentation, preparation, and much more. Her presentation of pre-WWII interpretation practice makes clear the 'bombshell' that was constituted by the simultaneous interpretation at Nuremberg, however primitive the equipment and conditions by today's standards. In that sense, certainly, "tout a commencé à Nuremberg" ('it all began at Nuremberg'; Skuncke 1989:5).

One of the most striking things about Nuremberg is that while it is rightly said that everything began there as far as the profession of conference interpreting in its modern form is concerned, simultaneous interpreting in this electronic form was for many years practically never again used in full-blown legal proceedings. The Tokyo Trials of Japanese war criminals did try to use simultaneous interpretation, but these proceedings foundered largely on the shoals of problems with written translations from Japanese. In Israel, the 1961 Eichmann and 1987 Demjanjuk war crimes trials made extensive use of simultaneous interpretation, but importantly used the consecutive technique for the provision of the Hebrew version, the language of the proceedings and the official record. Gaiba writes that simultaneous interpretation with electric/electronic equipment is seldom used in courts today because of its cost to the government. Her 1979 source for this statement is out-of-date: other possible reasons for the general absence from the courts of full-blown simultaneous interpreting include the greater difficulty of monitoring interpreted output and the concomitant reduced control over the interpreter by the court or lawyers. Another reason may well be conservatism on the part of most courts.

One of the few hilarious episodes of the trial involving interpretation is embodied in an anecdote quoted by Gaiba. One interpreter was reprimanded by the Presiding Judge because of a tendency to give truncated renditions of testimony during the questioning of a witness, Mr. Pine: "The judge got very cross about this on one occasion, and gave the interpreter a going-over in front of everybody saying, "Now look here, I want you to translate *everything* I say, *exactly*. Do you understand?" The interpreter nodded, and the judge signaled to me to proceed, saying, "Yes, Mr. Pine?," whereupon the interpreter said, "Ja, Herr Tannenbaum?"" (p. 107).

RUTH MORRIS

30/6 Haportsim Street, 92541 Jerusalem (Ezor 65 / Rova Bet), Israel.
morrir@mail.biu.ac.il

References

Herbert, Jean (1952) *The Interpreter's Handbook – How to Become a Conference Interpreter*, Geneva: Librairie de l'Université.

Skuncke, Marie-France (1989) 'Tout a commencé à Nuremberg...', *Parallèles* 11: 5-8.

Recent Publications

Agost, Rosa. *Traducción y doblaje: palabras, voces e imágenes*, Ariel, 1999. ISBN 84-344-2838-5.

Anderman, Gunilla and Margaret Rogers (eds). *Word, Text, Translation: Liber Amicorum for Peter Newmark*, Multilingual Matters, 1999. ISBN 1-85359-461-X (Hb), £49.95, 1-85359-460-1 (Pb), £16.95.

Awaiss, Henri and Jarjoura Hardane. *Al-Tarjama: Al-Muqarabat wa Al-Nazariyat/Traduction: Approches et Théories/Translation: Approaches and Theories*, Ecole de Traducteurs et d'Interprètes de Beyrouth, Université Saint-Joseph, 1999. ISSN 1561-8005, $22.

Ballard, Michel. *Les faux amis*, Ellipses, 1999. ISBN 2-7298-6880-1.

Beate, Hammerschmid und Hermann Krapoth (eds). *Übersetzung als kultureller Prozeß: Rezeption, Projektion und Konstruktion des Fremden*, Erich Schmidt, 1998. ISBN 3-503-03794-2, DM 84.

Boase-Beier, Jean and Michael Holman (eds). *The Practices of Literary Translation. Constraints and Creativity*, St. Jerome Publishing, 1999. ISBN 1-900650-19-3, £22/$38.50.

Bueno García, A. and J. García-Medall (eds). *La traducción de la teoría a la práctica*, Universidad de Valladolid, 1999.

Cabré, Maria Teresa. *La terminologie. Théorie, méthode et applications*, trans. Monique Cormier and John Humbley, Les Presses de l'Université d'Ottawa, 1998. ISBN 2-7603-0459-0, $38 (Cdn).

Corbett, John. *Written in the Language of the Scottish Nation. A History of Literary Translation into Scots* (Topics in Translation), Multilingual Matters, 1999. ISBN 1-85359-431-8 (Hb), £29.95/$59.

Delisle, Jean (ed). *Portraits de traducteurs* (Collection Traductologie), Les Presses de l'Université d'Ottawa & Artois Presses Université, 1999. ISBN 2-7603-0486-8/2-910663-39-6.

Delisle, Jean and Hannelore Lee-Jahnke (eds). *Enseignement de la traduction et traduction dans l'enseignement*, Les Presses de L'Université d'Ottawa, 1998. ISBN 2-7603-0480-9, $32 (Cdn)/FF 192.

Delisle, Jean, Hannelore Lee-Jahnke and Monique C. Cormier (eds). *Terminologie de la traduction/Translation Terminology/Terminología de la traducción/ Terminologie der Übersetzung*, John Benjamins, 1999. ISBN 90-272-2423-4, NLG 75.

de Regt, L. J. *Participants in Old Testament Texts and the Translator: Reference Devices and their Rhetorical Impact*, Van Gorcum, 1999.

Dollerup, Cay. *Tales and Translation. The Grimm Tales from Pan-Germanic Narratives to Shared International Fairytales*, John Benjamins, 1999. ISBN 90-272-1635-5 (Hb), NLG 170.

Esselink, Bert. *A Practical Guide to Software Localization*, John Benjamins, 1998. ISBN 90-272-1953-2 (Hb), NLG 126/90-272-1954-0 (Pb), NLG 50.

Foz, Clara. *Le Traducteur, l'Église et le Roi*, Les Presses de l'Université d'Ottawa & Artois Presses Université, 1998. ISBN 2-7603-0462-0/2-910663-25-6, $26 (Cdn).

Furuli, Rolf. *The Role of Theology and Bias in Bible Translation: With a Special Look at the New World Translation of Jehovah's Wintesses*, Elihu Books, 1999.

Gaiba, Francesca. *The Origins of Simultaneous Interpretation. The Nuremberg Trial*, University of Ottawa Press, 1998. ISBN 0-7766-0457-0.

Garre, Marianne. *Human Rights in Translation. Legal Concepts in Different Languages*, Copenhagen Business School Press (Handelshøjskolens Forlag), 1999. ISBN 87-16-13435-4, £18/$30/DKK 186.

Gouanvic, Jean-Marc. *Sociologie de la traduction*, Artois Presses Université, 1999. ISBN 2-910663-36-1, FF120.

Helgason, Jón Karl. *The Rewriting of Njáls Saga: Translation, Politics and Icelandic Sagas*, Multilingual Matters, 1999. ISBN 1-85359-457-1 (Hb), £29.95.

Hermans, Theo. *Translation in Systems. Descriptive and Systemic Approaches Explained* (Translation Theories Explained 7), St. Jerome Publishing, 1999. ISBN 1-900650-11-8, £19.50/$34.

Jürgen, Gercken. *Kultur, Sprache und Text als Aspekte von Original und Übersetzung: Theoretische Grundlagen und Exemplifizierung eines Vergleichs kulturspezifischer Textinhalte*, Peter Lang, 1999. ISBN 3-631-34471-6, DM 54.

Kalina, Sylvia. *Strategische Prozesse beim Dolmetschen: Theoretische Grundlagen, empirische Fallstudien, didaktische Konsequenzen* (Language in Performance 18), Gunter Narr, 1998. ISBN 3-8233-4941-4, DM 78.

Katan, David. *Translating Cultures. An Introduction for Translators, Interpreters and Mediators*, St. Jerome Publishing, 1999. ISBN 1-900650-14-2, £25.50/$44.40.

Lafarga, F. (ed). *La traducción en España, 1750-1830. Lengua, Literatura, Cultura*, Universitat de Lleida, 1999. ISBN 84-8409-983-0.

Martins, Marcia A. P. (ed). *Tradução e Multidisciplinaridade*, Editoria Lucerna, Rio de Janeiro, 1999. ISBN 85-86930-06-7.

Metzger, Melanie. *Sign Language Interpreting: Deconstructing the Myth of Neutrality*, Gallaudet University, 1999.

Mueller-Vollmer, Kurt and Michael Irmscher (eds). *Translating Literatures, Translating Cultures: New Vistas and Approaches in Literary Studies*, Stanford University Press, 1998.

Pekka, Kujamäki. *Deutsche Stimmen der Sieben Brüder: Ideologie, Poetik und Funktionen literarischer Übersetzung*, Peter Lang, 1998. ISBN 3-631-34038-9, DM 89.

Porter, Stanley and Richard Hess (eds). *Translating the Bible. Problems and Prospects*, Sheffield Academic Press, 1999.

Risku, Hanna. *Translatorische Kompetenz: Kognitive Grundlagen des*

Übersetzens als Expertentätigkeit (Studien zur Translation 5), Stauffenburg, 1998. ISBN 3-86057-244-X, DM 86.

Roland, Ruth A. *Interpreters as Diplomats. A Diplomatic History of the Role of Interpreters in World Politics*, University of Ottawa Press, 1999. ISBN 0-7766-0501-1.

Salevsky, Heidemarie. *Über die Sprache hinaus: Beiträge zur Translations-wissenschaft*, TEXTconTEXT Verlag, 1998. ISBN 3-9805370-7-2.

Santoyo, J. C. *Historia de la Traducción: 15 Apuntes*, Universidad de León, 1999. ISBN 84-7719-755-5.

Schmitt, Peter A. *Translation und Technik* (Studien zur Translation Band 6), Stauffenburg Verlag, 1999. ISBN 3-86057-245-8, DM 124.

Setton, Robin. *Simultaneous Interpretation. A Cognitive-pragmatic Analysis*, John Benjamins, 1999. ISBN 90-272-1631-2 (Hb), NLG 158.

Snell-Hornby, Mary, Hans G. Hönig, Paul Kußmaul and Peter Schmitt (eds). *Handbuch Translation*, Stauffenburg Verlag, 1998. ISBN 3-86057-990-8, DM 98.

Sohár, Anikó. *The Cultural Transfer of Science Fiction and Fantasy in Hungary 1989-1995*, Peter Lang, 1999. ISBN 3-631-35037-6, DM 84.

Stark, Susanne. *"Behind Inverted Commas". Translation and Anglo-German Cultural Relations in the Nineteenth Century* (Topics in Translation 15), Multilingual Matters, 1999. ISBN 1-85359-376-1 (Hb), £49/$85; 1-85359-375-3 (Pb), £16.95/$29.95.

Teubert, Wolfgang, Elena Tognini Bonelli and Norbert Volz (eds). *Translation Equivalence*, Proceedings of the Third European Seminar, Montecatini Terme, Italy, October 16-18, 1997, The TELRI Association (Trans-European Language Resources Infrastructure), 1998. ISBN 0-9528026-1-X.

Théorie et pratique de la traduction III: La traduction littéraire (*Cahiers Internationaux de Symbolisme*, Numéros 92-93-94), Centre Interdisciplinaire d'Etudes Philosophiques de l'Université de Mons-Hainaut, 1999. ISSN 0008-0284.

La Traduzione. Saggi e Documenti (IV), Istituto Poligrafico e Zecca dello Stato, 1999.

Tunç Özben, Riza. *A Critical Re-Evaluation of the Target-Oriented Approach to Interpreting and Translation*, Centre for Foreign Language Teaching and Research, Marmara University, Turkey, 1999. ISBN 900-400-196-0.

Tymoczko, Maria. *Translation in a Postcolonial Context. Early Irish Literature in English Translation*, St. Jerome Publishing, 1999. ISBN 1-900650, £22.50/$39.50.

Wechsler, Robert. *Performing without a Stage. The Art of Literary Translation*, Catbird Press, 1998. ISBN 0-945774-38-9.

Wilss, Wolfram. *Translation and Interpreting in the 20th Century. Focus on German*, John Benjamins, 1999. ISBN 90-272-1632-0 (Hb).

Conference Diary

10-11 November
Translating and the Computer
ASLIB, Staple Hall, Stone House Court, London, EC3A 7PB
Fax +44 171 903 0030

11-13 November
L'éloge de la différence: la voix de l'Autre
Université Saint-Joseph, Beirut. Email: hawaiss@usj.edu.lb

12-14 November
Translation Competence
Johannes-Gutenberg-Universität Mainz, Germersheim, Germany
leskopf@nfask2.Uni-mainz.De. http://www.fask.uni-mainz.de/inst/gi/tk/symposium

16-17 November
New Media Localisation – Challenge or Opportunity
European Foundation, Loughlinstown, Co. Dublin
Fax +353-61-330876. Email: LRC@ul.ie. http://lrc.csis.ul.ie

25-27 November
Translating and Training Translators for Changing Markets
Comenius University, Bratislava
Fax +421 763 826 615. Email: ucts@rec.uniba.sk

26-27 November
Aspects of Specialised Translation
University of North London, School of European and Language Studies
Fax +31 43 3466 649. Email: n.rahab@unl.ac.uk

1-3 December
Localization at the Millennium. Industry Performance and Evaluation
Hungary. Fax +41 21 821 3219. lisa@lisa.unige.ch. http://www.lisa.org

2-4 December
11th European Television and Film Forum
Hilton International, Prague
Fax +49 211 90 104 56. masius@eim.de. http://www.eim.de

16 December
Translation as/at the Crossroads of Culture
Faculty of Letters, University of Lisbon
Fax +351 1 7960063. Email: cec@mail.fl.ul.pt

17-19 December
Gender and Translation
British Centre for Literary Translation, University of East Anglia, UK
Fax +44 (0)1603 592737. Email: p.bush@uea.ac.uk

27-30 December
Translation in Context
American Philological Association, Dallas, Texas
e-vandiver@nwu.edu OR richarda@bayou.uh.edu
http://www.hfac.uh.edu/transcontext/

17-18 February **2000**
The Translator and the New Technologies. Redefining the Translator's Task
University of Alcala, Madrid, Spain
Fax +34 91 885 44 45
Email: fmcvg@filmo.alcala.es / isabel.cruz@alcala.es

17-19 February
La traduction juridique
l'Université de Genève, Switzerland
Fax +41 22 705 87 39. grejut@eti.unige.ch

2-4 March
The First International Conference on Specialized Translation
Facultat de Traducció i Interpretació, Universitat Pompeu Fabra, Barcelona
Fax +34 935 421 617. Email: congres.trades@grup.upf.es
http://www.upf.es/dtf/index.htm

23-24 March
Linguistique, Traductologie et Traduction
Centre de Recherches en Traductologie de l'Artois, l'Université d'Artois, France
9 rue du Temple, BP 665, 62030 Arras Cédex, France

23-26 March
Global Links, Linguistic Ties: Forging a Future for Translation & Interpreting
School of Continuing and Professional Studies, New York University
Fax +1 212 995 4139. Translation.2000@nyu.edu

7-8 April
Terminology and Law. 7th Symposium of the German Terminology Society
Fax +49 2066 370 999. johngraham@t-online.de

8-9 April
Annual Conference of the Institute of Translation & Interpreting
Imperial College, London
Fax +44 171 713 7650. Email: info@iti.org.uk. http://www.ITI.org.uk

26-29 April
Translation and Meaning
Hogeschool Maastricht, The Netherlands
Fax +31 43 346 6649. Email: m.m.g.j.thelen@hsmaastricht.nl

28-30 April
Research Models in Translation Studies
Centre for Translation Studies, UMIST, Manchester, UK
Fax +44 161 200 3099. Email: maeve@ccl.umist.ac.uk
http://www.ccl.umist.ac.uk/events/conf.htm

24-26 May
La traduction comme relation: identité, altérité, équivalence
ESIT, Université Paris III, Paris
Tel. +33 1 44 05 42 12. Fax +33 1 44 05 41 43

29-31 May
V Jornadas Internacionales de Historia de la Traducción
Universidad de León, Spain
Fax +34 987 29 10 99. Email: dfmlsf@isidoro.unileon.es

1-3 June
III Congreso Internacional sobre Trasvases Culturales Literatura, cine y traducción
Universidad del Pais Vasco, Spain
Fax: +34 945 144290. Email: fipmealr@vc.ehu.es; fipsaloj@vc.ehu.es

13-19 August
International Comparative Literature Association World Conference
Translation Themes: *The Legacy of Descriptive Translation Studies; Encounters with Otherness: New Context Formation by Translations and Translators*
University of South Africa (UNISA), Pretoria, South Africa
Email: GHB01144@nifty.ne.jp; jmilton@usp.br

28-30 August
Association of Professors of English & Translation at Arab Universities
University of Jordan, Amman. Tel. +962 6 5349 959. Fax +962 6 5355 599

20-24 September
39th American Translators' Association (ATA) Annual Conference
Buena Vista Palace Hotel, Orlando, Florida
Fax +1 703 683 6122. Email: conference@atanet.org. http://www.atanet.org

21-24 September
Translation and Meaning
University of Łódz, Poland
Fax +48 42 36 63 37. Email: duoduo@krysia.uni.lodz.pl

31 October-4 November **2001**
40th American Translators' Association (ATA) Annual Conference
The Regal Biltmore Hotel, Los Angeles
Fax +1 703 683 6122. Email: conference@atanet.org. http://www.atanet.org

The Translator. Volume 5, Number 2 (1999), 361-380   ISBN 1-900650-21-5

Course Profile

Relay Interpreting
A Solution for Languages of Limited Diffusion?

HOLLY MIKKELSON
Monterey Institute of International Studies, USA

Abstract. *Clients of public service agencies are often speakers of minority languages or languages of limited diffusion (LLDs) for which it is difficult to find interpreters. If no interpreter is available in a given language combination, relay interpreting may provide a solution. This profile describes an attempt to address the shortage of indigenous language interpreters in the United States by training selected speakers of these languages to work in a relay situation with certified Spanish-English interpreters in a variety of settings. The course, 'Indigenous Relay Interpreter Training', was presented to two different groups by the International Interpretation Resource Centre in conjunction with two other agencies, under a grant from Oxfam America. Participants heard lectures about the different settings in which dialogue interpreters work and the role of the interpreter, collaborated on subject-matter glossaries in indigenous languages, and practised relay interpreting with English-Spanish interpreters. The first group of trainees worked in the field for several months and then served as facilitators for the second training session.*

No one knows exactly how many languages are spoken in the world, partly because linguists cannot agree on what constitutes a language and what a dialect or variant of a language (Crystal 1997a), and partly because some languages cease to be spoken as minority groups are assimilated into surrounding societies. One estimate puts the number of languages actively spoken in the world today at 6000 (Crystal 1997b). Most countries have only one official language, and the languages spoken by minority groups may or may not be recognized in government, social, educational and cultural spheres.

Usually, the official language of a country is used as a lingua franca among minority groups, even though it is a second language for them. In the Philippines, for example, English is one of the two official languages but no Filipino claims English as a native language. In China, Mandarin is the official language but many different languages are spoken throughout the country. In

ISSN 1355-6509

the tiny Russian republic of Dagestan, 28 languages are shared by a population of two million. Although dozens of languages are spoken throughout Russia, 90 per cent of its citizens claim to speak Russian at home (*The Economist* 1997). French is the lingua franca in much of Africa, while English is often used for inter-ethnic communication in the Indian subcontinent. When speakers of minority languages emigrate to another country, they may find it easier to communicate in one of these major international languages than in their mother tongue.

The United Nations has declared 1994-2004 the Decade of Indigenous Peoples, in recognition of the existence of many ethnic groups that have survived invasion, colonialism and oppression. Members of indigenous ethnic groups are still frequently subjected to mistreatment or neglect in their home countries, and as a result, many of them emigrate. Much has been written about the need for quality interpretation services for immigrants in host countries' public institutions, such as courts, hospitals, social service agencies and schools. The focus of such writing tends to be on providing interpretation services in major languages such as Spanish, Arabic and Russian, no small task in itself. A few writers mention the added difficulty of finding qualified interpreters in less commonly spoken languages, often known as minority languages. The present article specifically addresses the issue of providing trained interpreters in indigenous languages through relay interpreting.

1. Definition of terms

A **minority language** is defined by Crystal (1997a:244) as

> A language used in a country by a group which is significantly smaller in number than the rest of the population, also called a linguistic or language minority. Those who speak the language may be nationals of the country but they have distinguishing ethnic, religious or cultural features which they wish to safeguard.

Often minority languages are suppressed by the government, which impedes their dissemination through formal instruction or publications. Some minority languages have survived only due to the tenacity of a few speakers who continue to use and teach them in secret. Examples include Catalan in Spain under the Franco regime and Gaelic in Ireland under British rule.

Indigenous languages are minority languages spoken by ethnic groups that predate the arrival of the group currently in power. Examples are Inuktitut in Canada and Maori in New Zealand.

Languages of Limited Diffusion (LLD) are spoken by relatively small numbers of people, in contrast to languages that are spoken in several different countries and are widely taught as foreign languages. An LLD may be the official language of a small country, such as Laos or Estonia, or it may be a minority or indigenous language, such as Hmong (spoken in Laos and now in immigrant communities in the United States and elsewhere) or Navajo (spoken by Native Americans in the southwestern United States). It is rare for an LLD to be the official language of an international organization such as the United Nations or the World Bank, but LLDs are frequently used in the daily work of these organizations. Because LLDs are spoken by relatively few people, it may be difficult to find publications written in them. Dictionaries may be scarce or non-existent, and there may be no university-level courses or trained teachers in these languages. As a result of these constraints, there are very few interpreter training programmes in LLDs.

Relay Interpreting is necessary when more than two languages are involved in an interpreted event and no single interpreter commands all of the languages, or when no interpreter can be found in a given language combination. Matheson (1997:17) illustrates the process by describing a hypothetical conference of widget makers in which the working languages are French, English, and Spanish:

> Let us say that the French CEO of Widget Makers de France is addressing the audience in French. Booth #1 is interpreting from French into Spanish for all conference attendees and panel members from Spain. Booth #2 does not listen directly to the speaker, but instead, using the relay switch, is listening to the interpreter in Booth #1, who is interpreting into Spanish. Then the interpreter in Booth #2 proceeds to interpret from Spanish into English for conference attendees and panel members who need to listen to the English interpretation.

Relay interpreting has been employed throughout history when explorers, traders or conquerors have come into contact with previously unknown groups. For example, Karttunen (1994) mentions the use of relay interpreting between Totonac, Nahuatl, Maya and Spanish during Cortes's conquest of Mexico. Today, this expedient is used extensively in large international organizations such as the European Union, which has 11 official languages (Matheson 1997). It would be impossible to find interpreters in every language combination (e.g. French to German, English, Spanish, Portuguese, Italian, Greek, Swedish, Finnish, Danish, and Dutch; Greek to French, German, English, Spanish, Portuguese, Italian, Swedish, Finnish, Danish, and Dutch, etc.), so the interpreters relay from other booths. Experienced conference interpreters are accustomed to relay interpreting and the conference halls and meeting rooms of international organizations are equipped with the appropriate electronic connections to make simultaneous relay interpreting a relatively seamless operation. The delegates are usually unaware that the version they are listening to is not being interpreted from the floor but from one of the other booths.

Another application of the relay system is found in sign language interpreting (New Jersey Court Interpreting Section 1997). When a Deaf individual does not know the standard sign language of the country (ASL in the case of the United States, or BSL in Britain), a Deaf interpreter may be asked to interpret what are known as "home signs" (informal sign language) into, say, ASL and the ASL version is then interpreted into English by a hearing interpreter.

Relay interpreting is obviously much more cumbersome than two-way interpreting, even when performed in the simultaneous mode. If an immigrant is bilingual in his native tongue (a minority or indigenous language) and the official language of his home country (a major world language such as Spanish, French, Russian, Hindi or Mandarin), he or she will have to rely on an interpreter in one of the latter languages, because English/minority-language interpreters are rare. But many immigrants speak only a minority or indigenous language. In the community interpreting settings of the United States (courtrooms, hospitals, etc.), there are no interpreting booths or elaborate electronic connections. As a result, relay interpreting in spoken languages must be performed consecutively. Thus, the service provider will make a statement in English, and the statement will be interpreted simultaneously into a major language (Spanish, for example) but the Spanish version will have to be interpreted consecutively into the minority language (Mixtec, for example). Then the Mixtec speaker will make a statement, which will be interpreted consecutively or simultaneously into Spanish; the Spanish version will then be interpreted consecutively into English.

2. Background of the Indigenous-Language Interpreter Project

In the United States, the language spoken by the largest number of immigrants, and therefore the language most frequently requested for interpretation, is Spanish (U.S. Immigration & Naturalization Service 1998). Mexico is the country that contributes the most immigrants to the United States and it is also a country where many indigenous languages are spoken. Another country that has recently seen many of its citizens emigrate to the United States, primarily because of a devastating civil war, is Guatemala, where 60 per cent of the population speaks an indigenous language (*Caribbean Update* 1997). Immigrants from these two countries in the 1980s and 1990s have included far more speakers of indigenous languages than in the past (McDonnell 1997). As a result, public institutions are faced with an urgent need to find qualified interpreters in Mexican and Guatemalan indigenous languages.

The most common indigenous languages spoken by Mexican immigrants are Mixtec and Zapotec (Kearney 1995, Alvarez 1995, Cearley 1997, Bedell 1997), each of which is actually a large family that includes dozens of mutually unintelligible dialects that could actually be categorized as separate languages. Thus, two people who claim to speak Mixtec may not be able to understand each other well if they are from different villages. The principal Guatemalan languages spoken by immigrants are Mam, Quiche, Kanjobal, Chuj, Quechi, Aguateco and Kacchiquel (Nugent 1998). Again, many speakers of these languages do not know Spanish, much less English. When they appear at a hospital, court or social service agency, they may be mistakenly assigned a Spanish interpreter whom they cannot understand. Once the language barrier is discovered, the search begins for an English/indigenous-language interpreter.

The rare person who is fluent in both English and an indigenous language is unlikely to be trained in the specialized skill of interpreting in the legal, medical or social services setting. As has been amply demonstrated elsewhere (Roberts 1994, Gentile *et al.* 1996), interpreting in these community settings is a complex task that requires extensive training to develop proficiency. Incidents of misdiagnosed patients, wrongfully convicted defendants and exploited workers have proliferated in recent years as the number of indigenous Mexican and Guatemalan immigrants has grown in the United States. Stories have appeared in the press describing injustices that have arisen because speakers of indigenous languages were provided with either no interpreter, a Spanish interpreter or an untrained and incompetent indigenous language interpreter (Alvarez 1995, Bingham 1997, O'Malley 1997, Bedell 1997). One such case was that of Santiago Ventura, a Mixtec speaker who was charged with murder and was provided with a Spanish interpreter throughout his prosecution. Ventura's conviction was eventually overturned, and he was released from prison. By the time of his exoneration and release, he had become fluent in English, and he became an advocate for the rights of indigenous-language speakers. His story was told in a documentary shown on the public broadcasting network throughout the United States.

The *Frente Indígena Oaxaqueño Binacional* (Binational Oaxacan Indigenous Front – Oaxaca being the state in Mexico where most indigenous immigrants come from) was founded to protect the human and labour rights of indigenous Mexicans and to promote solidarity with their cause. California Rural Legal Assistance (CRLA), a legal aid firm whose primary clientele are Mexican farmworkers, had seen first-hand the difficulties encountered by its indigenous clients in their dealings with public agencies, employers and landlords. Because inadequate interpreting was evidently one of the biggest barriers to meeting indigenous immigrants' needs, the *Frente* and CRLA decided to work together to seek funding for a programme to train interpreters. They obtained a grant from Oxfam America and contracted with the International Interpretation Resource Center (IIRC) at the Monterey Institute of International Studies to design and present a training course for indigenous-language interpreters. The IIRC determined that, given the limited formal education and English skills of the indigenous-language speakers, the most pragmatic and cost-effective approach would be to train them to interpret in a relay situation with experienced Spanish-English interpreters. Accordingly, a screening instrument and curriculum were designed to train indigenous-language relay interpreters to work in health, educational, social-service and legal settings.

3. Phase One

3.1 Recruitment and screening

The *Frente* and CRLA already had extensive contacts among the indigenous Mexicans living in California, and they set about publicizing the programme through newsletters, radio stations, and social organizations in Mexican immigrant communities, and by word of mouth. The *Frente* was flooded with enquiries about the course (Nugent 1997). All interested individuals filled out an application that asked for information about their legal status, educational background, language proficiency, current and past employment, availability for training and interpreting assignments, and reasons for wanting to participate in the programme. Those who lacked proper documentation to work in the United States had to be turned away, which had the unfortunate effect of eliminating many otherwise promising candidates. The trainees had to be able to leave their families and jobs for ten days to go through the training programme, a requirement that eliminated additional qualified candidates. The potential interpreters lived in many different parts of the state, an additional problem which required extensive travel for most of the trainees regardless of where the training took place. Candidates who were not literate in Spanish had to be rejected as well, since much of the work of a community interpreter involves reading written instructions and filling out forms (in California, most documentation in public agencies is translated into Spanish). Literacy in the indigenous language was not required.

Originally, the programme was intended to encompass three Mexican indigenous languages: Mixtec, Zapotec and Triqui. Unfortunately, no Triqui speakers came forward and only a few Zapotec speakers applied. The planners had also hoped to recruit equal numbers of men and women, but very few women met the initial requirements.

Applicants who satisfied the requirements of this first phase of screening were asked to take an oral and written qualifying exam. This exam consisted of several parts: (i) a group session in which applicants were encouraged to talk about their reasons for wanting to participate in the programme and their expectations about working as interpreters; (ii) an interview with a specialist in their indigenous language to determine oral fluency; (iii) a reading comprehension test in Spanish; and (iv) an oral exam designed to test their listening comprehension, memory, analytical skills and lexical resourcefulness in Spanish. The texts of the exams are included in Appendix A. Most applicants appeared in person for the exams; a few were interviewed by telephone.

Out of a total of 39 candidates, 15 were selected for the training programme. The languages represented were various dialects of Mixtec (a total of 13 who spoke various dialects of *mixteco alto* and *mixteco bajo*), and Zapotec (one speaker each of *zapoteco del valle* and *zapoteco de la sierra*) (Nugent 1997). Although Oxfam wanted to encourage as many women to participate as possible, only one woman was able to attend the training.

3.2 First training session

The first training session, entitled Indigenous Relay Interpreter Training, took place at a retreat centre over a period of six days (February 2-8, 1997). The curriculum was designed according to a classic model of introducing content first by using a subject-matter expert to present the topic, having the students develop language-specific glossaries related to the subject and then providing practice materials for the students to implement what they have learned in actual interpreting. Because the *Frente* and CRLA had detected a need for indigenous-language interpreting in a variety of settings, the curriculum was designed to cover interpreting for social services, state agencies and administrative hearings, education, health care, criminal law and civil law (see Appendix B for course syllabus). Each day focused on a different topic, with guest speakers who were either attorneys or government officials working in the particular setting, or interpreters with extensive experience in that area. All presentations were given in Spanish.

For example, on the day devoted to state agencies, a bilingual community worker who represents CRLA clients in administrative hearings conducted by various social service agencies provided an overview of how claims are filed and adjudicated in these agencies. To demonstrate administrative hearing procedures and the role of the interpreter, the guest speaker and two CRLA attorneys staged a mock hearing to allow the trainees to play the roles of interpreter and claimant. The proceedings were conducted in English and interpreted into Spanish and an indigenous language, and the "claimant" testified in the indigenous language. After the lecture and demonstration, the trainees met in language groups and began compiling indigenous-language glossaries based on Spanish word lists prepared by the IIRC. Then the students were given scenarios that served as prompts for improvisational role-playing in which they acted the parts of judge or attorney, client and interpreter in language-specific groups (examples of scenarios can be found in Appendix C). If any member of the group had sufficient English proficiency, the trainees practised relay interpreting. If no one spoke English fluently, the trainees interpreted between Spanish and the indigenous language. At the conclusion of the practice session, a plenary session was held to discuss issues related to procedure, ethics and terminology.

Using scenarios designed for improvisation enabled the trainees to practise dialogue interpreting in a multitude of languages and dialects for which no written materials existed. Moreover, role-playing allows students to work with spontaneous speech, which is more realistic than prepared scripts. In some cases (such as public assistance, hospitals and criminal courts) participants were also given some documents for practice in sight translation from Spanish into the indigenous languages.

The curriculum emphasized peer evaluation as well as guidance from the instructors. After each student finished interpreting, he or she received feedback from colleagues who shared the indigenous language, particularly on language-specific issues, and from the instructors, who focused on interpreting technique and protocol. With respect to relay interpreting in particular, the trainees had difficulties in three main areas. They had trouble remembering long utterances (in the simulated dialogue interpreting, questions and answers ranged from one to three sentences in length, perhaps three to one hundred words), and often needed to ask for repetitions. Exerting situational control was also difficult for them, as it is not customary in Mexico to question authority or assert individual needs. Thus, they had to overcome their reluctance to ask speakers to slow down or speak in shorter phrases or to seek clarification of terms. In addition, terminology posed problems: often they would simply use a Spanish term when they did not know the equivalent in the indigenous language, and because of the varying degrees of proficiency among the participants it was unclear whether (i) equivalents simply do not exist in the language in question, and the Spanish term is in fact widely used and understood by speakers of the indigenous language, or (ii) there is an equivalent term in the indigenous language but the trainee did not know it.

In addition to the topics mentioned above, an anthropologist addressed the group on the indigenous languages of Mexico. The purpose of including this subject was to instill pride in the students, since many of them had grown up in environments in which speaking an indigenous language was a source of shame. The participants were also given some tips on identifying the different dialects of their languages and dealing with intelligibility issues. Another lecture covered the code of ethics and the role of the interpreter in different settings. A well-known interpreter trainer, Alee Alger-Robbins, introduced the code of ethics in an interactive session that provided practical examples of ethical dilemmas and introduced the students to proper interpreting protocol (how to ask for clarification or repetitions, for example). During their role-playing exercises, the participants were encouraged to follow this protocol so that it would become automatic. By the end of the session, they appeared more comfortable with asserting themselves to request repetitions or clarifications to ensure accurate interpreting.

Given the multiplicity of languages, it was not possible to give the students a standardized interpreting exam at the conclusion of the course. Instead, they were asked to write an essay on the role of the interpreter and each language group gave a final demonstration of interpreting techniques before the whole class. The training session concluded with an emotional ceremony at which participants were awarded certificates of completion. One interpreter read a poem he had written about the experience, and several sang songs in their native languages.

One of Oxfam's aims in funding the training programme was to select potential leaders in the group who could in turn train other indigenous-language speakers as interpreters after they gained experience in the field. Accordingly, a few individuals with natural leadership abilities and strong interpreting skills were identified for a future training-of-trainers session, which would take place after they had been interpreting for about one year. In fact, these interpreters were used as small-group facilitators in the subsequent course that was offered for Guatemalan indigenous-language interpreters.

3.3 Results of first training

According to a report written by one of the course organizers (Nugent 1997:3),

> The trainees' progress was remarkable in the course of the exercises. They increasingly grew in self-confidence and skills in interpreting, e.g. learning how to interject diplomatically to the Judge for clarification; interpreting in the first person rather than third; maintaining compassion but impartiality towards clients; explaining to clients their limited role and ethical duties as an interpreter. The interpreters also developed a strong esprit de corps and respect for one another, bolstered by their time and (the) work they did together as well as the project's mission.

As soon as the course was over, press releases announced the availability of the interpreters, and the *Frente*, CRLA and the IIRC began receiving calls from court officials seeking indigenous-language interpreters. The interpreters themselves participated in press conferences and outreach efforts in indigenous Mexican communities throughout the state, and some were interviewed for newspaper articles and news programmes in California and Mexico. The goal was not only to alert state institutions to the need for and availability of indigenous-language interpreters, but also to make indigenous-language monolinguals aware of their right to an interpreter.

The number of interpreting assignments received varied considerably among the interpreters, depending on their location, language and employment status (some had full-time jobs that made it difficult for them to take time off for interpreting). In September 1997 the interpreters held a meeting at which they assessed their progress. Although they were pleased with the training they had received, some problems were identified (Nugent 1997:4):

> The difficulties we have contended with in generating, securing and maintaining a solid flow of contracts for the interpreters have been: a) the competition for services from other untrained interpreters Courts have become accustomed to using; b) the fact that Courts prefer to contact the interpreters directly rather than through our service; c) the fact that many indigenous [people] remain unaware of their language and interpreter rights or else erroneously believe that they are proficient in Spanish; and d) the need for expanded outreach to administrative agencies, schools, hospitals and the federal system.

These conclusions were confirmed by a follow-up telephone survey of the indigenous-language interpreters conducted by the IIRC in December 1997. Nine of the 15 trainees responded to questions about their opinion of the training and their experiences in the ensuing months. The respondents reported that they were not hired very frequently for interpreting assignments (only two reported more than 10 assignments) and that it was difficult for them to take time off from their regular employment to accept the few jobs that came their way. Sometimes they had to travel long distances to perform services. A few stated that they still felt pressure to provide interpreting services on a voluntary basis rather than receiving pay. None of those surveyed was making a living exclusively from interpreting (Mikkelson 1998).

4. Phase Two

In October 1997, another grant was secured from Oxfam America to train indigenous-language speakers in relay interpreting. This time the grant recipients were The Chicano Federation (replacing CRLA), the *Frente Indígena Oaxaqueño Binacional*, and the IIRC. There was some urgency in scheduling this training session, because tens of thousands of Guatemalan refugees were now facing asylum interviews and immigration removal proceedings. Because a large percentage of the refugees were monolingual indigenous-language speakers, there was an urgent need for relay interpreters. Accordingly, screening of applicants took place in December 1997 for a training session planned for February 1998.

4.1 Recruitment and screening

The recruitment effort took much the same form as the previous effort for Mexican indigenous-language speakers, through announcements in Spanish media outlets targeting immigrant communities, as well as word of mouth. Interested persons were asked to fill out a questionnaire indicating their languages, educational and employment background and immigration status. Those who were fluent in at least one Guatemalan indigenous language, literate in Spanish and legally present in the United States were asked to appear in person for screening tests.

The screening was very similar to that which had been applied to the Mexican indigenous-language speakers. The same instruments were used to measure Spanish reading comprehension, listening comprehension and memory and analytical skills. The candidates' indigenous-language skills were evaluated by experts from the *Academia de Lenguas Mayas* in Guatemala City, who conducted telephone interviews. Of the 70 candidates who were screened, 30 were selected for training (Nugent 1998). The languages represented were Quechi, Chuj, Kacchiquel, Mam, Aguateco, Zapotec, Kanjobal and Quiche. In general, the Guatemalans proved to be stronger candidates than the Mexicans had, because they had more years of formal education and thus were more literate in Spanish (many had been teachers in Guatemala before being forced to flee). In addition, the Guatemalan immigrants had lived in the United States for longer periods than their Mexican counterparts and had better employment because of their education level and refugee status. Unfortunately, job commitments prevented many of the most qualified candidates from signing up to become interpreters.

4.2 Training

Because of the narrower scope of the training and the urgent need for interpreters, the Guatemalan indigenous-language speakers were given only two days of instruction. The venue was once again a retreat centre, where the interpreter trainees spent a weekend. Mexican indigenous-language interpreters who had participated in the previous training were invited to act as facilitators for this second training session.

On Friday evening the participants were addressed in Spanish by an immigration judge and an interpreter on court procedure in the immigration courts. They learned about the different types of hearings that take place in this jurisdiction (e.g. exclusion, rescission, deportation or asylum) and about legal concepts such as 'order to show cause' and 'adjustment of status'. On Saturday morning they heard from a Spanish-speaking attorney specializing in representing clients in the immigration courts, who went into detail on various options available to immigrants seeking permanent residency and citizenship. Then the participants were shown a Spanish video on asylum cases. After a review of important terminology, the participants divided into language groups for glossary building. On Saturday afternoon they were given a lecture on the code of ethics and courtroom protocol and they heard a presentation from Berlitz Interpretation Services, the agency that hires all contract interpreters for the immigration courts. Once again, all instruction was in Spanish.

On Saturday evening the interpreter trainees held an organizational meeting at which they discussed some of the practical issues that would arise in providing interpreting services. They elected leaders and arranged regional follow-up sessions for further practice and glossary building. On Sunday morning, two Mexican interpreters gave a demonstration of relay interpreting and talked about their experiences. Then the participants spent three hours interpreting role-playing scenarios in their respective languages, with the Mexican interpreters acting as facilitators. It should be noted that the role-playing exercise was particularly traumatic for the Guatemalan interpreter trainees, because they had to describe incidents of persecution, torture and murder that coincided with their own experiences. At the conclusion, each group gave a demonstration of an interpreting scene involving its particular indigenous language. Participants were then given certificates of completion, and many of them expressed their heartfelt thanks for receiving the training to enable them to provide a much-needed service. The weekend ended on a high note with songs, gift-giving and pledges of solidarity.

5. Conclusions and recommendations

This writer embarked upon the Indigenous-Language Interpreter Project with great trepidation, given the multitude of languages and dialects involved, the participants' lack of formal education, the factors that precluded some of the most qualified candidates from participating, the limited time and resources available to invest in the project and the uncertain job market in which the interpreter trainees would be working. The participants had to overcome many obstacles to receive the training: obtaining leaves of absence from their regular employment, leaving family behind and going to a strange place for a week and suddenly being asked to demonstrate proficiency in a language which in the past may have been treated as a source of shame rather than pride. Thus, the trainees were preoccupied by other concerns during the session and it was difficult for them to concentrate. Because indigenous languages have been suppressed for so long and very few reference works are available, they had no definitive resource to determine what was correct usage and they had to rely on each other. Many vowed to consult further with relatives about terminology and usage when they returned home. Consecutive relay interpreting is by nature a time-consuming process and, given that we had only a week to cover a great variety of topics, the trainees were not able to spend as much time as they should have on glossary-building and interpreting practice. Those who did not share a dialect with anyone else did not receive any language-specific feedback.

Despite all those concerns, the project can be considered a qualified success. The trainees came away with a better understanding of what interpreters can and cannot do and a sense of professionalism that encouraged them to seek help from colleagues and strive for constant improvement. The publicity surrounding the training project heightened awareness among the public, government institutions and professional interpreters of the presence of indigenous-language speakers in our midst and the need to provide interpreters for them.

To be sure, crash courses and relay interpreting itself are mere band-aid solutions to a serious and long-term problem. Eventually, as the children of indigenous-language speakers come of age and receive a solid education in English (or the official language of whatever host country they may reside in), they will be able to undergo formal training so that they can interpret for their elders and newcomers alike in traditional two-way interpreting. It is unrealistic to expect, however, that migration by speakers of minority languages will cease, and as long as there are monolingual speakers of languages of limited diffusion immigrating to host countries, there will be a need for such expedients as short-term courses in relay interpreting. Such courses can be effective with proper screening, adequate resources for materials development and training facilities, language-specific instruction and outreach to educate the users of interpreter services about the appropriate ways to avail themselves of this resource.

HOLLY MIKKELSON
International Interpretation Resource Center, Monterey Institute of International Studies, 425 Van Buren Street, Monterey, CA 93940, USA. hmikkelson@miis.edu

References

Alvarez, Fred (1995) 'The Mixtecs: a Grim Life in the Fields', *Los Angeles Times*, July 27.

Bedell, Christine (1997) 'Tongues Lagging: Newly Arrived Languages Create New Challenges', *Santa Maria Times*, November 30.

Bingham, Janet (1997) 'Some Face Double Barrier: Differences in Cultures an Obstacle, Too', *The Denver Post*, May 18.

Caribbean Update (1997) 'Business Opportunities after Peace Accords: Education', October 1, Information Access Company.

Cearley, Anna (1997) 'Crossing Language's Barriers', *San Diego Union Tribune*.

Crystal, David (1997a) *A Dictionary of Linguistics and Phonetics*, Oxford, UK & Cambridge, Mass.: Blackwell.

------ (1997b) (ed) *Cambridge Encyclopedia of Language*, New York: Cambridge University Press.

The Economist (1997) 'Russia: Speak, Memory', March 1.

Gentile, Adolfo, Uldis Ozolins and Mary Vasilakakos (1996) *Liaison Interpreting: A Handbook*, Melbourne: Melbourne University Press.

Kartunnen, Frances (1994) *Between Worlds: Interpreters, Guides, and Survivors*, New Brunswick, NJ: Rutgers University Press.

Kearney, Michael (1995) 'The Effects of Transnational Culture, Economy, and Migration on Mixtec Identity in Oaxacalifornia', in Michal Peter Smith and Joe R. Feagin (eds) *The Bubbling Cauldron: Race, Ethnicity, and the Urban Crisis*, Minneapolis & London: University of Minnesota Press.

Matheson, Agnes Subiros (1997) 'The Amazing Relay Switch', *ATA Chronicle*, July.

McDonnell, Patrick J. (1997) 'Group Calls for Indian-Language Interpreters', *Los Angeles Times*, March 14.

Mikkelson, Holly (1998) *Indigenous-Language Interpreter Survey*. Unpublished report, Monterey, CA: Monterey Institute of International Studies.

New Jersey Court Interpreting, Legal Translating, and Bilingual Services Section (1997) *Standards for Court Interpreting, Legal Translating, and Bilingual Services*, Trenton, NJ: Administrative Office of the Courts.

Nugent, Chris (1997) *Mexican Indigenous Farmworker Interpreter Project: Progress Report to Oxfam America*. Unpublished report, September 11.

------ (1998) 'Nuevos intérpretes en las cortes', *El Latino*, February.

O'Malley, Michael (1997) 'Refusing to Let Hate Take Hold: Tuscarawas County Residents Band to Help Guatemalan Refugees Settle into Amish Country', *Plain Dealer Reporter*, December 7.

Roberts, Roda (1994) 'Community Interpreting Today and Tomorrow', in Peter Krawutschke (ed) *Proceedings of the 35th Annual Conference of the American Translators Association*, Medford, NJ: Learned Information.

United States Immigration & Naturalization Service, <*http://www.ins.usdoj.gov/stats/299.html*> (April 19, 1998).

Appendix A. *Screening Test* (conducted in Spanish; presented here in English translation)

1. Initially, candidates were divided into language groups, consisting of five or six persons each, and spent about 30 minutes discussing language issues and the role of the interpreter. Each person was asked to introduce himself or herself, including place of origin, current residence and occupation.

Then the facilitator asked the following questions of each person, and encouraged others to comment:

- What languages do you speak? How did you learn them, and where do you speak them now (at home, at work, etc.)? How often do you speak each language?
- Which languages do you read in? How often do you read, and what kinds of materials?
- Tell us something about your people and your culture (music, food, customs). How do they differ from Mexican culture? How is your language different from Spanish? Can you give any examples of differences?
- Why do you want to be an interpreter? What does an interpreter do? Do you have any hesitation about your ability to work as an interpreter?

The remaining parts of the screening test were administered individually, in Spanish.

2. Listening comprehension and memory

Instructions: Listen to the story and try to repeat as many details as you recall.

[recorded passage is played]

> Every day in the wintertime, the little Italian mountain village of Orasso, near the Swiss border, experiences two dawns and two dusks. This phenomenon is caused by a nearby mountain that has two peaks spaced far apart. When the sun appears for the first time, it comes up over one of the slopes. At about noon, it goes behind the first peak, causing the first dusk, and all the lights come on in Orasso. The sun reappears after reaching the valley between the peaks, allowing natural light to come in and causing the roosters to crow once again. When the sun reaches the second peak in the afternoon, the sun disappears for the rest of the night.

3. Reading comprehension, vocabulary, analysis

Instructions: Read the paragraph aloud. Replace the underlined words or phrases with another word or phrase that has the same meaning. After reading the paragraph, summarize it in your own words.

According to officials of the National Police who <u>fight crime</u> in the capital, about 20 pickpockets go out every day to <u>empty someone's pockets</u>. These assertions are backed up by confidential reports <u>compiled</u> by specialists in criminal investigation and by the number of complaints filed at <u>police stations</u>. Experts in crime prevention have devised a plan that has been <u>implemented successfully</u> over the past few months. The police tactic consists of accumulating evidence on subjects <u>with prior convictions</u> for pickpocketing. Suspects are detained as part of a <u>well-coordinated</u> operation carried out at bus stops, which reports indicate are the most common <u>sites of robberies</u>. Investigators have <u>confiscated</u> jewelry and other property belonging to the <u>victims</u> in the homes of some of these individuals. The seized property is then used as evidence for <u>criminal prosecution</u>.

4. Reading comprehension

Instructions: Read the text and answer the questions that follow.

Memories of Earthquake Live On in Mexico

Maria Elena Gonzalez, her face disfigured by constant crying and her voice full of anguish, says she will never forget what happened that fateful morning of September 19, 1985, the day when she lost her two children forever. They were two of the many children who were killed by the earthquake in Mexico City that day. As she lights a candle at the foot of the now restored building and tries in vain to hold back her tears, Maria Elena travels back in time to 11 years ago, the period she considers the saddest time of her life.

It was 7:19 am when the ground began to shake violently. At that time, Maria Elena was returning home from walking her oldest daughter to school. She was crossing the street, holding the hand of her other daughter, hurrying because of the quaking ground. She arrived too late; the building fell right before her eyes. In her apartment on the 11th floor, she had left her mother-in-law, her servant, and her two younger children asleep.

The earthquake caused the Nuevo Leon Building to collapse, leaving an official death toll of 472; according to residents, the real total was 1,100 dead. Eleven years after the quake, at least 700 homeless families are still living in 27 camps scattered around Mexico City. The tremendous housing shortage will not be solved with the 500 dwellings the city government plans to have completed by the end of this year to make available to the families made homeless in the '85 earthquake.

With approximately 9 million inhabitants and a transient population of a similar number, vast industrial areas, and myriad underground tunnels, quake-prone Mexico City is very vulnerable. The earthquake of September 1985 made it obvious that government agencies are ill-equipped to respond to the population's needs in a large-scale emergency.

Questions:
1. What was Maria Elena doing when the earthquake began?
2. Who else was in the apartment with the two children who died?
3. According to the government, how many people were killed when the building collapsed?
4. Have all of the homeless families found new housing by now?
5. What did the 1985 earthquake tell us about Mexico City?

5. Listening comprehension, analysis (cloze)

Instructions: Listen to the passage, and when the reader pauses, supply the missing words.

Children and Discipline

Every month at my sons' school, there is one day when no homework is assigned. On that day, rather than doing school work when they come home, the children are supposed to engage in a "family task" in which they discuss an issue such as respect, consideration for others, forgiveness, or truth and _____.

The purpose of the family task is to stimulate dialogue between parents and _____ about human values and how members of the family apply them in their relations with _____. For example, this week we talked about respect. My husband and I started the dialogue by asking the children to give us examples of what they considered an act of respect and an act of _____. They both mentioned acts that showed a lack of respect for themselves or for us, and they promised to be better about correcting _____. As parents, we also accepted that there are times when we have behaved _____, and we promised not to do it again.

We parents should not ignore the importance of teaching our children from a young age to treat others with _____, especially their teachers and _____. Any discourtesy, no matter how insignificant, distracts the class and disrupts _____. For example, if a child enters the room making a lot of _____, or is constantly talking _____ and interrupting the teacher, or takes things that do not _____, all of these acts could be prevented if the parents helped their children learn to practice at school the obedience and respect they are taught _____.

Appendix B. *Syllabus for First Training Course*

International Interpretation Resource Center, Relay-Interpreter Training

Course Outline

Monday

  9:00 Welcome, introductions, overview
10:00 Interpreter ethics, role of the community interpreter
       Speaker: Alee Alger-Robbins
12:00 Lunch
  1:00 Role playing of ethical issues
  3:00 Dialect intelligibility criteria
       Speaker: Alejandro Avila
  4:00 Interpreting exercises (impromptu speeches)
  5:00 Adjourn

Tuesday

  8:30 Interpreting in civil cases, state agency hearings – terminology
       Speakers: Hector de la Rosa, Luis Jaramillo
10:00 Interpreting exercises (role-playing scenarios – social services,
       unemployment)
12:00 Lunch
  1:00 Labor and employment (video) – terminology
  2:00 Interpreting exercises (employment, unemployment, ALRB)
  4:00 Sight translation of social services, unemployment documents
  5:00 Adjourn

Wednesday

  8:30 Interpreting in an educational setting (video) – terminology
       Speaker: Abel Valdez, Principal, El Sausal Middle School
10:00 Interpreting exercises (educational)
12:00 Lunch
  1:00 Motor vehicle and traffic law (video) – terminology
       Speaker: Hollister Police
  2:00 Interpreting exercises (traffic stops, DUI)
  4:00 Sight translation of education, motor vehicle documents
  5:00 Adjourn

Thursday

8:30 Hospital interpreting (video) – terminology
       Speaker: George Donald
10:00 Interpreting exercises (hospital admissions, surgery, release)
12:00 Lunch
 1:00 Health care settings (video) – terminology
 2:00 Interpreting exercises (medical exams)
 4:00 Sight translation of medical documents

Friday

8:30 Legal settings (video) – family law terminology
       Speaker: Lydia King
10:00 Interpreting exercises (landlord-tenant, child support, domestic
       violence)
12:00 Lunch
 1:00 Criminal law (video) – terminology
       Speaker: Ofelia Cuenca
 2:00 Interpreting exercises (court proceedings)
 4:00 Sight translation of court documents
 5:00 Adjourn

Saturday

8:30 Sex offenses – terminology
       Speaker: Estela Aguayo
10:00 Interpreting exercises (domestic violence, child molestation)
12:00 Lunch
 1:00 Review of ethical issues
 3:00 Awards ceremony, conclusion

Appendix C. *Sample Scenario for Role-Playing*

Civil Law – Scenario No. 3

You have had problems with your landlord. The apartment needs a lot of repairs: The roof leaks, the toilet is broken, and the front door does not lock properly. You have complained several times to the landlord, but he does nothing. You had to buy a new toilet and pay a friend to install it, and the landlord refused to reimburse you the $400 it cost you. He keeps promising to fix things, but he doesn't do it. In addition, he says your family is too big for the apartment, because it only has two bedrooms and there are eight of you. In spite of everything, you always pay the rent on time, $570 a month. The landlord says he wants to raise the rent, but you think $570 is already too high. Then, on April 15, the landlord shows up with a letter written in English, which you don't understand. He tells you you have to vacate the apartment within 15 days, and if you don't get out, he'll call the police to evict you. You don't want to leave the apartment because you live in the neighborhood and you get along well with the neighbours. You go to Legal Aid to request the help of an attorney.

Attorney

1. Do you rent a house or an apartment? How many bedrooms does it have?
2. Have you signed a lease?
3. When you rented the apartment, were you given anything in writing that imposed any restrictions on how many people could live there?
4. How many people are living in the apartment?
5. Have you had any problems with the apartment?
6. How much have you spent on repairs?
7. Have you asked the landlord for reimbursement?
8. Have you ever been late in paying the rent?
9. When did the landlord give you the eviction notice?
10. Have there ever been any complaints about noise in your apartment?

The Translator. Volume 5, Number 2 (1999), 381-385   ISBN 1-900650-21-5

Dialogue Interpreting
A Selective Bibliography of Research

Compiled by Ian Mason, UK

Altano, W. B. (1990) 'The Intricate Witness-Interpreter Relationship', in David Bowen and Margareta Bowen (eds) *Interpreting – Yesterday, Today and Tomorrow*, ATA Vol. 4, Binghamton: State University of New York.

Anderson, R. Bruce W. (1976) 'Perspectives on the Role of Interpreter', in Richard W. Brislin (ed) *Translation: Applications and Research*, New York: Gardner Press, 208-28.

Baker, Mona (1997) 'Non-Cognitive Constraints and Interpreter Strategies in Political Interviews', in Karl Simms (ed) *Translating Sensitive Text: Linguistic Aspects*, Amsterdam: Rodopi, 113-31.

Barsky, Robert F. (1993) 'The Interpreter and the Canadian Convention Refugee Hearing', *TTR* 6(2): 131-57.

------ (1996) 'The Interpreter as Intercultural Agent in Convention Refugee Hearings', *The Translator* 2(1): 45-63.

Berk-Seligson, Susan (1988) 'The Impact of Politeness in Witness Testimony: The Influence of the Court Interpreter', *Multilingua* 7(4): 411-39.

------ (1990a) 'Bilingual Court Proceedings: The Role of the Court Interpreter', in J. N. Levi and A. G. Walker (eds) *Language in the Judicial Process*, New York: Plenum Press, 155-201.

------ (1990b) *The Bilingual Courtroom: Court Interpreters in the Judicial Process*, Chicago & London: The University of Chicago Press.

Bowen, Margareta (1994) 'Negotiations to End the Spanish-American War', in Mary Snell-Hornby, Franz Pöchhacker and Klaus Kaindl (eds) *Translation Studies. An Interdiscipline*, Amsterdam & Philadelphia: John Benjamins, 73-81.

Brennan, Mary (1994) 'Cross-examining Children in Criminal Court: Child Welfare under Attack', in John Gibbons (ed) *Language and the Law*, London & New York: Longman.

------ (1997) 'Seeing the Difference: Translation across Modalities', in Karl Simms (ed) *Translating Sensitive Text: Linguistic Aspects*, Amsterdam: Rodopi, 97-108.

------ and Richard Brown (1997) *Equality before the Law: Deaf People's Access to Justice*, Durham: Deaf Studies Research Unit, University of Durham.

Brown, S. (1993) 'Access to Justice: the Role of the Interpreter', *Judicial Officers Bulletin* 5(3): 17-18.

Carr, Silvana, Roda Roberts, Aideen Dufour and Dini Steyn (eds) (1997) *The Critical Link: Interpreters in the Community*, Amsterdam & Philadelphia: John Benjamins.

ISSN 1355-6509

Chapman, R. C. (1990) 'How American Courts View Defendants' Rights to Interpreters', in David Bowen and Margareta Bowen (eds) *Interpreting – Yesterday, Today and Tomorrow*, ATA Vol. 4, Binghamton: State University of New York.

Colin, Joan and Ruth Morris (1996) *Interpreters and the Legal Process*, Winchester: Waterside Press.

Cooper, M. (1974) *Rodrigues the Interpreter. An Early Jesuit in Japan and China*, New York: Weatherhill.

De Jongh, E. M. (1992) *An Introduction to Court Interpreting*, Lanharn, MD: University Press of America.

Downing, B. and K. Helms Tillary (1992) *Professional Training for Community Interpreters: A Report on Models of Interpreter Training and the Value of Training*, Minneapolis: Center for Urban and Regional Affairs, University of Minnesota.

Duncan, S. and D. W. Fiske (1977) *Face-to-face Interaction: Research, Methods and Theory*, Hillsdale, NJ: Erlbaum.

Edmondson, W. J. (1986) 'Cognition, Conversing and Interpreting', in Juliane House and Shoshana Blum-Kulka (eds) *Interlingual and Intercultural Communication*, Tübingen: Gunter Narr.

Edwards, Alicia (1995) *The Practice of Court Interpreting*, Amsterdam & Philadelphia: John Benjamins.

Englund Dimitrova, B. (1993) 'Turntaking in Interpreted Discourse: Interplay of Implicit and Explicit Rules', in K. Cankov (ed) *Problemi na sociolingvistikata. Ezikovata situacija v mikro- i makrosocialnite obstnosti*, Veliko Târnovo: Universitetsko izdatelstvo, 15-21.

------ (1995) 'Omissions in Consecutive Interpretation: Evidence of a Decision Component', in P. Ambrosiani, B. Nilsson and L. Steensland (eds) *Podobaet "pamjat's" tvoriti. Essays to the Memory of Anders Sjöberg* (Acta Universitatis Stockholmiensis. Stockholm Slavic Studies 24), Stockholm: Stockholm University, 67-76.

------ (1997) 'Degree of Interpreter Responsibility in the Interaction Process in Community Interpreting', in Silvana Carr, Roda Roberts, Aideen Dufour and Dini Steyn (eds) *The Critical Link: Interpreters in the Community*, Amsterdam & Philadelphia: John Benjamins, 147-64.

Fenton, Sabine (1997) 'The Role of the Interpreter in the Adversarial Courtroom', in Silvana Carr, Roda Roberts, Aideen Dufour and Dini Steyn (eds) *The Critical Link: Interpreters in the Community*, Amsterdam & Philadelphia: John Benjamins, 29-34.

Gentile, Adolfo, Uldis Ozolins and Mary Vasilakakos (with Leong Ko and Ton-That Quynh-Du) (1996) *Liaison Interpreting: A Handbook*, Melbourne: Melbourne University Press.

González, R. (1994) 'The Federal Court Interpreter Certification Project: Defining World Class Standards for Court Interpretation', in *Proceedings of MET 4*, Brisbane: University of Queensland.

González, Dueñas Roseann, Victoria Vásquez and Holly Mikkelson (1991) *Fundamentals of Court Interpretation: Theory, Policy and Practice, Durham, North Carolina: Carolina Academic Press.

Hale, Sandra (1997a) 'The Treatment of Register Variation in Court Interpreting', *The Translator* 3(1): 39-54.

------ (1997b) 'The Interpreter on Trial: Pragmatics in Court Interpreting', in Silvana Carr, Roda Roberts, Aideen Dufour and Dini Steyn (eds) *The Critical Link: Interpreters in the Community*, Amsterdam & Philadelphia: John Benjamins, 201-211.

------ and John Gibbons (1999) 'Varying Realities: Patterned Changes in the Interpreter's Representation of Courtroom and External Realities', *Applied Linguistics* 20(2): 203-220.

Harris, Brian (1981) 'Observations on a Cause Célèbre: Court Interpreting at the Lischka Trial', in Roda Roberts (ed) *L'Interprétation auprès des tribunaux*, Ottowa: University of Ottawa.

------ (1990) 'Norms in Interpretation', *Target* 2(l): 115-19.

------ (1993) 'Un intérprete diplomático inglés en el siglo XIX en Japón', *Livius. Revista de Estudios de Traducción* 3: 115-36.

------ and Bianca Sherwood (1978) 'Translating as an Innate Skill', in D. Gerver and W. H. Sinaiko (eds) *Language, Interpretation and Communication*, Oxford & New York: Plenum.

Jansen, Peter (1995) 'The Role of the Interpreter in Dutch Courtroom Interaction: The Impact of the Situation on Translational Norms', in Jorma Tommola (ed) *Topics in Interpreting Research*, Turku: University of Turku, 11-36.

Karttunen, Frances (1994) *Between Worlds. Interpreters, Guides, and Survivors*, New Brunswick: Rutgers University Press.

Kauffert, Joseph and William Koolage (1984) 'Role Conflict Among Cultural Brokers: The Experience of Native Canadian Medical Interpreters', *Social Science and Medicine* 18(3).

Keith, Hugh A. (1984) 'Liaison Interpreting: An Exercise in Linguistic Interaction', in Wolfram Wilss and Gisela Thome (eds) *Die Theorie des Ubersetzens und ihr Aufschlusswert für die Ubersetzungs- und Dolmetschdidaktik*, Tübingen: Gunter Narr, 308-317.

Knapp-Pothoff, Annelie and Karlfried Knapp (1986) 'Interweaving Two Discourses – The Difficult Task of the Non-Professional Interpreter', in Juliane House and Shoshana Blum-Kulka (eds) *Interlingual and Intercultural Communication*, Tübingen: Gunter Narr.

------ (1987) 'The Man (or Woman) in the Middle: Discoursal Aspects of Nonprofessional Interpreting', in K. Knapp, W. Enninger and A. Knapp-Potthoff (eds) *Analyzing Intercultural Communication*. Berlin: De Gruyter, 181-211.

Lang, Ranier (1976) 'Interpreters in Local Courts in Papua New Guinea', in W. M. O'Barr and J. F. O'Barr (eds) *Language and Politics*, The Hague-Paris: Mouton, 327-65.

------ (1978) 'Behavioral Aspects of' Liaison Interpreters in Papua New Guinea: Some Preliminary Observations', In D. Gerver and H. W. Sinaiko (eds) *Language Interpretation and Communication*, New York & London: Plenum, 231-44.

Laster, K. (1990) 'Legal Interpreters: Conduits to Social justice?', *Journal of Intercultural Studies* 11(2): 16-32.

------ and V. Taylor (1994) *Interpreters and the Legal System*, Leichhardt, NSW: The Federation Press.

Linell, Per, Cecilia Wadensjö and Linda Jönsson (1992) 'Establishing Communicative Contact through a Dialogue Interpreter', in Annette Grindsted and Johannes Wagner (eds) *Communication for Specific Purposes*, Tübingen: Narr, 125-42.

Marcos, Luis (1979) 'Effects of Interpreters on the Evaluation of Psychology in Non-English Speaking Patients', *American Journal of Psychiatry* 136(2): 171-74.

Metzger, Melanie (1999) *Sign Language Interpreting: Deconstructing the Myth of Neutrality*, Gallaudet University.

Meyer, Bernd (1998) 'What Transcriptions of Authentic Discourse Can Reveal about Interpreting', *Interpreting* 3(1): 65-83.

Mikkelson, Holly (1998) 'Towards a Redefinition of the Role of the Court Interpreter', *Interpreting* 3(1): 21-45.

Morris, Ruth (1989) 'Court Interpretation: The Trial of Ivan Demjanjuk. A Case Study', *The Interpreters' Newsletter* 2: 27-37.

------ (1993) 'Nobs and Yobs – the Provision of Interpreters for Legal Proceedings Involving High-status Foreigners and Others', in Catriona Picken (ed) *Translation – the Vital Link* (Proceedings of the XIII FIT World Congress), Volume 2, London: Institute of Translation & Interpreting, 356-66.

------ (1995) 'The Moral Dilemmas of Court Interpreting', *The Translator* 1(1): 25-46.

Müller, F. (1989) 'Translation in Bilingual Conversation: Pragmatic Aspects of Translatory Interaction', *Journal of Pragmatics* 13: 713-39.

Niska, Helge (1990) 'A New Breed of Interpreter for Immigrants: Contact Interpretation in Sweden', in Catriona Picken (ed) *Proceedings of the Institute of Translation and Interpreting 4*, London: ASLIB, 94-104.

Roberts, Roda (1993) 'Community Interpreting in North America', in Catriona Picken (ed) *Translation – The Vital Link*, 2, London: Institute of Translation & Interpreting.

Roland, Ruth A. (1999) *Interpreters as Diplomats. A Diplomatic History of the Role of Interpreters in World Politics*, Ottawa: University of Ottawa Press.

Roy, Cynthia (1990) 'Interpreters, their Role and Metaphorical Language Use', in A. L. Wilson (ed) *Looking Ahead: Proceedings of the 31st Annual Conference of the American Translators Association*, Medford, NJ: Learned Information, 77-86.

------ (1992) 'A Sociolinguistic Analysis of the Interpreter's Role in Simultaneous Talk in a Face-to-Face Interpreted Dialogue', *SLS* 74: 21-61.

------ (1993) 'A Sociolinguistic Analysis of the Interpreter's Role in Simultaneous Talk in Interpreted Interaction', *Multilingua* 12(4): 341-63.

------ (1996) 'An Interactional Sociolinguistic Analysis of Turn-taking in an Interpreted Event', *Interpreting* 1(1): 39-67.

Schäffner, Christina (1995) 'Establishing Common Ground in Bilateral Interpreting', in Jorma Tommola (ed) *Topics in Interpreting Research*, Turku: University of Turku, 91-108.

Shlesinger, Miriam (1989) 'Monitoring the Courtroom Interpreter', *Parallèles: Cahiers de l'Ecole de Traduction et d'Interpretation* 11: 29-36.

------ (1991) 'Interpreter Latitude vs. Due Process. Simultaneous and Consecutive Interpretation in Multilingual Trials', in Sonja Tirkkonen-Condit (ed) *Empirical Research in Translation and Intercultural Studies*, Tübingen: Gunter Narr, 147-55.

Tebble, Helen (1992) 'A Discourse Model for Dialogue interpreting', in *AUSIT Proceedings of the First Practitioners' Seminar*, Canberra: Australian Institute of Interpreters and Translators.

Tommola, Jorma (ed) (1995) *Topics in Interpreting Research*, Turku: University of Turku.

Wadensjö, Cecilia (1992) *Interpreting as Interaction: On Dialogue Interpreting in Immigration Hearings and Medical Encounters*, Linköping: University of Linköping Department of Communication Studies.

------ (1993) 'Dialogue Interpreting and Shared Knowledge', in Yves Gambier and Jorma Tommola (eds) *Translation and Knowledge*, Turku: Centre for Translation and Interpreting, University of Turku.

------ (1995) 'Dialogue Interpreting and the Distribution of Responsibility', *Hermes: Journal of Linguistics* 14: 111-29.

------ (1997) 'Recycled Information as a Questioning Strategy: Pitfalls in Interpreter-Mediated Talk', in Silvana Carr, Roda Roberts, Aideen Dufour and Dini Steyn (eds) *The Critical Link: Interpreters in the Community*, Amsterdam & Philadelphia: John Benjamins, 35-54.

------ (1998) *Interpreting as Interaction*, London & New York: Longman.

Wande, E. (1994) 'Translating Machine or Creator? On Finnish-Swedish Community Interpreting in Sweden', *Hermes: Journal of Linguistics* 12: 109-26.

Zimman, Leonor (1994) 'Intervention as a Pedagogical Problem in Community Interpreting', in Cay Dollerup and Annette Lindegaard (eds) *Teaching Translation and Interpreting 2: Insights, Aims, Visions*, Amsterdam: John Benjamins, 217-24.

Translation Studies Abstracts

Published as one volume of two issues per year
(approximately 200 pages, June and December)
ISSN 1460-3063. Available from St. Jerome Publishing

TSA is a new initiative designed to provide a major and unique research tool, primarily for scholars of translation and interpreting. It is the first abstracting service of its kind, focusing on and covering all aspects of research within the domain of translation studies, including translation theory, literary translation, bible & religious translation, audiovisual translation, technical & legal translation, interpreting studies, community/dialogue interpeting, conference interpreting, court interpreting, signed language interpreting, history of translation & interpreting, translator/interpreter training, process-oriented studies, corpus-based studies, translation and gender, translation and cultural identity, translation policies, research methodology, evaluation/quality, machine(-aided) translation, terminology & lexicography, translation and issues of crosscultural communication, translation and language teaching, translation and the language industry.

Translation studies has many points of contact with other disciplines, especially linguistics, pragmatics, comparative literature, cultural studies, gender studies, postcolonial studies, corpus linguistics, anthropology, ethnography, and any field of study concerned with the history of ideas. Scholars working in any of these fields will find much of direct relevance in *TSA*.

TSA Editor: Maeve Olohan, UMIST, UK

Consulting Editors:
Andrew Chesterman (Finland)
Birgitta Englund Dimitrova (Sweden)
Adolpho Gentile (Australia)
Theo Hermans (UK)
Rosa Rabádan (Spain)
Ronald Sim (Kenya)
Gideon Toury (Israel)
Maria Tymoczko (USA)

Subscription to Volume 3 (2000)
Institutional: £62/$109(UK & Europe) / £65/$114 (Outside Europe), inc. p&p
Individual: £32/$56 (UK & Europe) / £35/$62 (Outside Europe), inc. p&p

Bibliography of Translation Studies (Companion to *TSA*)
ISBN 1-900650-13-4

Available free for subscribers to TSA
Price for non-subscribers: £15/$26.50, inc. postage & packing